SOUND Foundations

A source of reference and a guide for aspiring composers

James Rae & Mike Cornick

www.universaledition.com
vienna · london · new york

UE 21483
ISMN 979-0-008-08092-0
UPC 8-03452-06450-3
ISBN 978-3-7024-6731-9

CD Recorded at Simon Painter Production, Farnham, Surrey, U.K.
Recording Engineer: Simon Painter

Live CD tracks:

Pentafunk
Keyboard: Mike Cornick
Bass Guitar: Dave Olney
Drums: Dave Barry

Mix and Match Blues
Bass: Dave Olney
Drums: Dave Barry

Cover Design: Lynette Williamson
Cartoons: Wendy Sinclair
Layout: Ingrid Zuckerstätter
Edited by Anne Handley

© Copyright 2009 by Universal Edition A.G., Wien

Contents

Introduction		8
Acknowledgements		11
Preface		12
Section 1	**Notation – the Basics**	13
1.1	Introduction	13
1.2	Duration	13
1.3	The notation of pitch	15
1.4	A few tips	17
Section 2	**Composition: Getting Started**	19
2.1	Introduction	19
2.2	Placing your melody within a scale	20
2.3	The importance of rhythm in a melody	20
2.4	Melodic structure	21
2.5	Using sequence in a melody	22
2.6	Phrase and answer – call and response	23
2.7	Improvisation	24
2.8	Making some important decisions	25
2.9	Where to look for help	26
2.10	Conclusion	27
Section 3	**Understanding Pulse, Time Signatures and Rhythm**	28
3.1	Introduction	28
3.2	Writing a rhythm and using software	29
3.3	To begin with the basics – notating a regular pulse	29
3.4	Simple time signatures	30
3.5	The metronome	32
3.6	Table of common simple time signatures	33
3.7	Dividing the beat in simple time	33
3.8	Compound time signatures	36
3.9	Table of common compound time signatures	39
Section 4	**Understanding Key Signatures**	40
4.1	Introduction	40
4.2	Major keys	41
4.3	Minor keys	43
4.4	Choosing a key	46

	4.5	Some other scales	48
	4.6	The chromatic scale	48
	4.7	Modes	49
	4.8	The whole-tone scale	51
	4.9	The pentatonic scale	52
	4.10	The blues scale	53
	4.11	The diminished or octatonic scale	54

Section 5 — Understanding Harmony 56
- 5.1 Introduction 56
- 5.2 Historical background 56
- 5.3 The 'nuts and bolts' of tonal harmony 58
- 5.4 Harmonising a melody 60
- 5.5 Chord inversions 63
- 5.6 Cadences 64

Section 6 — The Composer's Tool Kit 68
- 6.1 Introduction 68
- 6.2 The physical tool kit 68
- 6.3 The mental tool kit 71
- 6.4 Some analogies 72
- 6.5 Some common musical forms 73
- 6.6 Other approaches to form 74
- 6.7 Development 77
- 6.8 Conclusion 79

Section 7 — Thinking Horizontally 80
- 7.1 Introduction 80
- 7.2 Towards a horizontal approach 81
- 7.3 A two-part invention 85
- 7.4 Descants and countermelodies 87
- 7.5 Counterpoint in jazz and jazzy styles 90
- 7.6 Conclusion 95

Section 8 — Instruments and their Characteristics 97
- 8.1 Introduction 97
- 8.2 The woodwind family: 98
    - *The recorder family* 99
    - *The flute family* 100
    - *The oboe family* 102
    - *The clarinet family* 103

		The bassoon family	105
		The saxophone family	106
8.3	The brass family:		109
		The trumpet	110
		The french horn	111
		The tenor trombone	111
		The bass trombone	112
		The tuba	112
8.4	The string family:		113
		The violin	113
		The viola	114
		The cello	114
		The double bass	115
8.5	Plucked stringed instruments:		115
		The harp	116
		The acoustic guitar	116
		The electric guitar	117
		The bass guitar	117
8.6	The percussion family:		118
	Pitched percussion:	The timpani / kettledrums	118
		The xylophone	118
		The glockenspiel	119
		The marimba	119
		The vibraphone	120
		The celeste	120
		Tubular bells	120
		Steel pans	121
	Unpitched / pitched percussion:	Metal	121
		Wood	122
		Skin	122
		The drum kit	122
8.7	Keyboard instruments:		123
	Acoustic:	The acoustic piano	123
		The harpsichord	124
		The pipe organ	124
		The accordion	124
	Electric:	The electric piano	125
		The electronic keyboard	125
		The synthesizer	125
		The electronic organ	125
8.8	The Scottish Highland bagpipes		126

Section 9		**Writing for the Piano**	127
	9.1	Introduction	127
	9.2	Piano notation	128
	9.3	Dealing with more than one part/voice	130
	9.4	A few other issues	131
	9.5	Indicating use of the pedals	131
	9.6	The modern piano:	132
		The grand piano	132
		The upright piano	133
	9.7	Some stylistic 'snapshots':	135
		The 'Classical' period	133
		Romanticism and the piano	135
		Late Romanticism	136
		Diversity in the reaction against romanticism and the movement away from tonality	137
		Nationalism	138
	9.8	The roots of jazz piano:	140
		Barrelhouse and boogie	140
		Ragtime	141
		The evolution of jazz piano	142
	9.9	Modernism: an experiment with the piano	142
	9.10	Piano duet and piano for 6 hands	143
	9.11	A few starting points	143
	9.12	The electronic keyboard	146
Section 10		**Writing for Voices**	148
	10.1	Introduction	148
	10.2	Which comes first? The melody or the lyrics?	148
	10.3	Word-setting	151
	10.4	Vocal ranges	156
	10.5	Scoring	157
	10.6	Interpreting the lyrics	160
	10.7	An so, in conclusion …	161
Section 11		**Adding Important Instructions to Your Score**	163
	11.1	Introduction	163
	11.2	Where words or symbols may be needed	163
	11.3	Tempo and changes of tempo	164
	11.4	A few other useful tempo-related words and symbols	165
	11.5	Dynamics	166
	11.6	Changes of dynamic	167

11.7	Articulation	168
11.8	How *legato* and *staccato* is achieved on different instruments	170
11.9	Further effects possible on some instruments	170
	Arpeggiation	170
	The glissando	171
	Tremolo / Tremolando	171
	Con sordino / sordini	171
	Special effects for bowed strings	172
11.10	Repeats and 'shorthand' signs and symbols	173
11.11	Some Italian terms which indicate style or mood	175

Section 12   Breaking the Rules 177

12.1	Introduction	177
12.2	Changing time signatures during the course of a melody	177
12.3	Introducing 'rogue' notes into a melody	178
12.4	Sudden dynamic changes	179
12.5	Incorporating large interval leaps	179
12.6	Ending on a note other than the tonic	180
12.7	Using chord substitutions	181
12.8	Using parallel intervals	182
12.9	Using chords without 3rds	182
12.10	Using quartal harmony	183
12.11	Using unprepared and unresolved suspensions	184
12.12	Doubling 3rds in major chords	185
12.13	Conclusion	185

Appendices 187

Appendix 1   Understanding Intervals 187
Appendix 2   Commonly Used Chords and Chord Symbols 193
Appendix 3   Understanding Arpeggios 194
Appendix 4   Composing and Arranging Assignments –
                        Some Suggestions 198

Select Bibliography 208

Postscript 209

Glossary 210

Sound Foundations: Introduction

The way in which each of us approaches the process of composing music is probably unique and will depend on a host of factors. Some of these are obvious: our own musical experience, for instance, including our individual cultural background and, not least, our accumulated musical knowledge and expertise.

There are many other factors, of course, and these might include our improvisational skills, whether we are attempting to compose within certain parameters which might dictate form, style or the duration of the piece, or we may be simply producing coursework in order to pass an examination. Whichever is the case we are all, hopefully, highly motivated and our greatest reward [leaving aside the attainment of a good exam grade] will probably be to hear our own music performed and to receive the approval of others.

In Western culture, the word 'composer' tends to summon up a host of preconceptions among those who are 'out of the loop'. Many children, by virtue of their educational experiences, may instantly visualise a bewigged 18th-century gentleman, scratching away with a quill in a candlelit room, on the edge of bankruptcy, and a slave to his art: Mozart, perhaps. All composers in this preconception are dead and seem always to be men.

Part of the purpose of this book, therefore, is to replace misconception with a degree of reality. Mozart is without doubt dead; that much is true, although the products of his intellect are very much alive. He may have relied on candles and quills too, although he did not wear a wig, being financially quite successful enough in his earlier years in Vienna to pay for the daily services of someone else to assist with hairdressing[1]. He also needed to be fashion-conscious and was certainly motivated by financial reward, both of which should sound familiar enough to those who are striving for success in the world of pop and rock today. Professional composers, like everyone else, need to pay the rent or mortgage and eat and drink from time to time!

The truth is that composing is very much alive. The work of today's composers is with us everywhere we go and whatever we do! It is heard in advertising jingles, in film themes and incidental music and in the form of signature tunes for TV shows. Music is composed for video games and for the multimedia presentations of international corporations. It is heard in supermarkets and shopping malls and even in the lift. In fact, high quality reproduction of music is now totally portable through mp3 players and car radios/CD players. Leaving aside the question of the actual artistic value of much of what we are sometimes compelled to hear, it is probably true to say that never has there been more music in the world than there is today!

---

[1] Mozart's letter to his sister: Vienna, 13th February, 1782.

At the height of his success, Mozart might be compared to, say, today's Andrew Lloyd Webber, although this comparison should not be extended too far. Andrew Lloyd Webber has written many highly successful musicals which have brought considerable financial rewards: Mozart was composing, amongst a great deal of other music, successful operas and there is evidence that he was making, at the very least, a reasonable living at one stage of his life. The main point, however, about both of these individuals, and by far the majority of other successful composers is that, apart from their obvious abilities [their talents, for want of a better term], both experienced a thorough grounding in their craft. And this leads us to another purpose of this book which is to provide some of the technical and theoretical 'know-how' which will certainly make the process of composing a lot easier, and which might prove essential if we want others to perform our ideas.

Consequently, a great deal of this 'know-how' is, of necessity, concerned with the notation of music, with or without the aid of music software. A problem encountered by many of us is that we may think of what seems to be a terrific phrase, chord sequence or melody but later, when we re-visit our moment of inspiration, it's gone! For one reason or another, some of the best ideas seem to arrive late at night but when we wake in the morning, we've either forgotten them or we are distracted by another more pressing task – getting ready for school or college or, perhaps, calling the plumber or trying to get the car started. If only we'd written it down on a scrap of manuscript paper or played it into a musice software programme!

Not all music is written down, however. In fact, one could probably argue quite successfully, that by far the majority of music has never been notated or has only been notated after the process of composition had been accomplished. Examples of such un-notated music might include the entire folk repertoire, every form of genuinely improvised music [jazz comes to mind as a good example] and a great deal of studio-evolved rock and pop music where ideas are often contributed by musicians and others involved in the session. One example of this is the piano introduction to the *Beatles*' track *Money*, where George Martin provided the powerful 'R & B'-styled opening. Interestingly, sometimes this multi-composer approach has led to legal battles when a recording has subsequently proved to be lucrative.

So, don't be disheartened if you find yourself struggling with the whole business of notating music. Although we associate the notated copy of a piece of music with the actual music itself [in English we even use the same word to describe both] it's worth bearing in mind that it is what we *hear* that is important! Music notation is the written version of a language which serves many of the same purposes as writing in any other language.

Two further aspects of the composer's 'know-how' are also addressed in this book. The first is contained in a reference section which deals with the capabilities and aural qualities of the vast range of musical instruments which exist today as well as some discussion of how they may work in combination. The sounds of many of these instruments have been included on the CD although, of necessity, these are sampled. Two further specialist sections have also been included which deal with composing for the piano and writing for voices.

Most of us would accept that, although we may well have acquired facility in performing on one or more instruments, none of us can play every instrument. Consequently, details are included on the range of instruments and voices as well as the peculiarities of notating what they play under varying circumstances. In these sections, and elsewhere in the book, we have also provided 'suggested listening' examples. Undoubtedly, there is no substitute for learning through the ear when it comes to gaining musical experience.

The other kind of 'know-how' consists of the composer's tool kit – the devices which can be employed, very often, to extend and develop musical ideas. Many of us will have found that we can think of very attractive musical ideas but are at a loss to handle their evolution in order to create a complete and coherent piece. Early examples of instrumental music exhibit a lack of such developmental devices, resorting to a series of variations on a theme using notes of ever shorter and shorter duration! Mention of this glimpse of musical history brings us, finally, to a number of other aspects of this book.

Firstly, where appropriate, some historical context has been included. This is not, however, primarily a book about musical history and readers who have an interest in historical background will find a wealth of publications to help them extend their knowledge.

Secondly, although many aspects of the theory of music are discussed and explained, such content, within a book of this size and scope, cannot be exhaustive. Again, further reference can readily be obtained from specialist publications or from *reliable* internet sites.

Nevertheless, it is to be hoped that *Sound Foundations* will answer many of the questions which novice composers frequently ask and that it will provide some useful teaching too. Perhaps the most valuable gift that any teacher can give their pupil is inspiration, not only in terms of specific ideas or starting points, but also in helping the pupil to value what they create, no matter how simple.

We would hope that among the many suggestions and musical examples included in this book, the reader will find the inspiration to begin or continue their journey towards fulfilment as a composer.

And remember, if *you* like the sound of what you compose, then maybe others will too.

James Rae and *Mike Cornick*
April, 2009

Acknowledgements

We would like to thank the following who all willingly assisted in the writing of this book:

Tim Barry, Ben Costello, Flora Death, Linda Evans, Simon Gay, Jeremy Gough, Paul Harvey, Ian Haysted and Maitreya Jani.

We would especially like to thank Anne Handley and Mike Breneis of Universal Edition who have offered their advice and editorial skills as well as guiding this project through to completion.

Photographs:
Page 69. Wenger Music Lab Workstation, photo courtesy of Black Cat Music Europe
Page 127. Grand piano photo used with kind permission of Yahama-Kemble (UK) Ltd.

Preface

Although the various sections of this book contain much in the way of advice as well as many suggested exercises and assignments, it has been designed primarily as a source of reference for those who are starting out on the road to becoming composers as well as for those who have already made some progress in that journey. As such, it can be 'dipped into', as and when required, and we hope that answers to many of the reader's questions can easily be found.

We have tried to take very little for granted but, inevitably, a book of this size and scope cannot hope to take account of the various starting points of every imaginable reader. Nevertheless, the real basics of music theory and musical notation have been included and, in many instances, this theoretical knowledge has been extended to a level which goes far beyond the basics.

We have taken the view that composers learn most effectively by studying the works of other composers and, to this end, we have included a great number of notated musical excerpts which can serve as starting points. Many of these notated examples are also recorded on the accompanying CD.

A number of icons appear throughout the book:

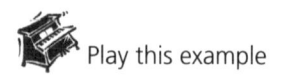

Suggested listening

Play this example

Play the relevant track on the CD

Try this experiment

A glossary has also been included which contains definitions/explanations of technical terms and foreign words and this can be used independently or in conjunction with the text. Words which are included in the Glossary are printed in bold italics.

Finally, it should be kept in mind that, as long as we continue to 'push the boundaries' in our music, the process of learning to compose is likely to last a lifetime. And therein lies its great fascination: there is always something new to achieve and, once we are 'bitten by the bug', the excitement which we feel when embarking on a new piece never goes away.

Notation – the Basics

1.1 Introduction

[N.B. The content of the following subsections on Duration through to Dividing the Beat is substantially reiterated and expanded in Section 3: Understanding Pulse, Time Signatures and Rhythm]

Music, when written down, can at first appear to be a very tough code to crack but, if broken down into its basic elements, is very simple to read and write. Initially, we only need to deal with the first seven letters of the alphabet and counting up to four.
Each note conveys two vital pieces of information:

- How long it sounds – *duration*
- How high it sounds – *pitch*

1.2 Duration

To begin with, we will deal with very basic note values and initially take the crotchet as the unit of *beat* or *pulse*. Therefore:

♩   A crotchet [USA quarter-note] will last for one beat

𝅗𝅥   A minim [USA half-note] will last for two beats

𝅝   A semibreve [USA whole-note] will last for four beats

Extending the duration of the note

There are two basic ways of doing this:

- By using a *tie* which is a curved line connecting two notes of the same pitch:

- By adding a *dot* after the note which extends its length by fifty percent. In this example, the minim which is worth two beats, when dotted, is now worth three:

Dividing the beat

As well as notes which have values that are multiples of the beat, there are also notes which last for fractions of the beat:

♪   The quaver [USA eighth-note] has a duration of half a crotchet [USA quarter-note]

♬   The semiquaver [USA sixteenth-note] has a duration of a quarter of a crotchet [USA quarter-note]

There are notes of shorter duration which you are unlikely to need in the early stages.

Time signatures

Before attempting to write down a rhythm, it is important to think of it in the context of a regular pulse.

Notated music is usually divided into **bars** or **measures** of equal length, marked off with vertical lines called **barlines**. The barlines serve as a visual aid and have no duration in themselves. The length of each bar is determined by the **time signature** which, in turn is, determined by the frequency of the strongly stressed beats.

e.g. If a strong accent or stress occurs on the first of every four beats, then we notate the rhythm in 4-time. If each beat is a crotchet, then this will require a $\frac{4}{4}$ time signature:

4 indicates the number of beats in the bar
4 indicates the note value of the beat, *i.e.* crotchets [USA quarter-notes].

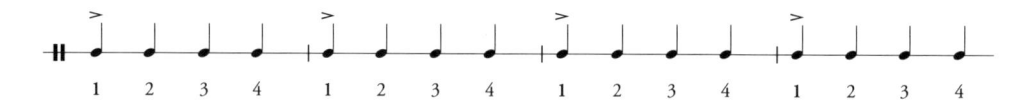

By the same token, the upper figure could be 2, denoting two beats in a bar, or 3 which denotes three beats in a bar and so on.

The lower figure could be 2 denoting minims [USA half-notes], 8 denoting quavers [USA eighth-notes] and so on.

This type of time signature is known as '*simple time*' because the note value of the beat is an un-dotted note rather than a dotted note. For a more detailed examination of time signatures including **compound time**, see *Section 3: Understanding Pulse, Time Signatures and Rhythm*.

Rests

It is equally important to be able to notate silences of equivalent duration to the notes previously shown and for this purpose *rests* are used:

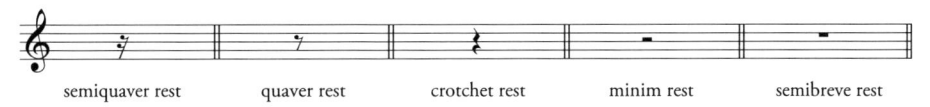

    semiquaver rest   quaver rest   crotchet rest   minim rest   semibreve rest

N.B. Rests, like notes, may also be dotted, thus increasing their value by fifty percent.

e.g. a dotted crotchet rest:

1.3 The notation of pitch

Music has evolved to be written on five parallel lines known as the *staff* or *stave*. Noteheads can be placed on each one of the five lines:

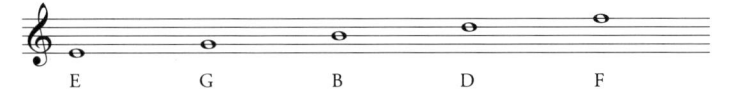

    E   G   B   D   F

Or, in each one of the four spaces:

    F   A   C   E

The pitch of the notes represented on the lines or in the spaces depends on a symbol known as a *clef* which is placed at the beginning of each stave. The clef determines the pitch of the notes on the lines and spaces. The clef used in the previous two examples is known as the *treble* or *G clef*. As its name implies, this clef is generally used to notate pitches from about middle **C** up.

From about middle **C** down, notes are generally written in the *bass clef*.

Lines:

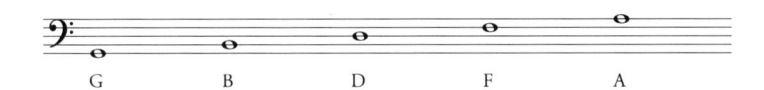

    G   B   D   F   A

Spaces:

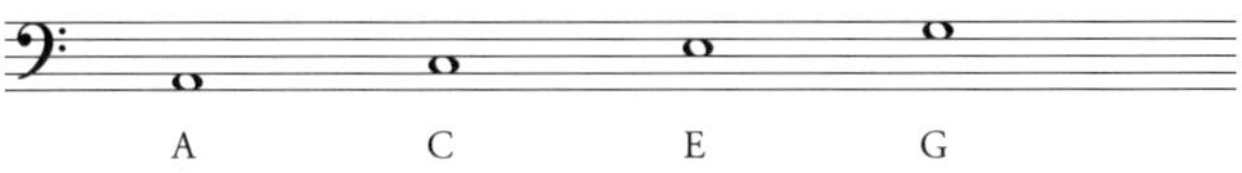

    A   C   E   G

Other clefs exist but these need not concern us in the early stages.

Using a piano stave, we can show how the notes on the bass and treble clefs relate to middle **C** and also to one another:

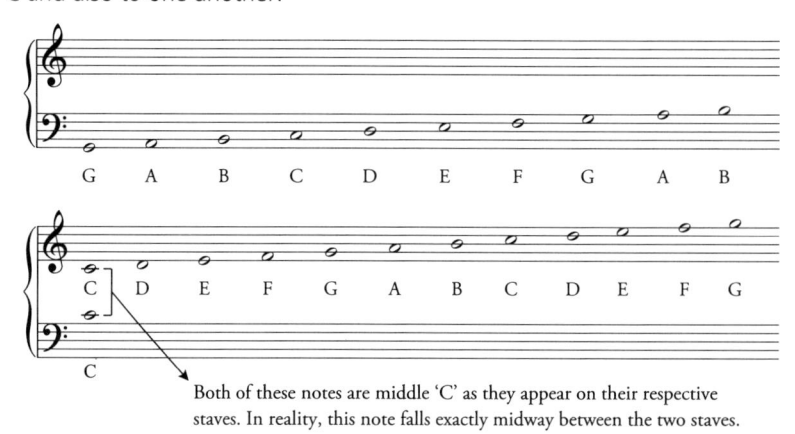

Both of these notes are middle 'C' as they appear on their respective staves. In reality, this note falls exactly midway between the two staves.

Using the stave provides a very convenient means of notating different pitches but, with only five lines and four spaces [together with the possibility of placing a note resting on the top line or hanging from the bottom line] we are limited to eleven pitches. In order to write notes which do not fall on the stave, we can use additional short stave lines specifically for each note which effectively extend the stave up or down. These lines are called *ledger* or *leger lines*.

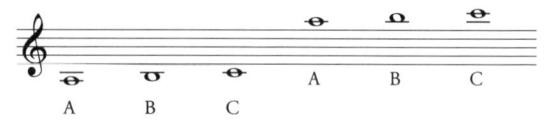

If we want to avoid the excessive use of ledger lines, we can write the relevant passage an octave lower [for notes which would otherwise be on ledger lines above the treble clef] or an octave higher [for notes which would otherwise be on ledger lines below the bass clef] and add an *8va* or *8vb* symbol, followed by a dotted line to indicate how far the instruction extends, as shown below:

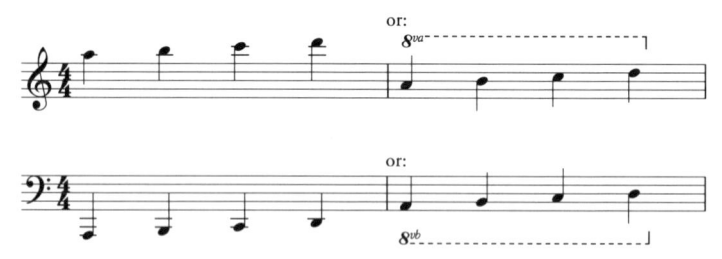

In each of these examples, the first and second bars would sound the same. When we reach the end of an *8va* or *8vb* passage, we use the word *loco* to show that we must return to playing the notes at their written pitch.

Sharp, flat and natural signs

The pitch of a note can be raised or lowered by placing a symbol before it. The following symbols alter the pitch by one *semitone* [*i.e.* the smallest step on an instrument of fixed pitch such as a piano from one note to the next, immediately above or below]:

♯   Sharp sign, which raises the pitch of a note by a semitone

♭   Flat sign, which lowers the pitch of a note by a semitone

♮   Natural sign, which cancels the effect of a sharp or flat sign

These signs are referred to as **accidentals** and stay in effect for the duration of the bar in which they appear unless cancelled by a natural or another accidental.

When sharps or flats appear at the beginning of each line of music, they are described as a **key signature**. Refer to *Section 4: Understanding Key Signatures* for further information. Key signatures remain in force throughout the piece and are not cancelled by barlines.

1.4 A few tips

- When writing musical notation by hand, composers do not generally try to imitate the graphic perfection of printed music by attempting to form perfect noteheads, for instance. With increasing practice, you will evolve your own style of musical 'handwriting', but remember that your intentions must always remain clear.

- When buying manuscript paper, choose a style which has well-spaced staves. Some types of 12-stave manuscript allow insufficient space between the staves for notating piano music very easily.

- When drafting notation, work with a soft pencil and an eraser so that alterations can be made easily. Final copies, which are to be read by performers, may need to be bolder for which an italic-style fibre-tip pen makes a suitable choice.

- When making final handwritten copies, use a ruler to draw lines and try to place barlines underneath one another as you move down the page.

- Take the trouble to observe basic conventions of notation. This might include writing note stems in the correct direction wherever possible [up – if the notehead is below the middle stave line, or down if the notehead is above the middle line; notes on the middle line offer the choice of stems up or down]. *Beaming* [the lines connecting the stems of pairs or groups of quavers, semiquavers, *etc.*] should also follow the direction of the notes and will help the player to see at once whether a passage is ascending or descending.

- There are also well-established conventions concerning the addition of other instructions to your musical notation and many of these are fully explained in *Section 11: Adding Important Instructions to Your Score.*

Finally, it would certainly be well worth looking at printed music copy to see how these conventions should be followed and many of the 'rules' will also be fully explained in a suitable music theory book.

> *Did you know ...*
>
> ... that the round *Sumer is Icumen In* is thought to be the earliest written piece of music, dating from about 1240?
> It is sometimes known as the *Reading Rota* because its manuscript originated at Reading Abbey.

Composition: Getting Started

2.1 Introduction

Very frequently, the starting point for a composition is a melodic idea [*i.e.* a tune]. The melody may not be complete and it may exist without reference to a particular instrument or voice. The composer may or may not be aware of its harmonic implications and sometimes, not even its eventual style or mood. In the mind of the composer, it may not even belong to a particular key or scale, but the important thing is – that it exists!

It is at this point when students frequently make a remark such as, 'I can't compose!'

Don't despair! You already *have* composed, even if it's only a fragment. Your problem may be that you can't finish or extend your idea or, perhaps, because your fragment of a melody is not attached to a musical context, you may be finding it difficult to imagine how it could take its place in a finished piece. Some students attempt to carry their musical idea around in their heads which might be fine for an accomplished composer, but makes progress very difficult for the relative beginner.

Our first task, then, is to record the idea, either quite literally as an audio recording, or to try to notate it; otherwise, it may soon be gone! This is a point of such fundamental importance that it is reiterated at several key points in the book.

If you can't notate it [*i.e.* write it down] yourself, then try to get someone to do it for you. Eventually, you will need to develop the skills to notate music yourself and, for this purpose, it may be helpful to look at *Section 1: Notation – the Basics* to get you started. If you can persuade a teacher or a friend who has a good grasp of musical notation to go through this with you, then so much the better.

If you are fortunate enough to have access to a music IT workstation and have developed some skill in its use, then this first stage of recording your work may not be too much of an obstacle. Frequent reference to the usefulness of such a set-up is made throughout this book and the subject is discussed in greater detail in *Section 6: The Composer's Tool Kit*.

But the important thing is that, once recorded, and especially if it's notated, you and others can access your idea and build on it.

2.2 Placing your melody within a scale

Although you may have arrived at your melody or fragment quite intuitively [or, indeed, through improvising vocally or on an instrument – an approach which is discussed later in this section], it may still be very useful to adopt a slightly more analytical approach to melody. Admittedly, many great melodies have been 'written' by composers who have never read a theory book or received any tuition in their lives. And that's fine, just as long as your intuitive approach is serving you well. But even an entirely intuitive approach can only be strengthened by the acquisition of some knowledge, and it is certainly worthwhile taking a look at how melodies can be constructed.

So, first of all, what is a melody? An obvious question you might think, but quite a difficult word to define. Nevertheless, here is a possible definition:

A melody is a succession of notes of various pitches which makes musical sense to the listener.

Why a melody should make musical sense is really the key point in this rather incomplete definition. The answer to that question really lies in the composer and the listener sharing their musical culture to some extent. Western musical culture has evolved, at least until comparatively recently, so that it uses the language of *tonality*, and that implies, as far as pitch is concerned, the predominance of *major* and *minor* scales. In fact, tonality continues to rule in the world of Western popular music and in a great deal of other music too. If you are not familiar with major and minor scales, this subject is discussed in detail in *Section 4: Understanding Key Signatures* and in *Section 5: Understanding Harmony*.

So, looking at your melody or fragment, one essential decision to make is whether its notes are drawn from a major or minor scale or, indeed, from some other scale altogether.

2.3 The importance of rhythm in a melody

Of equal importance to the succession of notes in a melody is its *rhythm*. Rhythm arises when sounds of different durations [lengths] follow one another. Very often, the character of a melody depends very much on the repetition of such patterns. The point is very easily demonstrated by taking the rhythm out of a well-known tune. For instance, identifying this example may be quite difficult:

Track 1

Equally, we may not recognise it from the rhythm alone:

[Track 1 - musical notation]

But when both pitch and rhythm are combined, we'll probably recognise it as Wagner's famous *Bridal March*:

[Track 1 - musical notation]

One of the reasons why this melody is so memorable is the repeated rhythmic phrase and this is true of many different styles of music ranging from **Baroque** to **Rock**.

So, a 'catchy' rhythm, when repeated, can give your melody a recognisable character. As we will mention again in later sections of this book, repetition helps the music to 'teach itself' to the listener.

2.4 Melodic structure

Another aspect of melody which will help to make it memorable and easily understood is its structure. To make this subject a little easier to discuss, it's usual to label sections of a melody with letter names: A, B, C, *etc*. The verse of the well-known tune *Rule, Britannia*, illustrates a commonly used structure which might serve as a useful model:

Rule, Britannia   Thomas Arne

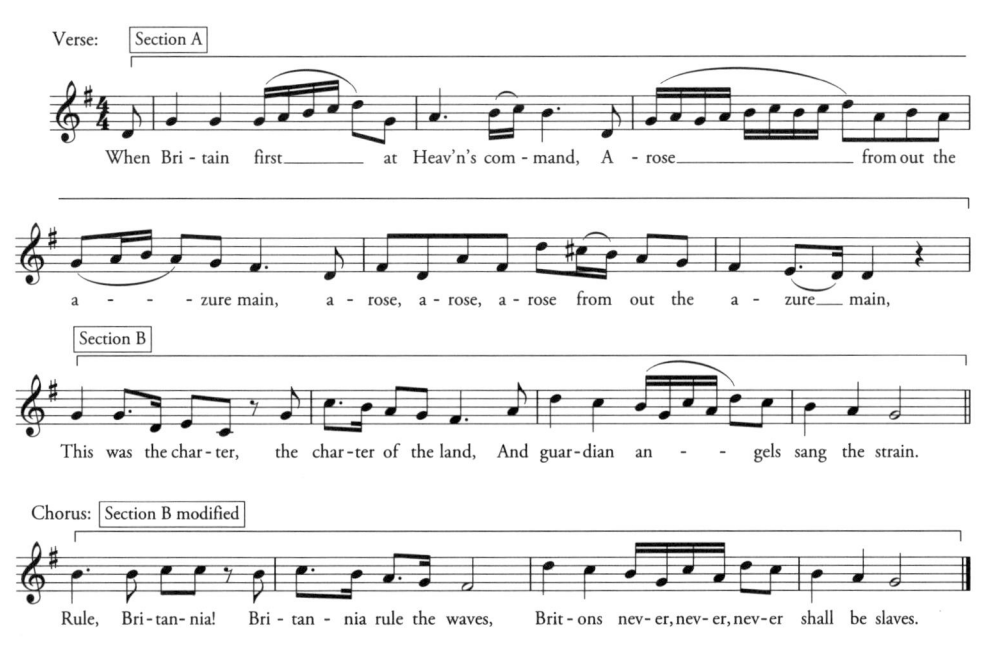

[Track 2 - musical notation]

Verse: Section A
When Bri-tain first___ at Heav'n's com-mand, A-rose___ from out the a - - - zure main, a-rose, a-rose, a-rose from out the a - zure___ main,

Section B
This was the char-ter, the char-ter of the land, And guar-dian an - - gels sang the strain.

Chorus: Section B modified
Rule, Bri-tan-nia! Bri-tan - nia rule the waves, Brit-ons nev-er, nev-er, nev-er shall be slaves.

21

- Section A begins in the *tonic* ['home'] key of **G** major and *modulates* [changes key] to **D** major – the *dominant* – a new key with **D** as its key note. The key of the dominant [*i.e.* the key which has the 5th note of the original key as its new tonic] is the most closely related to the tonic. Notice the added **C♯** in bar 5 which leads the melody into the new key.

All modulation will involve the use of one or more *accidentals*. Once again, the subject of key signatures is fully explained in Section *4: Understanding Key Signatures*

- Section B begins, once more, in the tonic, briefly visits the dominant [Bar 8] and then returns to the tonic.

- Sections A and B, together, make up the verse and can be described as *binary form*.

- The chorus consists of a modified Section B, starting and ending in the tonic key.

- The structure of verse followed by chorus is then repeated with changing words. This overall pattern is described by the word *strophic*.

Binary form is just one of many other more complex forms, some of which are referred to later in this book. Interestingly, song writers, especially of popular songs, have their own vocabulary to describe formal structure and, should you wish to explore this a little further, there are many websites which deal with the subject.

So, to sum up, a strong rhythmic idea, probably repeated in the context of a clear structure will help your melody to be effective and memorable.

2.5 Using sequence in a melody

A *sequence* is a specific kind of repetition where a phrase or fragment of a phrase is repeated, perhaps several times, at different pitches. The sequence may ascend or descend, and will almost certainly include some modification in each repetition. A very familiar use of sequence occurs in the refrain of the Christmas carol *Ding! Dong! Merrily on High*:

Ding! Dong! Merrily on High [refrain] Thoinot Arbeau [1520–1595]

Track 3

Sequence is a very useful melody-building tool and, once you are aware of the device, you will hear it in countless pieces of music in a variety of musical styles. The list of pieces would be a very long one, but here is just a start:

Flute Sonata V in F [Giga *e.g.* bars 3 & 4, 16–18] – G. F. Handel
Sonata in C, KV 545 [first movement; bars 4–8] – W. A. Mozart
Take Five [middle eight] – Paul Desmond
The Winner Takes It All [chorus] – ABBA
Ob-La-Di, Ob-La-Da [verse]– Lennon & McCartney
How Deep Is Your Love? [verse] – Barry, Robin & Maurice Gibb

A very sophisticated use of sequence can be seen in the following excerpt from Tchaikovsky's *Fantasy Overture: Romeo and Juliet*:

Love Theme from Fantasy Overture: Romeo and Juliet Pyotr Il'yich Tchaikovsky [1840–1893]

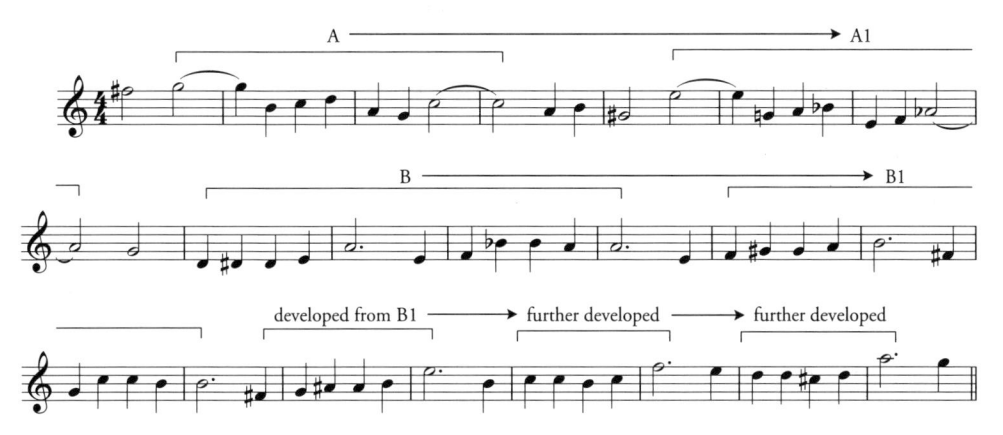

Here, sequential repetition is by no means exact, with modification and development occurring throughout. However, the listener is still aware of the sequential nature of the theme which, as a consequence, displays a kind of organic development.
This theme is referred to again in the context of programme music in *Section 6: The Composer's Tool Kit*.

2.6 Phrase and answer – call and response

Another way of looking at melody writing is to think in terms of *phrase* and answering phrase. Such a pattern occurs quite naturally and probably, originally, quite spontaneously in many Afro-American and Afro-Caribbean songs. Many of these songs originated as work songs or in religious celebrations where this style of singing can still be heard. In a religious context, a solo voice [the preacher] will sing the *call* and the *response* will be made by the congregation.

Mary Had a Baby Medium swing tempo; Trad. Afro-American

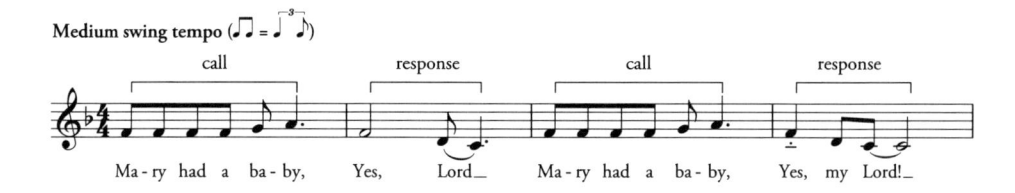

[Musical notation: "Mary had a baby, Yes, Lord. Mary had a baby, Yes, my Lord! Mary had a baby, Yes, Lord! Well the people keep a-comin' but the train done gone!" with call and response markings]

Not surprisingly, the call-and-response pattern is also frequently to be found in jazz which is a genre which evolved from the same roots. For example:

Suggested Listening:
Moanin' – Bobby Timmons
Don't Get Around Much Anymore – Ellington
Things Ain't What They Used to Be – Ellington
So What – Miles Davis

2.7 Improvisation

Although, as suggested earlier in this section, we may be lucky enough to think of melodies easily, very often the creative process may need a little stimulus. If we are composing a melody which is in a particular style, we may find it helpful to improvise our way in and this suggests some possible approaches:

- Playing along with an existing recording, or setting up a suitable accompaniment using software or an electronic keyboard set to the appropriate style will probably lead to some usable phrases and possibly some which we will reject.

- Competent pianists may be able to play an accompaniment with the left hand whilst improvising melodic ideas with the right.

- 'Jamming' along with other musicians in a live band session has certainly led to the origin of many jazz and rock compositions and is a great way to start if the opportunity arises.

For those who are keen to develop their improvisational skills, the following tracks have been included from two other publications.

Pentafunk from *Jazz Zone* by James Rae [© Copyright 2009 by Universal Edition (London) Ltd., UE 21 030]

This is a piano, bass and drums backing track for a modal extended blues piece with a rock feel in the key of **C** minor.

Use this C minor pentatonic scale as a basis for your improvisation over the track *Pentafunk*

Mix and Match Blues from *Jazz Improvisation for Piano and Keyboard* by Mike Cornick [© Copyright 1996 by Universal Edition (London) Ltd., UE 14050]

Track 7

This is a bass and drum backing track for a 12-bar blues in swing style in the key of **C**. There is a 2 bar 'lead-in' followed by 4 choruses of the blues chord sequence [see *Appendix 4: More Advanced Assignments 2*].

Use this blues scale on C as a basis for your improvisation over the track *Mix and Match Blues*

Jazz Zone [available for trumpet, flute, clarinet and saxophones] contains many more examples of pre-recorded backing tracks which are suitable for improvisation.

Jazz Improvisation for Piano and Keyboard is a step-by-step guide to playing the blues with pre-recorded backing tracks.

2.8 Making some important decisions

Once you have a complete melody it will be difficult to proceed any further without settling some rather important questions about the direction you want to take. Some of these decisions are interdependent, and might be taken in a number of different orders, but they may well include:

- How is the melody to be harmonised?

- Are you going to add lyrics and develop the piece into a song?

or:

- Is it going to become an instrumental piece?

and if so:

- Is it a solo piece or will you be combining instruments in a group?

if so:

- For what combination of instruments is it to be scored?

- Is there a real possibility of hearing a live performance of your piece?
- Will you need to extend the form of the piece by adding other sections?
- Will the piece contain any development of your original melody?
- Does your melody suggest a certain style?

and, if so:

- What are the main characteristics of that style and would it be helpful to listen to or, perhaps, look at some examples of that style?

or:

- Would it be a good idea to model your piece on an existing one?
- In straightforward notational or recording terms, how or, perhaps, even where are you going to build your piece? Do you already have the skills to write out your piece by hand?

or, if not:

- Will you have access to computer hardware and software to construct your piece?

and, in both cases:

- Can you get help when you need it?

2.9 Where to look for help

If you are a pupil or student in a school or college, then practical help may be at hand; your teacher/tutor will be able to offer advice or, if you're developing your skills yourself, you may find a friend who will share their knowledge with you. But, as a composer, you're very often 'on your own' when it comes to making many of the sorts of decisions which we have outlined above and the various sections of this book have been written to specifically address these questions.

So, here's a guide which should help you to find some answers:

Harmonising your melody:	go to *Section 5: Understanding Harmony*
Writing a song:	go to *Section 10: Writing for Voices*
Choice of instrument(s):	go to *Section 8: Instruments and Their Characteristics*
Form and development and how and where to build your piece	go to *Section 6: The Composer's Tool Kit* and *Section 12: Breaking the Rules*

Deciding on style: The many suggested listening examples will help you to develop a sense of style, and *Section 9: Writing for the Piano* contains a number of stylistic snapshots.

2.10 Conclusion

Remember, performing and composing are related activities. Don't be afraid of looking at the pieces you play, whatever their style, from a compositional angle.

And don't forget that every single piece of music which you hear or see began life in the mind of a composer or composers and may well have developed from the music which they played or heard.

> *Did you know …*
>
> … that Ludwig van Beethoven lived at about sixty addresses during his time in Vienna, all of them rented and sometimes more than one at a time?
> If you're visiting Vienna, go to the House of Music where you can see a map showing their locations.

Understanding Pulse, Time Signatures and Rhythm

3.1 Introduction

Pulse and rhythm are the lifeblood of music. Arguably, you could remove virtually any other element – melody, harmony or dynamics, for instance – and, as long as rhythm remains, you could still be left with a musical experience. 'Rap' is a genre which, in some instances, illustrates this. The essentials of 'rap' consist of a powerful underlying drum pattern, usually sequenced, with cross-rhythms arising through the spoken 'rap'. Admittedly, this is often relieved by the use of intermittent *riffs* and the drum pattern is reinforced with a powerful bass line.

An understanding of rhythm begins with the concept of a regular *pulse* or *beat*, and these words immediately suggest an analogy with the heartbeat and pulse of the human body.

A heartbeat rate and the speed or *tempo* of a piece of music are both measured in *bpm* – beats per minute.

Interestingly, the range of the human pulse or heartbeat rate compares, very roughly, with the range of tempi commonly heard in music:

e.g. [and don't take these figures too literally – in reality, there are reasons for considerable variation] an average adult resting heartbeat might fall into the range of 60–80 beats per minute.

During exertion, this rate will rise appreciably to, perhaps, 150–160 beats per minute, or maybe more in the case of a sprinter.

The main point to grasp here is that however much the number of beats per minute may vary, we would hope that those beats would be regular. That is to say, they will occur at equal time intervals. Of course, we know that this will not be strictly true because these rates are constantly adapting to the demands made on the heart and, similarly, a piece of music may slow down or speed up. But, for the moment, let's assume that the number of bpm remains constant, at least for a short period of time.

The pattern of a heartbeat can be shown as a graph [an ECG] like the one in the following ilustration and, although it would take a medical specialist to make sense of this in detail, we can see a regularity in its pattern.

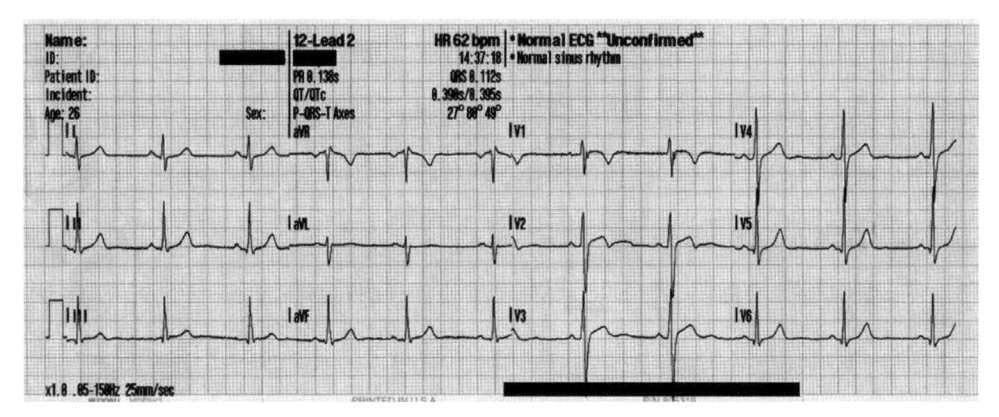

3.2 Writing a rhythm and using software

Writing down a rhythm can certainly be problematic but it is a skill which can be improved through practice. A music software programme can provide help here and will allow you to 'play in' a musical phrase against a *click track* [a regular pulse provided by the programme, the speed or tempo of which can be set by the user] but, as we have constantly reiterated throughout this book, it will not perform miracles.

If you are interested in the notated printout of your music, you may well need to determine the time signature beforehand and you will also need to play with great rhythmic accuracy, not only placing the notes precisely in time but maintaining their durations.

You can, of course, make corrections to your 'played-in' phrases afterwards, possibly by *quantizing* [i.e. deciding on the shortest duration that you want the programme to recognise] and/or correcting the notation as it appears on the screen.

However, whether or not you use music software as you compose, an understanding of time signatures and the standard practices of notating rhythm can only prove helpful in the long run.

3.3 To begin with the basics – notating a regular pulse

[N.B. Some of the information in this section is first discussed in *Section 1: Notation – the Basics* and readers with no previous experience of reading or writing musical notation may wish to study this earlier section again]

We can write a regularly recurring sound in musical notation using a sequence of notes of the same duration, and although, theoretically, these could be of any value, we'll choose crotchets [or in the USA, quarter-notes] in the first instance:

Track 8

If the playing of each of these crotchets is absolutely equal in all respects, then we have no time signature.

3.4 Simple time signatures

But if we begin to *accent* some of these crotchets in a regular pattern, say the first of every four, or three, or two, then we have produced a sequence of sounds which can be notated with a time signature, so that:

Track 8

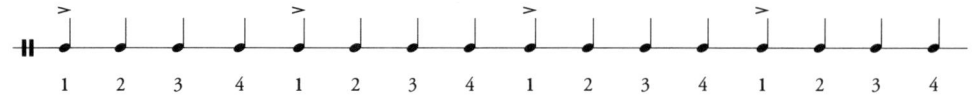

1 2 3 4 1 2 3 4 1 2 3 4 1 2 3 4

… suggests a time signature with a top figure of 4:

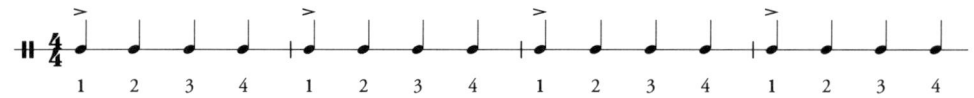

1 2 3 4 1 2 3 4 1 2 3 4 1 2 3 4

This pattern:

Track 8

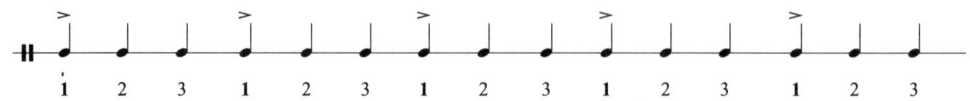

1 2 3 1 2 3 1 2 3 1 2 3 1 2 3

… suggests a time signature with a top figure of 3:

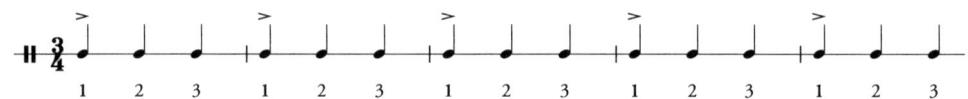

1 2 3 1 2 3 1 2 3 1 2 3 1 2 3

And this pattern:

Track 8

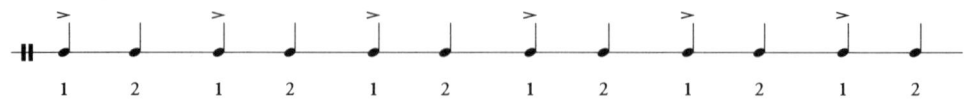

1 2 1 2 1 2 1 2 1 2 1 2

… suggests a time signature with a top figure of 2:

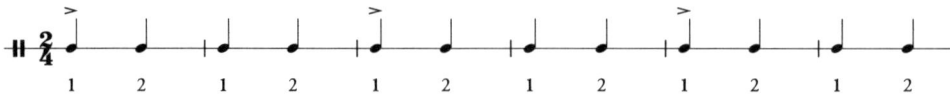

1 2 1 2 1 2 1 2 1 2 1 2

Understanding Pulse, Time Signatures and Rhythm

You will have noticed, too, that each of the sets of four, three or two crotchets has been separated with a vertical line. This is called a barline and marks off the notated music into equal bars [or in the USA: measures].

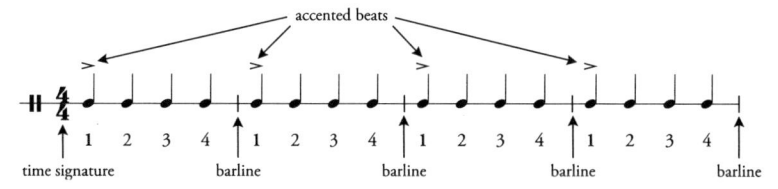

Now, each of these time signatures is described as being *simple*. This does not imply that they are necessarily simple to understand but that the beat or pulse is an un-dotted note – a crotchet in these instances.

The top figure tells us the number of beats in each bar or measure: some may also use the terminology *duple, triple* or *quadruple*.

But what about the bottom figure? This tells us which value of note has been chosen to represent the beat or pulse, as follows:

2 means a minimum beat

4 means a crotchet beat

8 means a quaver beat

So, why choose any note other than a crotchet to represent the value of the beat in simple time signatures? Given that the way in which we notate music should always be governed by the principle of making it as easy as possible to read, there are, sometimes, choices to be made when notating the same musical idea.

In the sphere of rhythmic notation, there is no aural difference between this example:

Away in a Manger W. J. Kirkpatrick

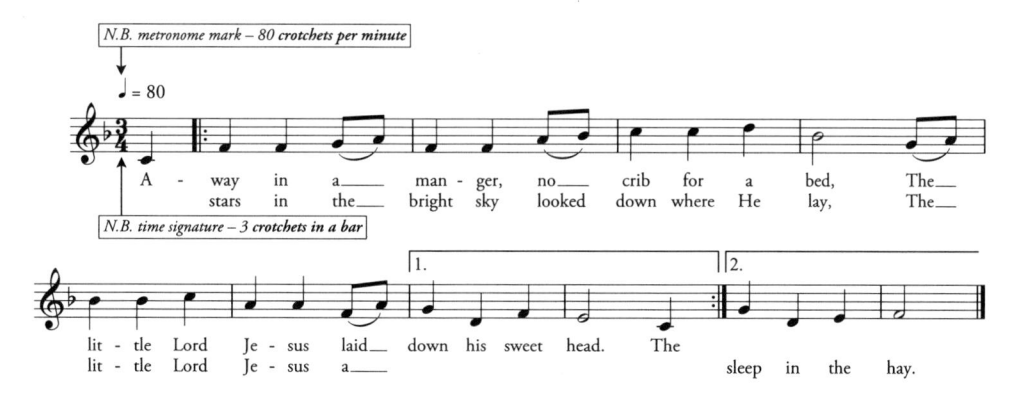

and this one ...

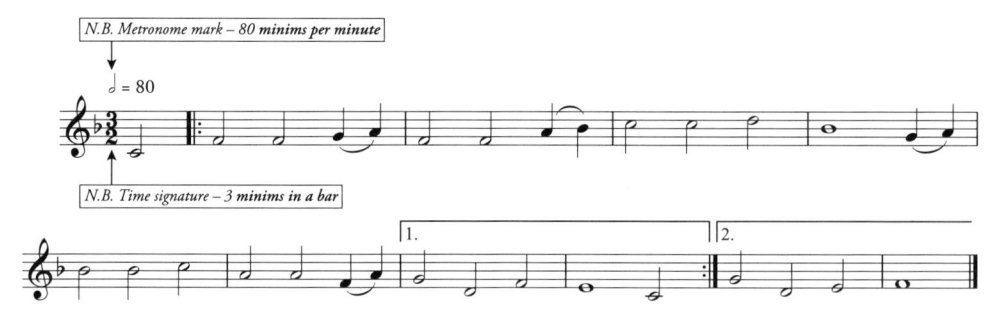

N.B. Metronome mark – 80 minims per minute

𝅗𝅥 = 80

N.B. Time signature – 3 minims in a bar

... provided that, in the case of the second example, we take the minim as our pulse/beat instead of crotchets.

3.5 The metronome

At this point, it would be useful to introduce a device known as the **metronome**. This device, invented by Johann Maelzel [1772–1838] in the time of Beethoven, provides the composer and performer with an exact measure of the tempo of a piece – *i.e.* the speed of the beat in bpm.

The clockwork version illustrated here has, of course, been superseded by electronic versions which don't need to stand on a level surface to work properly and some are almost as small as a credit card (although their sound may not be very loud). Many digital pianos and electronic keyboards now also have an in-built electronic click track which serves the same purpose.

With the use of a metronome mark [shown as M.M. ♩ = 120, for example, or more commonly these days, ♩ = 120] we can determine the exact tempo [the speed of the pulse or beat] whenever required.

The note which is chosen to be given a bpm value in a metronome mark is usually that of the bottom figure of a simple time signature. Occasionally, when the tempo of a piece is very slow, a note of half that value might be given. *e.g.* in $\frac{4}{4}$ where the value of the beat is a crotchet, the metronome mark might be given in quavers.

3.6 Table of common simple time signatures

So, to summarise, the following table gives the most commonly encountered simple time signatures.

N.B. the time signature $\frac{4}{4}$ is sometimes represented by the sign C, and $\frac{2}{2}$ by the sign: ¢

Value of beat	Common Simple Time Signatures		
	Duple	Triple	Quadruple
♪	$\frac{2}{8}$	$\frac{3}{8}$	$\frac{4}{8}$
♩	$\frac{2}{4}$	$\frac{3}{4}$	$\frac{4}{4}$ or C
𝅗𝅥	$\frac{2}{2}$ or ¢	$\frac{3}{2}$	$\frac{4}{2}$

Of course, other simple time signatures are used:

Signatures with odd-numbered upper figures like $\frac{5}{4}$ and $\frac{7}{8}$ are not unusual: $\frac{5}{4}$ tends to fall into $\frac{3}{4} + \frac{2}{4}$ or $\frac{2}{4} + \frac{3}{4}$ pattern and $\frac{7}{8}$ into $\frac{4}{8} + \frac{3}{8}$ or $\frac{3}{8} + \frac{4}{8}$ pattern.

Suggested Listening:

For those who enjoy jazz, Paul Desmond's *Take Five* [The Dave Brubeck Quartet – from the album: *Time Further Out*] is a good example of $\frac{5}{4}$ time. Tchaikovsky enthusiasts might prefer the 2nd movement of his 6th Symphony.

3.7 Dividing the beat in simple time

In simple time, the note duration chosen to represent the beat is always a straightforward un-dotted note – a quaver, crotchet or minim for instance. The division of these note values by 2, 4, 8 *etc.* can easily be notated.

In the following three examples, the crotchet beat is divided [by 2] into quavers. The quavers are joined together by a line connecting their stems which is called a **beam**. Joining notes of quaver or shorter duration is called *grouping*:

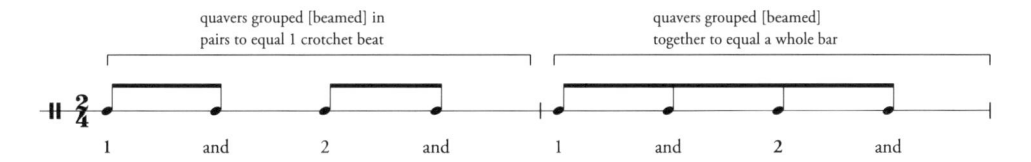

quavers grouped [beamed] in pairs to equal 1 crotchet beat

quavers grouped [beamed] together to equal a whole bar

1 and 2 and 1 and 2 and

Understanding Pulse, Time Signatures and Rhythm

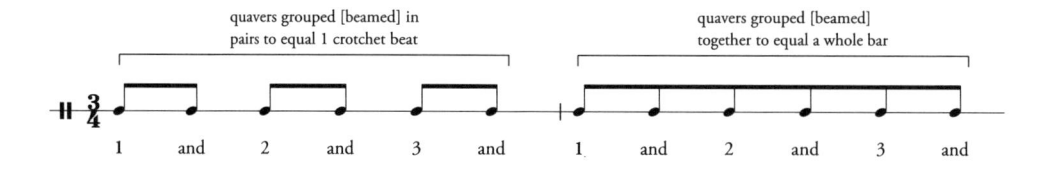

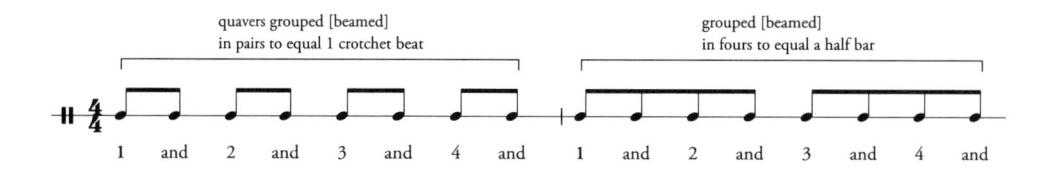

[Musical notation in 3/4 showing quavers grouped (beamed) in pairs to equal 1 crotchet beat, and quavers grouped (beamed) together to equal a whole bar, counted "1 and 2 and 3 and | 1 and 2 and 3 and"]

[Musical notation in 4/4 showing quavers grouped (beamed) in pairs to equal 1 crotchet beat, and grouped (beamed) in fours to equal a half bar, counted "1 and 2 and 3 and 4 and | 1 and 2 and 3 and 4 and"]

The quaver can be further subdivided [by 2 again] into semiquavers [two beams] and you may wish to write rhythms which use both:

[Musical notation in 4/4 showing semiquavers grouped (beamed) in fours to equal 1 crotchet beat, or mixed in various combinations of quavers and semiquavers with each group equalling one crotchet beat]

Similarly, the semiquaver can be further divided [by 2 once more] into demisemiquavers [three beams] and you may wish to notate rhythms using these, usually in combination with other fractional note values:

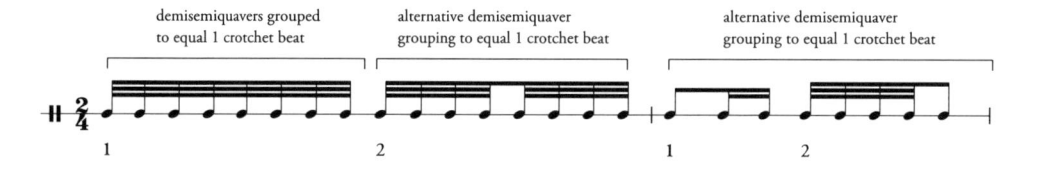

[Musical notation in 2/4 showing demisemiquavers grouped to equal 1 crotchet beat, alternative demisemiquaver grouping to equal 1 crotchet beat, and alternative demisemiquaver grouping to equal 1 crotchet beat]

There are conventions which govern the way in which fractional notes are grouped/beamed in simple time signatures and these are summarised as follows:

- In 2/4 and 3/4 time signatures, entire bars of quavers can be grouped or beamed together.
- In 4/4 time, group quavers to equal a minim – a half bar.
- Notes of shorter duration should be grouped to add up to one beat although demisemiquavers can be grouped to add up to a quaver which makes the notation easier to read.

Dotted rhythms are governed by the same rules and it is worth remembering that dotted notes should be used in preference to ties where possible, always aiming for ease of reading. For instance:

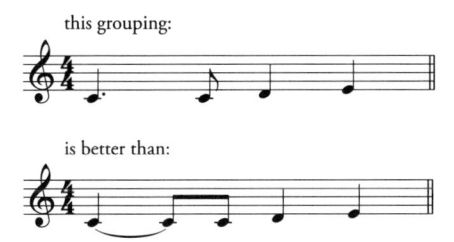

this grouping:

is better than:

The permutations which could arise in combining these notes of different values is vast, and a useful exercise is to write out a series of bars, in $\frac{4}{4}$ say, increasing the complexity of the rhythm from one bar to the next. However, you will probably want to restrict yourself to crotchets, quavers and semiquavers, although dotted rhythms will extend the range of possibilities considerably! [see *Appendix 4: Composing and Arranging Assignments* for a fuller description of this exercise]

Remember, too, that the silences in music are just as important as the sounds, so you could incorporate rests as well [see *Section 1: Notation – the Basics* for a reminder of how to notate rests of different durations].

It is equally important to keep in mind that notation represents real sounds – rhythms, in this instance – and that we should be able to clap or tap the rhythms which we are writing.

If, exceptionally, we want to notate a division of the beat by three in simple time [known as a *triplet*], we have to indicate this division as follows:

A crotchet divided by three:

A minim divided by three:

Other exceptional divisions of the beat can also be notated in a similar way, as, for example, in this excerpt from a Chopin *Nocturne* [No. 5 in F♯ major]:

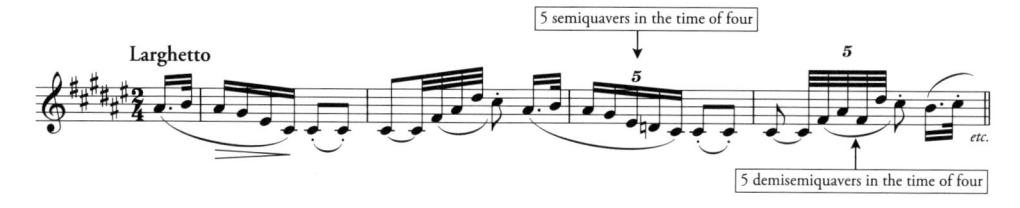

5 semiquavers in the time of four = one beat: a crotchet in this instance.

5 demisemiquavers in the time of four = half of a beat: a quaver in this instance.

3.8 Compound time signatures

In compound time, the note duration chosen to represent the beat is always a dotted note [thus, the term *compound*] – a dotted quaver, a dotted crotchet or a dotted minim. So, why do we need compound time signatures?

The answer, once again, lies in notating music so that it is most easily read and understood. If we are notating music where the beat is most frequently divided into halves, quarters, eighths, *etc.*, then we will probably choose a simple time signature. Exceptional divisions, such as the triplet, will then have to be indicated, as previously shown.

If, on the other hand, the piece principally involves divisions of the beat by three, six *etc.*, then the choice is probably going to be a compound time signature.

Therefore, a regular pulse or beat, in compound time, might well be notated in dotted crotchets:

Of course, we might equally well have chosen dotted minims or even dotted quavers for this example.

Now, just as with simple time signatures, the compound time signatures will also be determined by the pattern of accentuation of the pulse or beat – in twos = duple time, threes = triple time and fours = quadruple time [again, as an example, using dotted crotchets as the pulse or beat]:

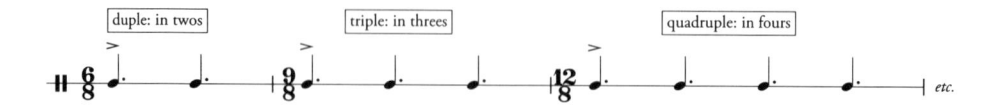

Understanding Pulse, Time Signatures and Rhythm

The difficulty in understanding compound time signatures arises from the fact that, unlike simple time signatures, the top figure does not usually tell us the number of beats in the bar and, similarly, the bottom figure does not usually tell us the value of the beat[1].

In a $\frac{6}{8}$ time signature, for instance, the bar will certainly contain six quavers [with, again, the lower figure of 8 = quavers] but, because these are accentuated and grouped in threes, this results in a duple time signature of two dotted crotchet beats in a bar.

It all sounds very difficult in theory, but very obvious when you hear it .

Take the well-known children's nursery rhyme *Hickory, Dickory Dock*, for example, which has a clear pulse of two beats in a bar. Because the pulse or beat is most frequently divided by three, the most obvious way to notate the song is in compound duple time:

If we were to notate this in simple duple time, we would need to mark the triple divisions of the beat as triplets which would be impractical:

Of course, if we were to notate the song in $\frac{3}{4}$ [simple triple time] we would produce a version which sounded like a waltz, which might make a nice variation, but is a different result altogether:

---

[1] In a very slow tempo, $\frac{6}{8}$ is counted in 6, $\frac{9}{8}$ in 9 and $\frac{12}{8}$ in 12 beats per bar.

[Musical notation: "Hickory dickory dock" in 3/4 time]

Returning, once more, to a duple compound time notation, we could also have chosen to notate the piece in $\frac{6}{4}$ or $\frac{6}{16}$, but these would be very unlikely choices and would almost certainly prove quite puzzling to the performer. The following example illustrates a $\frac{6}{4}$ notation [compound duple time with the dotted minim as the beat]:

[Musical notation: "Hickory dickory dock" in 6/4 time]

Just as in simple time, the beat will often be further divided [into semiquavers, *etc.*] and dotted rhythms will often occur. The general rule with regard to grouping is to beam notes together which belong to one beat [the dotted crotchet in $\frac{6}{8}$ time] – see example below.

The exceptional division of the beat in compound time is the *duplet* where the beat is divided by two. This is also illustrated in the following example:

[Musical notation in 6/8 time showing duplet and semiquavers]

3.9 Table of common compound time signatures

So, to summarise, the table below shows compound time signatures based on the dotted quaver, dotted crotchet and dotted minim:

Value of beat	Compound Time Signatures		
	Duple	Triple	Quadruple
♪.	6/16	9/16	12/16
♩.	6/8	9/8	12/8
𝅗𝅥.	6/4	9/4	12/4

> *Did you know …*
>
> … that the dramatic cantata *The Whale* by John Tavener [b. 1944] makes use of such diverse 'musical' elements as amplified metronomes, sanctus bells, pre-recorded tape and a football rattle?
>
> Several performers are also required to shout through loud hailers, one of whom on the 1970 Apple label recording was Ringo Starr who, according to the CD sleeve notes, calls out "… and cause suffocation".
>
> Incidentally, the blue whale is said to be the loudest living creature producing sounds that can reach 188 decibels and which travel for vast distances underwater.

4

Understanding Key Signatures

4.1 Introduction

Perhaps the easiest starting point for understanding key signatures is to look at the layout of the piano keyboard.

This layout was not invented at a stroke, of course, but evolved through pre-tonal times when *modes* served the purposes which, today, are fulfilled by a wide range of scales.

Early keyboards consisted only of the equivalent of the white keys on today's instruments, and consequently, it is possible to reproduce the modes on the modern keyboard.

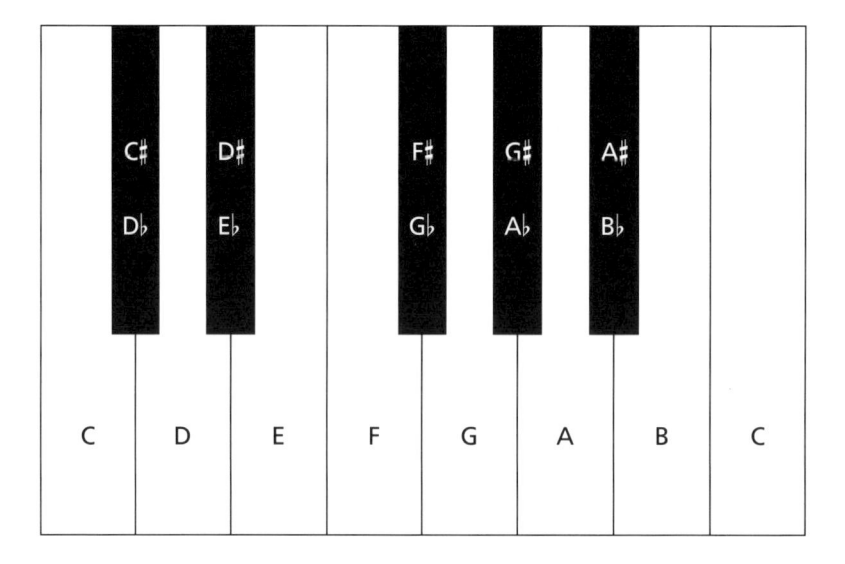

This present arrangement of black and white keys [as illustrated above] has been in existence since about the mid-15th century and represents a compromise between likely hand spans, the width of individual keys, and the assimilation of pitches to create 12 intervals.

And so, between middle **C**, say, and the **C** one octave higher, there are 12 intervals called *semitones*, as follows:

C to C♯/ D♭

C♯/ D♭ to D

D to D♯/ E♭

Understanding Key Signatures

D♯/ E♭ to E

E to F

F to F♯/ G♭

F♯/ G♭ to G

G to G♯/ A♭

G♯/ A♭ to A

A to A♯/ B♭

A♯/ B♭ to B

B to C

As the majority of the modes in most genres of Western European music gradually fell into disuse, two survived rising in prominence to become our major [Ionian] and minor [Aeolian] scales.

4.2 Major keys

The example given below is the major scale beginning on **C**:

N.B. an interval which encompasses two semitones is known as a ***tone.***

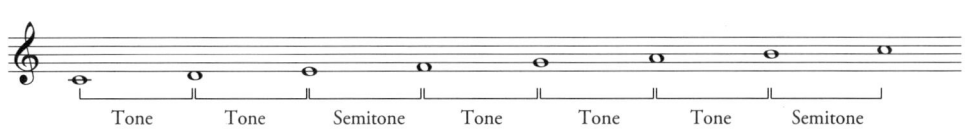

Tone   Tone   Semitone   Tone   Tone   Tone   Semitone

This sequence of tones and semitones is, therefore a kind of formula for the creation of a major scale.

Tone   Tone   Semitone   Tone   Tone   Tone   Semitone

And so, on whichever note we choose to begin a major scale, we will need to follow the formula – this exact sequence of tones and semitones.

For example, if we begin our major scale on the note **G**, we now need to substitute an **F♯** for the note **F**:

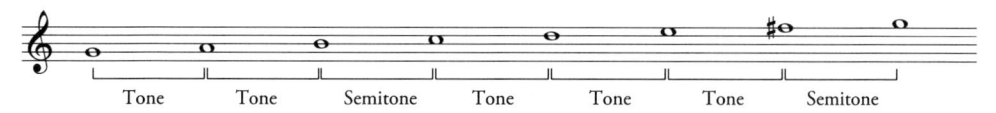

Tone | Tone | Semitone | Tone | Tone | Tone | Semitone

Similarly, if we begin our major scale on the note **F**, we need to substitute a **B♭** for the note **B**:

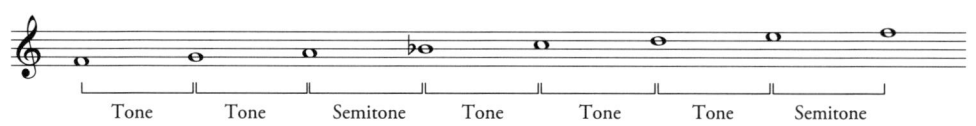

Tone | Tone | Semitone | Tone | Tone | Tone | Semitone

Since it would make the reading of notation unnecessarily complex to constantly place accidentals in front of every note which required one, the system of *key signatures* evolved so that the required sharp or flat signs are placed at the beginning of the music and the player is expected to hold this in mind.

The key signatures of all major scales are set out below as they would appear in notated music. The key of **C** major, of course, has no sharps or flats:

Sharp key signatures with their tonic [key] notes:

G major | D major | A major | E major | B major | F♯ major | C♯ major

Flat key signatures with their tonic [key] notes:

F major | B♭ major | E♭ major | A♭ major | D♭ major | G♭ major | C♭ major

In practice, although the sequence of sharps or flats in a particular key signature arise respectively in perfect 5ths or 4ths [see Appendix 1: *Understanding Intervals*], the layout is determined by convention and simply has to be learned.

Another way of looking at key signatures is illustrated by the following diagram, and this may help to make it clearer:

Understanding Key Signatures

Flat keys: rising steps of a perfect fourth

Sharp keys: rising steps of a perfect fifth

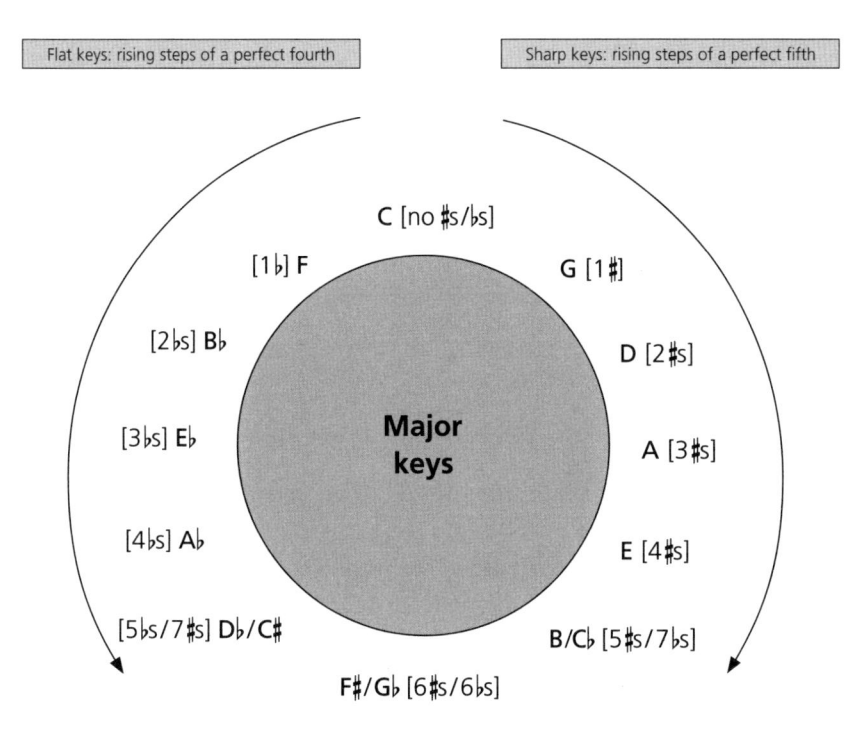

C [no #s/♭s]

[1♭] F

G [1#]

[2♭s] B♭

D [2#s]

Major keys

[3♭s] E♭

A [3#s]

[4♭s] A♭

E [4#s]

[5♭s/7#s] D♭/C#

B/C♭ [5#s/7♭s]

F#/G♭ [6#s/6♭s]

N.B. the keys of D♭ major and C# major sound the same and are described as *enharmonic*. Similarly, F# major and G♭ major are enharmonic as are B major and C♭ major.

This useful mnemonic gives the order of the sharps and when read in reverse, gives the order of the flats as they appear in key signatures.

#s ⟶

Father Charles Goes Down And Ends Battle

⟵ ♭s

4.3 Minor keys

The other most commonly used scale is the *minor*. This exists in a number of forms, the most frequently encountered being the melodic *minor*, in which the ascending and descending scales differ and the *harmonic minor* where ascending and descending scales are the same.

The melodic minor

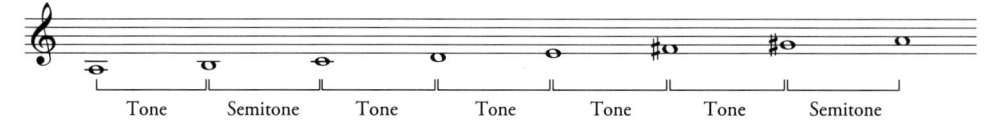

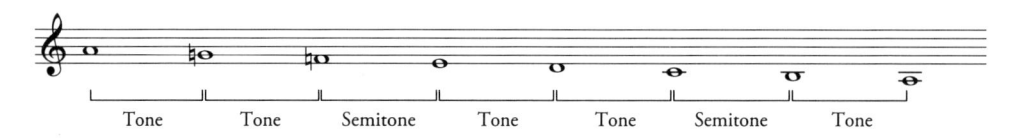

Which gives the formula:

Ascending: Tone   Semitone   Tone   Tone   Tone   Tone   Semitone

Descending: Tone   Tone   Semitone   Tone   Tone   Semitone   Tone

N.B. The sharpened 6th and 7th degrees in the ascending version of this scale appear as accidentals and not in the key signature.

The harmonic minor

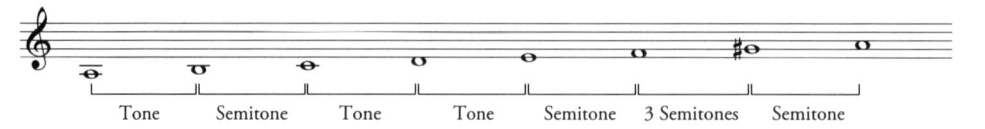

Which gives the formula:

Tone   Semitone   Tone   Tone   Semitone   Tone   3 Semitones   Semitone

N.B. As with the melodic minor, the sharpened 7th degree of the scale appears as an accidental and is not included in the key signature. In fact, the *interval* between the 6th [the *submediant*] and the 7th [*leading note*] in the harmonic minor is more accurately described as an *augmented* 2nd and contributes to the characteristic sound of the scale.

The key signatures of all minor scales are set out below as they would appear in notated music. The key of **A** minor, of course, has no sharps or flats:

Sharp key signatures with their tonic [key] notes:

E minor   B minor   F♯ minor   C♯ minor   G♯ minor   D♯ minor   A♯ minor

Understanding Key Signatures

Flat key signatures with their tonic [key] notes:

D minor   G minor   C minor   F minor   B♭ minor   E♭ minor   A♭ minor

Once again, another way of looking at these key signatures is illustrated by the following diagram, and this may help to make it clearer:

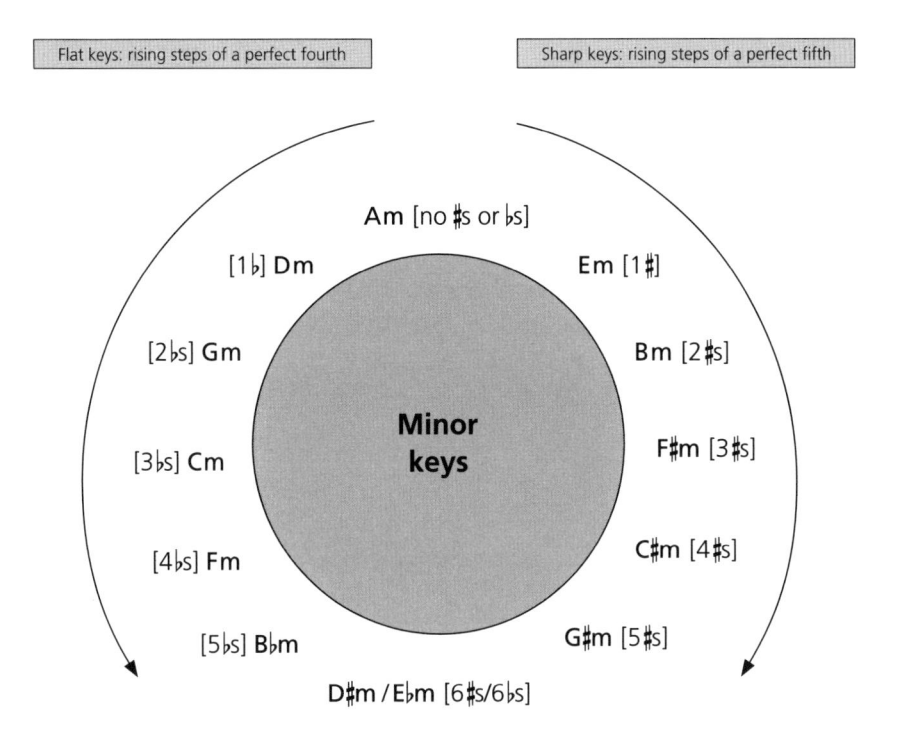

Flat keys: rising steps of a perfect fourth   Sharp keys: rising steps of a perfect fifth

Am [no ♯s or ♭s]

[1♭] Dm   Em [1♯]

[2♭s] Gm   Bm [2♯s]

[3♭s] Cm   **Minor keys**   F♯m [3♯s]

[4♭s] Fm   C♯m [4♯s]

[5♭s] B♭m   G♯m [5♯s]

D♯m / E♭m [6♯s/6♭s]

As with major keys, **D♯** minor and **E♭** minor are described as enharmonic, which means that they sound the same.

It is also important to realise that there is a relationship between major and minor keys; for any major key, the tonic of its *relative minor* [i.e. the minor key which shares the same key signature] is always the sixth degree of the scale. Conversely, in a minor key, the tonic of its *relative major* is always the third degree of the scale.

e.g. the relative minor of **C** major is **A** minor.

This relationship is easily worked out, of course, but is summarised for convenience in the table below:

Sharp keys:

Major key	Relative minor key
C major	A minor
G major	E minor
D major	B minor
A major	F♯ minor
E major	C♯ minor
B major	G♯ minor
F♯ major	D♯ minor

Flat keys:

Major key	Relative minor key
C major	A minor
F major	D minor
B♭ major	G minor
E♭ major	C minor
A♭ major	F minor
D♭ major	B♭ minor
G♭ major	E♭ minor

4.4 Choosing a key

In practice, of course, we are unlikely to venture into extreme keys. The choice of key for a particular piece is usually determined by considerations such as ease of playing or, in the case of song writing, finding the best fit to the comfortable range of a particular voice.

However, for those with so-called *perfect* (or absolute pitch), choice of key signature may have a greater significance. Perfect pitch is the ability to remember pitch without reference to a previously heard note. An individual with such a facility can identify any note which is sung or played to them or, conversely, can sing any note [within their vocal range, of course] on request. With this facility, for trained musicians at least, comes the ability to recognise the key signature of a piece of music aurally.

This ability is quite rare and seems to be either inherited or learned at an early age, unlike *relative pitch* which is the ability to sing or identify a note with reference to another known note which has just been heard.

We can deduce that certain composers may well have had the facility of perfect pitch – Mozart is a good example – mainly from anecdotal sources. For those such as Mozart, particular key signatures seem to have suggested certain qualities such as colour or brightness, or to have become associated with certain expressive qualities. For Mozart, it is evident that the key of **G** minor held a darker association, for instance.

So, to turn to an example from another composer, we might ask why Beethoven chose **C♯** minor as the tonic key of the opening movement of his Piano Sonata Op. 27, No. 2 [the so-called *Moonlight Sonata*].

Sonata quasi una Fantasia Op. 27, No. 2 Ludwig van Beethoven [1770–1827]

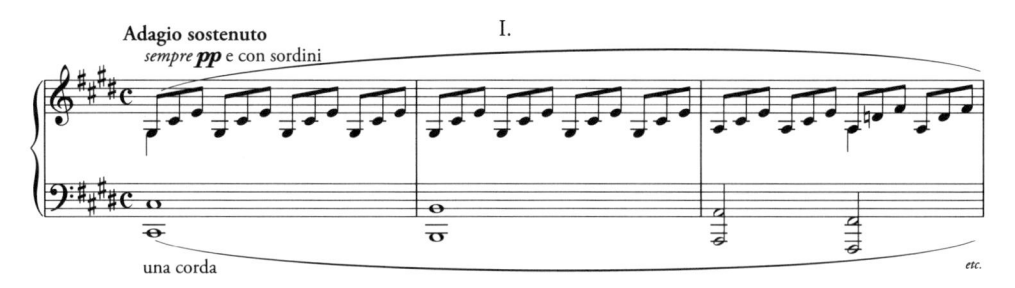

The temptation is to suggest that this particular minor key held a special significance for Beethoven, and very possibly, it might have done.

However, an equally viable suggestion derives from the way in which Beethoven named this sonata: not *The Moonlight Sonata* – a name which was given by someone else at a later date – but *Sonata quasi una Fantasia*, which suggests that the piece may have been intended to have an improvisatory quality.

In fact, the opening bars of this movement fall easily under the hands depending on the fingering which the player elects to use and we cannot know how Beethoven played it. It is the notation in four sharps which may lead to difficulties in reading rather than the actual execution of the piece. It seems likely that Beethoven found this initial idea whilst improvising at the piano and would have felt no compulsion to change the key.

Now, all of this is conjectural, we know. But what *is* certain is that the key of **C♯** minor which we hear today [with a standardised pitch of A = 440 cps[1]] is not the **C♯** minor that Mozart or Beethoven heard. Pitch in the latter half of the 18th century is known to have been lower

---

[1] cps is an abbreviation for cycles per second.

and Percy Scholes in the *Oxford Companion to Music* [9th edition] suggests that the note **A** at this time was pitched between 415 and 430 cps.

So, possibly, purists might bear this in mind when criticising the idea of transcribing pieces into more accessible keys.

4.5 Some other scales

Instrumentalists are inclined to think of scales as exercises which are prescribed by teachers to improve technique. But, as we have already begun to show, the structure of the scale from which each piece, or indeed genre, of music is created has a fundamental influence.

There are countless scales in existence, some of which have evolved, some scientifically deduced and others which have been contrived by composers. Some scales are a rationalisation of the pitches which are encountered in a particular style of music [like the blues scale] and many others, from non-Western cultures, involve the use of intervals which cannot be played on instruments with fixed semitone divisions.

However, the following section includes a few of the more commonly encountered examples, together with notated musical excerpts which illustrate their use.

4.6 The chromatic scale

The chromatic scale contains every available note on the keyboard, played consecutively, ascending or descending and it therefore consists only of semitone intervals. For this reason, there is only one chromatic scale which may begin on any of its notes.

Theorists debate the various ways of notating the scale, but historically, there is plenty of evidence that composers have and will continue to notate the scale in a variety of ways and will, in any case, consider the key of the musical context if this is relevant.

As a general rule, sharps are commonly used in the ascending scale and flats in the descending version, as follows:

Melodic notation

However, as this example from Beethoven's *Pathetique* piano sonata illustrates, practice and theory may well diverge.

Sonata Pathetique Op. 13 [Final bar of introduction] Ludwig van Beethoven [1770–1827]

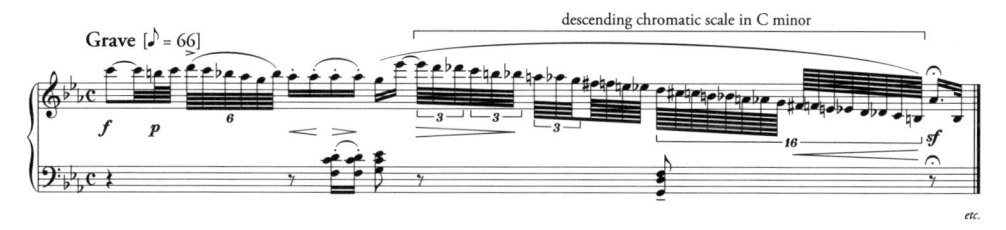

4.7 Modes

As referred to earlier in this section, modes formed the basis of Western European music before tonality became fully established. Although a complete analysis of the modal system is beyond the scope of this book, the following *authentic modes* and their *plagal mode* counterparts are given below as a basis for further study.

Authentic modes:

Dorian

Phrygian

Lydian

Mixolydian

Aeolian

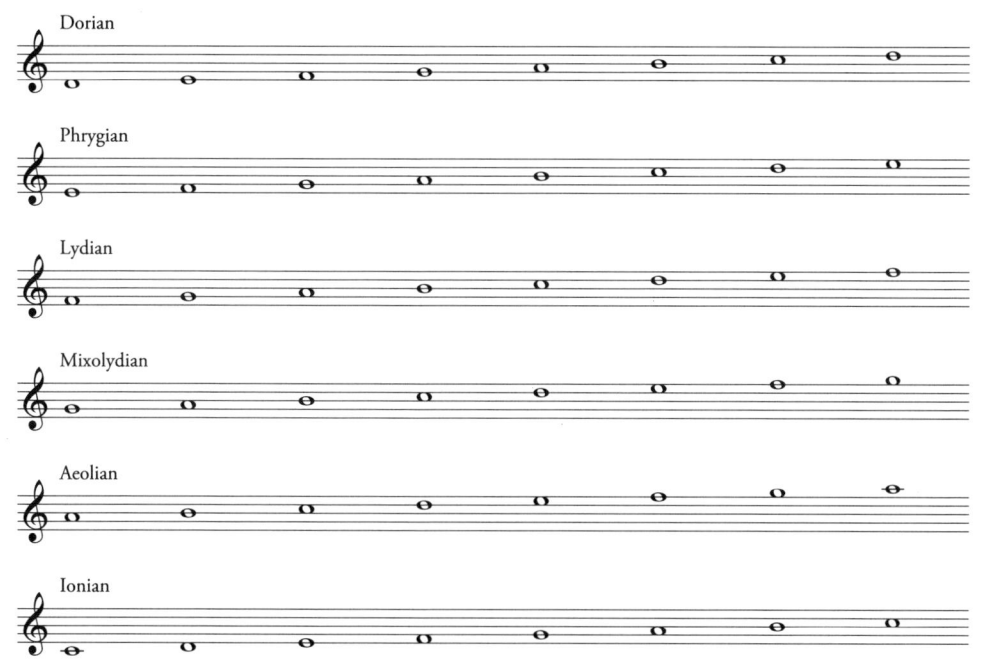

Ionian

Understanding Key Signatures

Plagal modes:

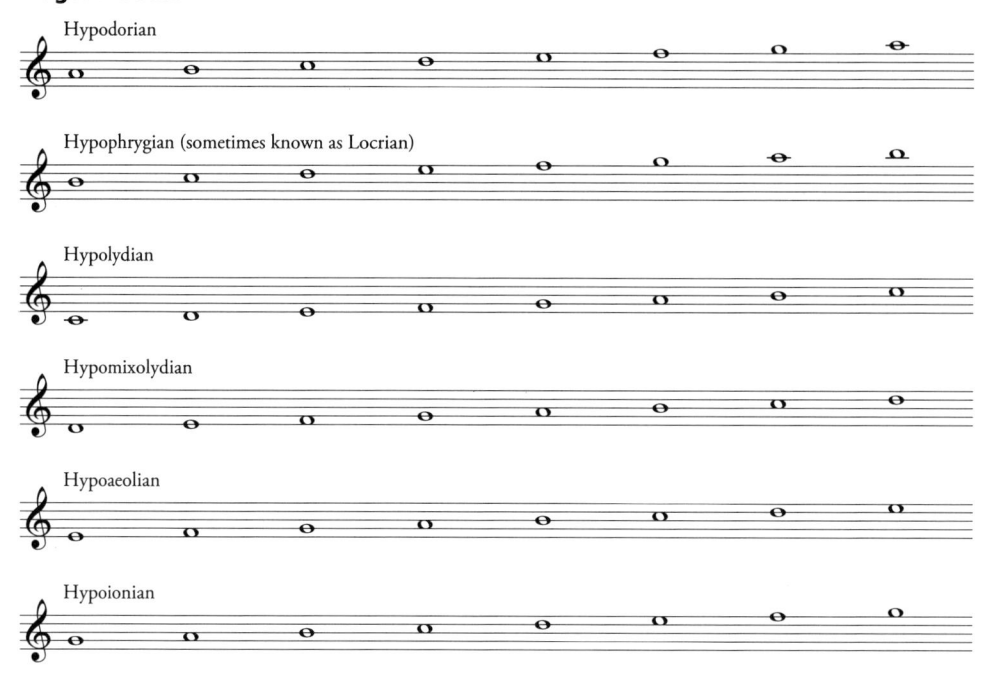

Hypodorian

Hypophrygian (sometimes known as Locrian)

Hypolydian

Hypomixolydian

Hypoaeolian

Hypoionian

Another way of thinking of these different modes is to transpose them all [except the *Ionian* which requires no transposition] so that they all begin on the note **C**:

Authentic modes transposed to begin on C:

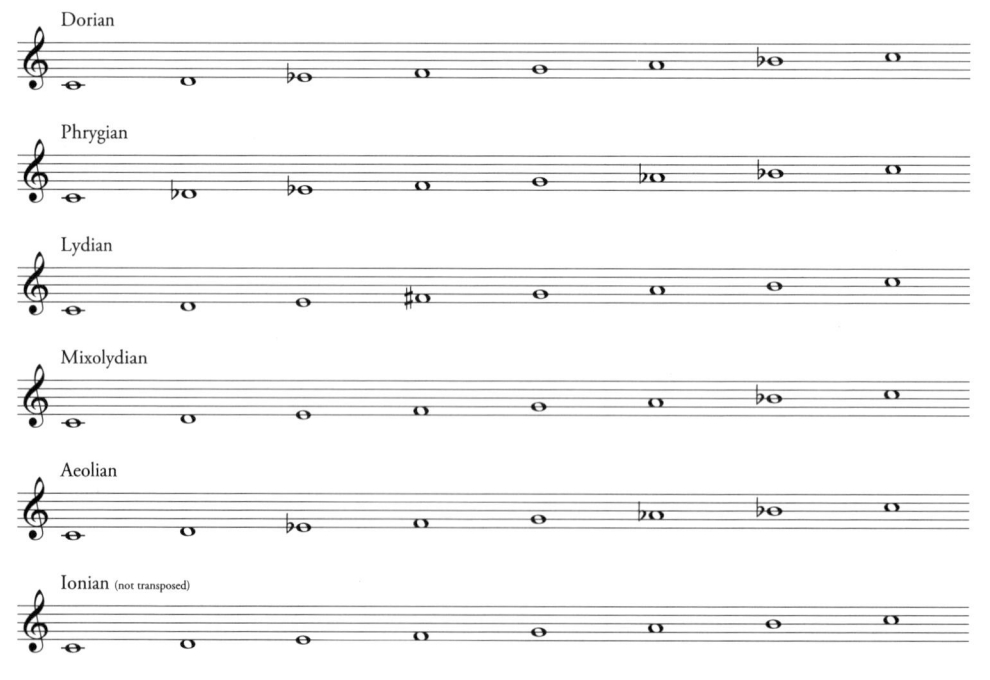

Dorian

Phrygian

Lydian

Mixolydian

Aeolian

Ionian (not transposed)

As this demonstrates, the fundamental character of a particular mode is not changed (except in pitch) by transposition and each one could begin on any chosen note. Like major and minor scales, it is the sequence of tones and semitones which is recognisable and so, for example, we could begin the Dorian mode on A:

Dorian on A

Modes have regained their status in modern music, not least through their use by jazz musicians and, of course, they also survive in folk music. By this means, they have even re-appeared in popular music as a result of folksong arrangements [Paul Simon and Art Garfunkel's use of the English folksong *Scarborough Fair* is an example which comes to mind].

The example notated below is in the Dorian mode [on **D**] and will probably be known to most readers. It is a work song of the sea – in other words, a sea shanty:

What Shall We do With The Drunken Sailor? Traditional

What shall we do with the drunk-en sail-or? What shall we do with the drunk-en sail-or?
What shall we do with the drunk-en sail-or? Ear-ly in the morn-ing. Hoo-ray and up she ris-es,
Hoo-ray and up she ris-es, Hoo-ray and up she ris-es, Ear-ly in the morn-ing.

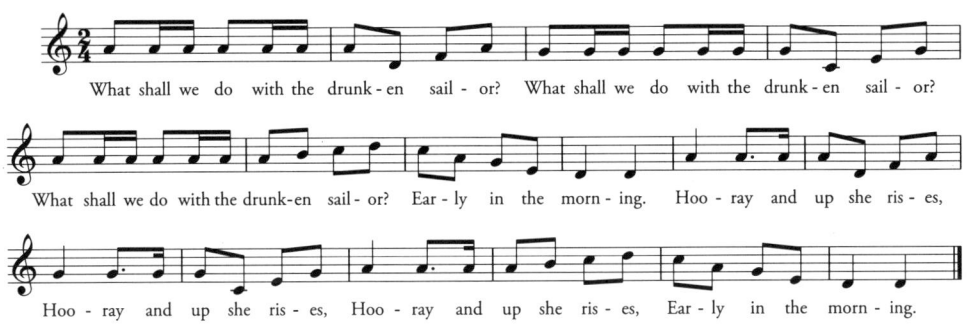

4.8 The whole-tone scale

This scale, as its name suggests, consists of any succession of whole-tone intervals. In fact, theoretically, there are only two possible whole-tone scales [beginning on either **C** or **D♭**], although the starting point might be chosen at any point in the scale:

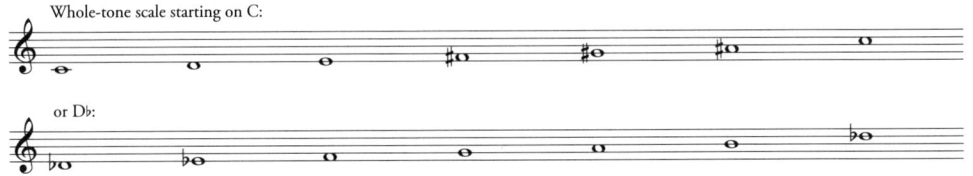

Whole-tone scale starting on C:

or D♭:

Because of the absence of any semitone steps, this scale has a vagueness of tonality which has been exploited by a number of composers, especially in the so-called 'impressionist' genre. One of the most frequently quoted examples is the following, by Claude Debussy:

from the piano prelude *Voiles* Claude Debussy [1862–1918]

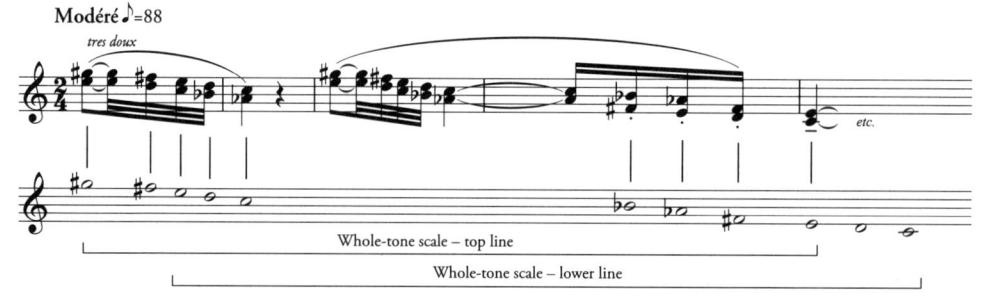

Whole-tone scale – top line
Whole-tone scale – lower line

In a suitably quiet environment, hold down the sustain pedal of a piano and fairly rapidly play a whole-tone scale in the mid- to upper-range of the instrument. Keep the pedal depressed and listen to the resulting accumulated sound which has an almost mystical effect.

4.9 The pentatonic scale

As its name suggests, this is a five-note scale, one major version of which is easily reproduced on the piano by playing the black keys: **F♯, G♯, A♯, C♯** and **D♯**. The same scale beginning on middle **C** is notated below:

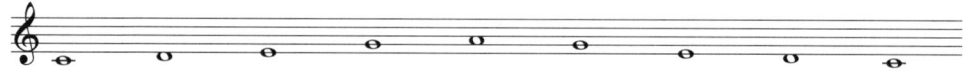

Referred to by some as a *gapped scale* for obvious reasons, it can appear in the minor form [which uses the same sequence of notes as the major example above but begins on **A**]:

If we take the major pentatonic scale and flatten the 3rd degree, we have a *minor 3rd pentatonic*, here shown beginning on **C**:

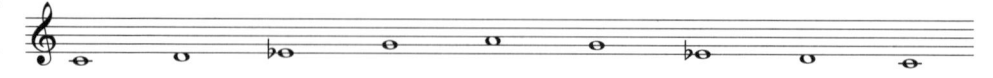

Understanding Key Signatures

In one guise or another, pentatonic scales, like modes, are encountered in the folk music of many cultures and have been explored by jazz musicians.

The following example of a major pentatonic melody [which, incidentally, appears in many variants] will probably be recognised by readers as the tune which has been most frequently adopted as a setting for John Newton's text *Amazing Grace:*

Amazing Grace Melody: Trad. U.S.A. / Words: John Newton

A - maz - ing— grace! How sweet the sound, That sav'd a— wretch like— me!—
— I— once was— lost, but now am found, Was blind but— now can see—

4.10 The blues scale

The blues scale is a rationalised version of the notes commonly used as the basis of many blues melodies. Because the blues was originally a vocal genre, the bending of pitches which is heard in this style cannot be achieved by instruments of fixed pitch. The flattened 3rd, 5th and 7th of this scale approximate to this vocal style. In fact, the blues scale is identical to the minor pentatonic with the addition of the flattened 5th, the most potent of all the so-called 'blue' notes.

Of course, the blues scale can begin on any note too, as long as the same sequence of intervals is retained. The following example shows the blues scale beginning on **D**:

The following example for piano substantially takes its melodic line from the blues scale beginning on **D**. In this excerpt, the melodic line falls within a one-octave compass of the scale, but blues melodies might well extend above and below this range.

Definitely Blue Mike Cornick [*1947]

Track 20

Very slow and bluesy ($\quarternote$ = 85, $\eighthnote\eighthnote$ = $\quarternote\eighthnote$)

from *Start Pianojazz* [UE 17 361, © Copyright 1997 by Universal Edition (London) Ltd., London]

4.11 The diminished or octatonic scale

This scale exists in two different forms: one which moves by a tone followed by a semitone:

Track 21

and one which does the reverse [semitone followed by a tone]:

Track 22

As you can see, the 1st, 3rd, 5th and 7th notes are common to both forms of this scale. When these notes are played individually, they form the diminished 7th arpeggio to which they are related [see Appendix 3: *Understanding Arpeggios*]:

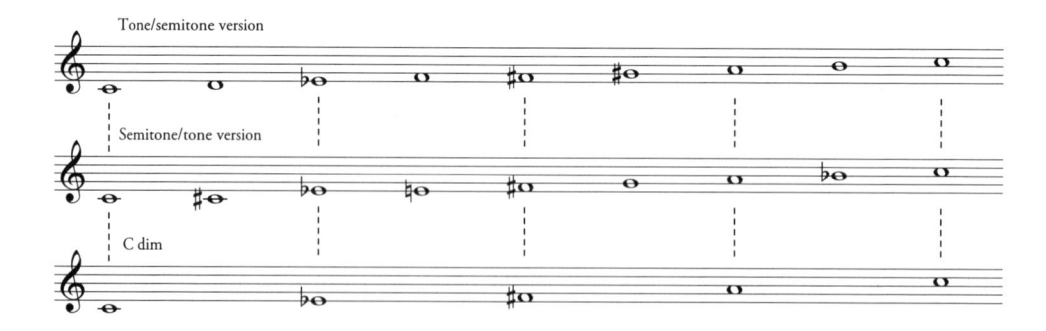

Tone/semitone version

Semitone/tone version

C dim

The following excerpt from *Diminishing Returns* explores the tone-semitone version of the scale:

Understanding Key Signatures

Diminishing Returns James Rae [*1957]

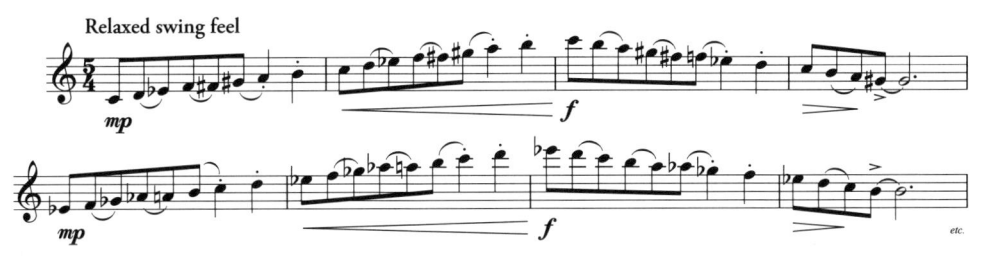

Relaxed swing feel

from *Jazz Scale Studies* [UE 21 351, © Copyright 2006 by Universal Edition (London) Ltd., London]

Did you know ...

... that the world's longest piece of music is expected to last for 639 years? It is based on the piano piece As Slow as Possible by the American composer John Milton Cage and is called Organ²/ASLSP (As SLow aS Possible). The piece, which is being performed on a church organ in Halberstadt, Germany began with a twenty-nine month pause on September 5th 2001 and then continued with a chord which lasted until July 5th 2005.

The duration of the piece was chosen because, in the year 2000 when this project was planned, it was 639 years since the original organ had been built.

When it finally finishes, will there be anyone around to ask for an encore?

Understanding Harmony

5.1 Introduction

One of the first problems in understanding harmony is to arrive at some kind of definition. And this can be more difficult than one might imagine.

In music which has evolved in Western European culture and which is *tonal*, harmony describes the addition of other notes to a *melody* which has the effect of enriching and usually strengthening the progression of that melody.

Readers who wish to move straight to the mechanics of tonal harmony may omit the following potted history of its evolution, but a deeper understanding of the subject will result from some exploration of the music of the past.

5.2 Historical background

The roots of Western European harmony lie in the evolution of vocal music in the church. In the singing of *plainsong chants* in the ninth or tenth centuries, it became common practice for voices with different vocal ranges to sing the same melody in parallel at an interval of a perfect fourth or fifth.

This use of parallel melodies is described as *organum* and gave rise to what we regard as the earliest form of four-part vocal harmony. *The Oxford Companion to Music* gives the following example[1]:

10th century organum from *Musica Enchiriadis*

Interestingly, the distinctive sound of this harmony, which does not use intervals of a 3rd or 6th has often been used to great effect by later composers. [see *Section 12: Breaking the Rules*]

The main points to grasp, however, are that the harmony in such music arises from the combination of melodic lines and that intervals of a perfect fourth, fifth and octave were felt to be the most *consonant*. Harmony at this time does not give the sense of tonal progression which we expect today and the singers were thinking of their music horizontally, as melodies

[1] See *Select Bibliography* for details of this publication

rather than in a vertical sense of a melody with chords added beneath or around it.

Polyphony

A growing freedom from the simple addition of parallel melodies arose for practical and artistic reasons in the following centuries and reached a degree of artisitic perfection in the 16th century in a style which we now call *polyphony* [meaning many sounds].

Suggested listening:
Any examples of the music of Palestrina, Lassus or Byrd.

We also hear a growing awareness of *harmonic progression* in this music although the establishment of *tonality* is still evolving.

The Baroque period

We tend to refer to the use of polyphony as *counterpoint* in discussion of music of the 17th and the first half of the 18th centuries and its evolution continued alongside the growing establishment of major/minor tonality and the development of contrapuntal forms.

This era, now referred to as the *Baroque* period was also a time of significant development in instrumental music.

During this period, we see the wider acceptance of *equal temperament*, a system of tuning instruments which divided the octave into twelve equal semitones. This allowed instruments of fixed pitch to play in any key, a facility which was celebrated by J. S. Bach in the writing of his *48 Preludes and Fugues* [also known as *The Well-tempered Clavier* – composed from 1722 onwards].

Suggested Listening:
Any examples of music by J. S. Bach, G. P. Telemann, G. F. Handel or A. Vivaldi

Rococo and Classical periods

As we progress into the time of J. S. Bach's sons and, subsequently, that of Mozart and Haydn, we see a movement away from the virtually sole use of *counterpoint* and evidence of a more vertical approach to the use of harmony emerges. Counterpoint is still a strong and significant feature, but what we could now describe as the functional use of harmony becomes completely established.

Suggested Listening:
Wolfgang Amadeus Mozart: *Symphonies 38, 39, 40 and 41.*

For the modern listener, we are now in familiar territory. Classical music displays a clear sense of key [*tonality*] within clearly established musical forms which rely heavily on a scheme of *modulation* [key change], and it is at this point that we can set the issues of musical history behind us for the moment and start to explore the theory and practice of harmony in our own music.

5.3 The 'nuts and bolts' of tonal harmony

It may be useful to think of the following process as *functional harmony* – i.e. harmony which reinforces the tonality of a melody and gives a sense of progression.

In learning to harmonise in this way we are, for the most part, thinking vertically – which means we are providing harmony beneath a melodic line, sometimes on a note-for-note basis, sometimes for each beat of the bar or perhaps, quite simply, when your ear tells you that a change of harmony is needed.

We begin with a **C** major scale:

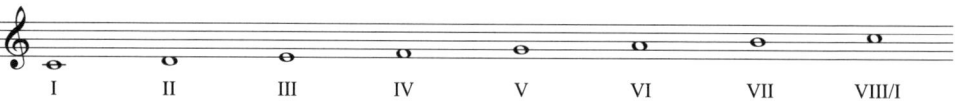

On each step of the scale, we can construct a *triad* which is a three-note chord using alternate letter-named notes, as follows:

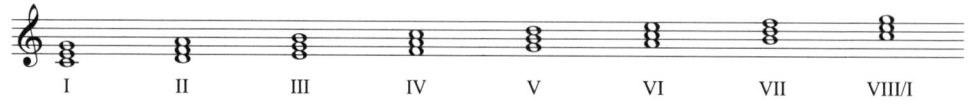

Notice that triads formed in this way are not identical. Listen to the differences in tonality:

- Triads constructed on notes I, IV and V are *major* chords. These are called *primary chords* and are the workhorses of basic harmony.

- Even though we are building triads on the steps of a major scale, triads constructed on notes II, III and VI are *minor*.

- The triad constructed on note VII is a diminished chord which we will leave aside for the moment.

You will have noticed that we have also numbered each step of the scale using roman numerals, so now we can refer to these triads or chords by number as well as by name.

e.g. In a **C** major scale, the triad constructed on note I [**C**] is chord I as well as being a **C** major chord. [The system of using roman numerals is useful when referring to triads or chords in the general context of any key.]

There is also another system of naming each degree of any major or minor scale which is useful in referring to the notes and their triads. These names reflect the relative importance of the notes in the scale:

I	tonic
II	supertonic
III	mediant
IV	subdominant
V	dominant
VI	submediant
VII	leading note

And VIII is, of course, the tonic once again, an octave higher.

Although it might, at first, seem very confusing to have three naming systems in use simultaneously, it may be helpful to try to get used to thinking of these alternative names until they become familiar.

And so, in a **C** major scale, the triad constructed on note I might be referred to as chord I, whilst also being a **C** major chord and the tonic chord.

We now have all the chords we need to harmonise any number of simple melodies, but before we proceed, it would be useful to be able to refer specifically to the notes which make up a triad:

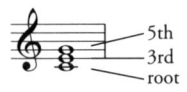

5.4 Harmonising a melody

Now, we come to the real business of harmonising a melody. Suppose we take the melody of a simple nursery rhyme like *Pop Goes the Weasel*:

Track 26

- Where do we need to add the chords?
- Where does our ear tell us that a change of harmony is needed?
- Mark the relevant places with an asterisk. You will probably have chosen the following scheme:

Now, we need to decide which chords/triads will be appropriate in each case. Limiting ourselves to primary chords [I, IV and V – C, F and G] we may, depending on experience, be able to hear in our 'mind's ear' which chords will work. The ability to do this depends largely on experience, although players of keyboard instruments and guitars, for instance, will probably have developed this facility to some extent already.

Alternatively, we may adopt a purely mechanical process, as follows:

- Each melody note to be harmonised can be found in three different triads.
- We write down the possibilities in each case, and then
- We select our chosen chord according to various criteria.

These include:

- Establishing the key with the tonic chord at the beginning.
- As we progress, looking at the melody notes which may strongly suggest a particular choice.
- Trying out the alternatives on a keyboard instrument and using our ear to make choices.
- Being aware of *cadences* at phrase endings – see explanation of cadences later in this chapter.

Understanding Harmony

In the following example, chord options have been added and the selected chords indicated with arrows:

[Musical notation with chord options:]

I ←	II	I ←	I ←	II	I ←
IV	V ←	IV	IV	V ←	IV
VI	VII	VI	VI	VII	VI

I ←	II	I ←	II	II	I ←
IV	V ←	IV	IV ←	V ←	IV
VI	VII	VI	VI	VII	VI

We can now proceed to make a simple piano arrangement of *Pop Goes the Weasel* by placing the melodic line on the treble stave of a standard piano score and adding the chosen triads in the bass clef for the left hand:

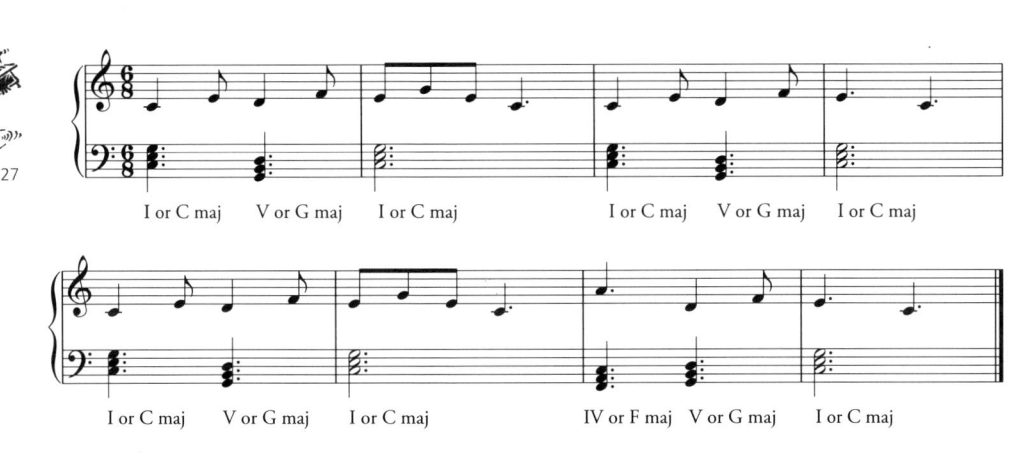

[Piano score with chord labels:]

I or C maj   V or G maj   I or C maj   I or C maj   V or G maj   I or C maj

I or C maj   V or G maj   I or C maj   IV or F maj   V or G maj   I or C maj

Now, although the choice of chords seems workable, this simple arrangement does not sound too good. There are a number of reasons for this, which include:

- Triads in **close position** – i.e. with their notes as closely spaced as possible – will not sound good in piano writing at lower pitch for acoustical reasons. We need to think about spacing out the notes of our triads to achieve what is known as better *voicing*.

- If we simply add triads below a melodic line, then we inevitably **double** one of the notes of the triad; i.e. we use one of the notes in the triad twice. Although doubling the **root** of a triad can work well in many instances, doubling the third of the triad, especially in a major chord will weaken its effect.

Understanding Harmony

- We have limited ourselves in this instance to using triads in root position. As a consequence, we hear the same chord at the beginning of Bar 3 as was heard at the end of the previous bar. We will need to explore the use of *inversions*, which will be explained following the next example.

- Our arrangement is also weakened by the *parallelism* which results from the unremitting use of closely spaced root-position triads.

In the following example, we have attempted to remedy some of these problems by placing one bass note in the left-hand part and two notes in the right hand. This at once simplifies the issue of doubling:

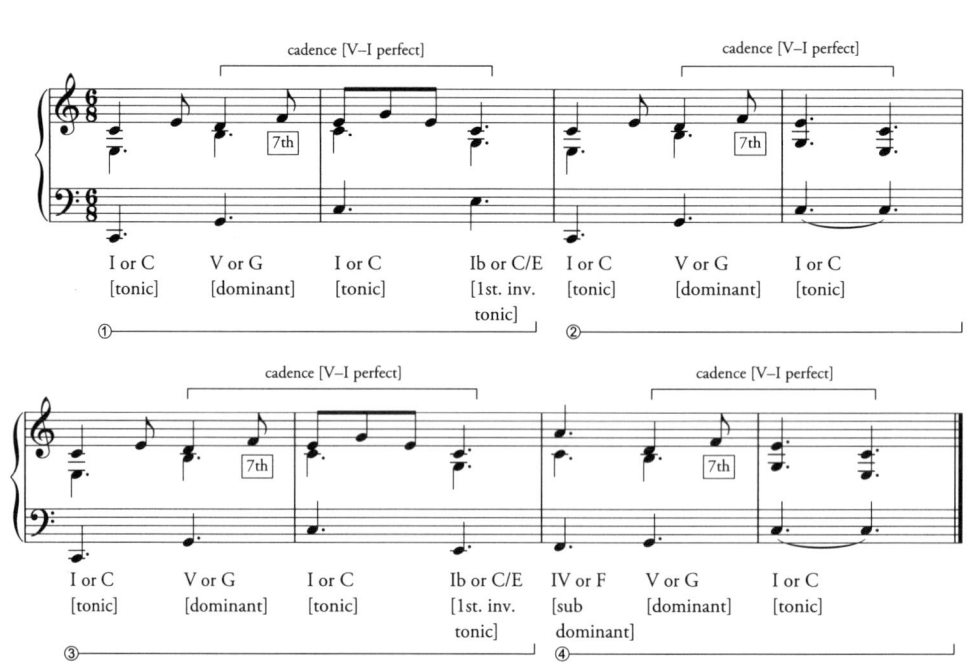

Track 28

Some observations on this revised arrangement

- Sometimes, the 5th has been omitted from some chords. The ear can accept this omission but could not accept the omission of the root or the 3rd.

- An inversion of the tonic chord has been used in bars 2 and 6 to offset the effect of repetition of the tonic chord. [see following notes on the inversion of chords].

- In bars 3 and 7, the last melody note is an F which does not belong to the dominant **G** triad and yet it seems to fit perfectly. Why is this? [see the following section on *added notes*].

5.5 Chord inversions

In so-called root position, the lowest note [the root] is found at the bottom of the harmony and is treated as the bass.

However, the fundamental nature of a triad is not altered by rearranging its constituent notes. If we take the root of a triad and move it to the top by raising it by an octave, we produce what is known as a first *inversion* chord.

In the following example, the chosen triad is chord I in the key of **C** major. In its first inversion, it is now described as Ib or **C/E** [In chord symbol notation, the first letter name denotes the chord and the second denotes the bass]. If the process is continued and the lowest note of this first inversion is taken to the top, we now have a second inversion chord, described as Ic or **C/G**. No further inversions are possible since they would return the triad to root position one octave higher:

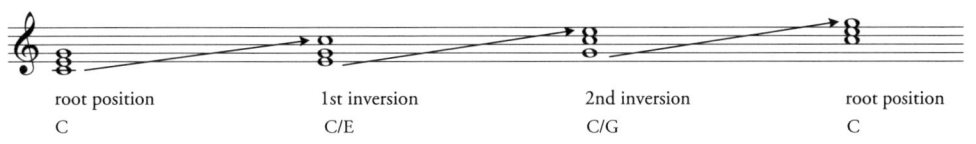

root position	1st inversion	2nd inversion	root position
C	C/E	C/G	C

Added notes

Other notes can be added to triads so making them into four-note chords. The added note is indicated in the chord symbol by the addition of a small number to the right [*e.g.* **C⁷**]. The most common addition is probably the 7th and this indicates the addition of a note at the interval of a 7th above the root of the chord. This added 7th, incidentally, is always at the interval of a minor 7th unless otherwise stated. *e.g.*

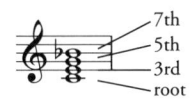

- 7th
- 5th
- 3rd
- root

Triads with an added note are capable of a further inversion as a consequence of containing four notes, as shown below:

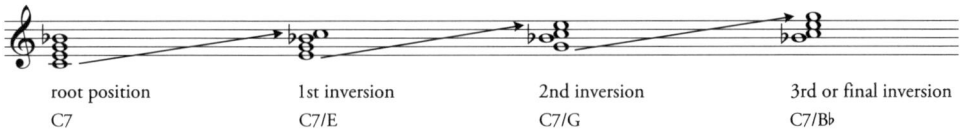

root position	1st inversion	2nd inversion	3rd or final inversion
C7	C7/E	C7/G	C7/B♭

In simple terms, added notes can further enhance the melodic line by providing us with a wider harmonic vocabulary.

5.6 Cadences

Any melody which is to be sung or played on an instrument which requires opportunities to breathe, will fall into *phrases*. At the end of each phrase, the melody will feel as if it has reached a destination – no matter how briefly or temporarily – and there will be a feeling of coming to rest or a slight release of tension.

Because instrumental music developed from vocal music, this grouping of notes into phrases is found in the vast majority of Western European music and has become part of its inherent structure. One stylistic exception which comes to mind is *minimalism* in which, very often, the music can be intentionally relentless and machine-like.

However, when harmonising a conventional melody, it will be found that a need for the use of cadences will naturally arise at the end of each phrase, and since this is such a well-established musical convention, these cadences should become part of your tool kit, known by name and by their constituent chords.

A definition of the cadence

A cadence is a two-chord progression which is used to harmonise a phrase ending.

Although it is possible to find cadences which fall outside the following descriptions, our harmony tool kit should certainly contain:

The perfect cadence:
[sometimes called the final cadence]   V ⟶ I

The imperfect cadence:
commonly   I ⟶ V

or   II ⟶ V
or   IV ⟶ V
or   VI ⟶ V

The plagal cadence: IV ⟶ I

The interrupted cadence: usually   V ⟶ VI

It might be useful to think of these four types of cadence in two groups: those which sound complete, Perfect and Plagal, because they end with the tonic chord and those which seem to be leading on, or which sound incomplete: Imperfect and Interrupted.

Understanding Harmony

In practice, these cadences [in four-part harmony] might be voiced in a variety of ways which will also depend on the melody notes being harmonised. The following notated examples suggest one possible arrangement of each cadence.

In the key of C major:

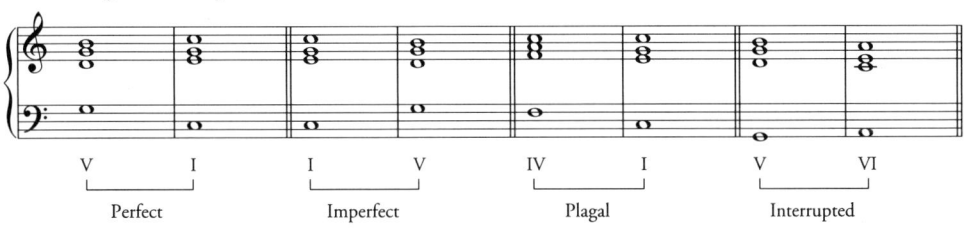

V – I	I – V	IV – I	V – VI
Perfect	Imperfect	Plagal	Interrupted

Experiment with different voicings of each cadence.

Cadences are with us whenever we listen to or perform tonal music. At a birthday party, we often sing *Happy Birthday to You* which, in fact, is based on the song *Good Morning to All*, the tune of which was written by Mildred J. Hill in 1893.

If harmony is provided, by other voices or a piano perhaps, we would expect to hear the following sequence of cadences [*N.B.* for the moment, we will disregard the third phrase since this modulates to a cadence in a new key – **F** major]:

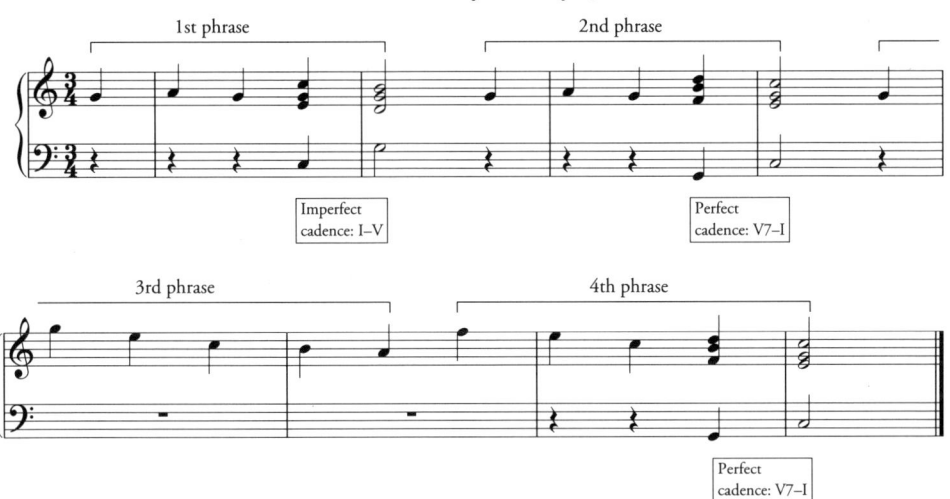

1st phrase — Imperfect cadence: I–V

2nd phrase — Perfect cadence: V7–I

3rd phrase

4th phrase — Perfect cadence: V7–I

Understanding Harmony

If we cheat a little and add an extra few bars at the end, we could also include an interrupted and a plagal cadence:

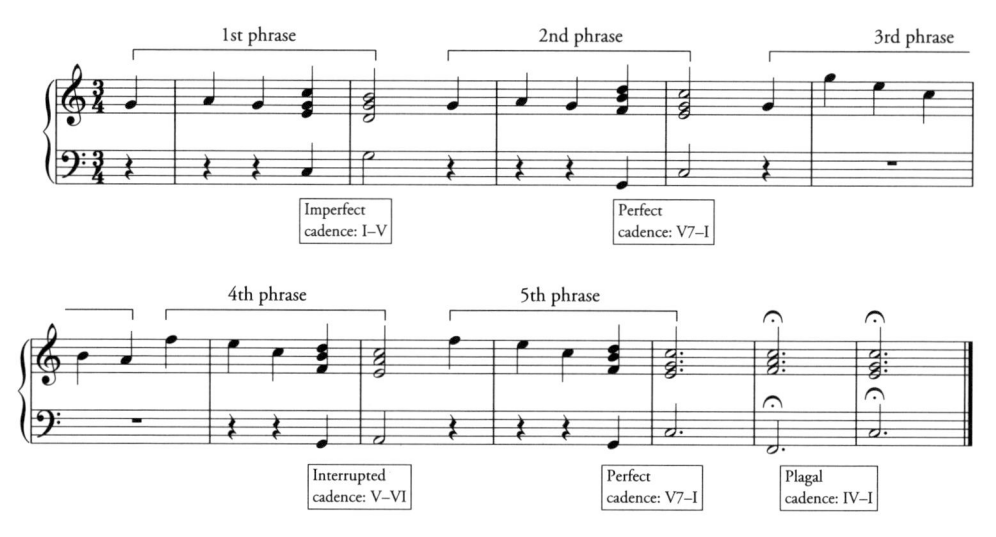

Track 33

1st phrase — Imperfect cadence: I–V
2nd phrase — Perfect cadence: V7–I
3rd phrase

4th phrase — Interrupted cadence: V–VI
5th phrase — Perfect cadence: V7–I
Plagal cadence: IV–I

And now, finally, the following example is a fully harmonised version. It includes a few features which are worth noting:

- A cadence is supplied at the end of the third phrase – a perfect [V-I] cadence in the key of **F**.

- Some *passing notes* are included. Passing notes, quite literally, pass between harmony notes and are accepted by the ear principally because they are moving to the next harmony note.

- The melody note at the beginning of the 6th bar is a **B** which then moves to the final note of the phrase which is **A**. The note **B** is treated as an *appoggiatura*; that is to say, although it forms a *dissonance* with the chord of **F**, it *resolves* immediately by a downward step onto the note **A** which belongs to the chord.

Understanding Harmony

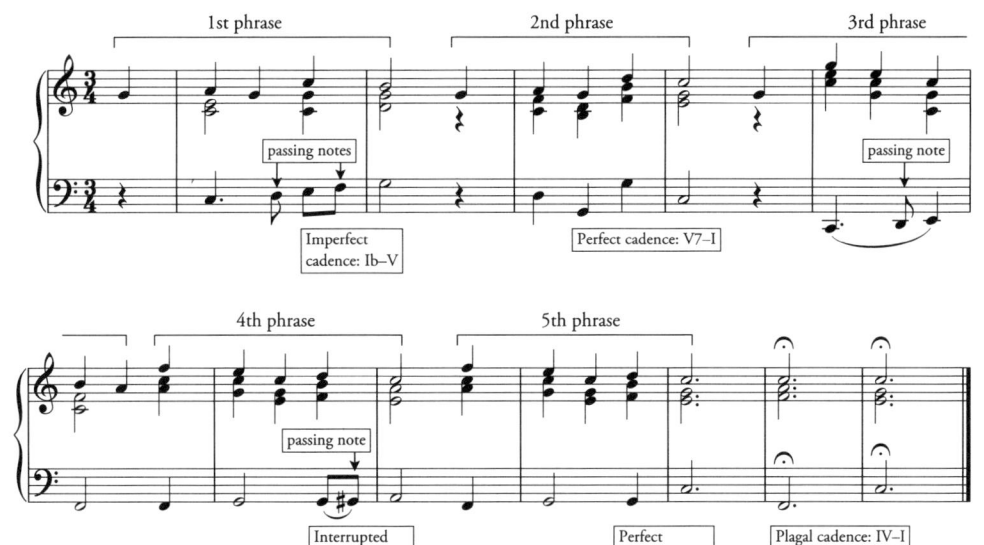

[Musical score with phrase markings: 1st phrase, 2nd phrase, 3rd phrase, 4th phrase, 5th phrase. Annotations include: passing notes, Imperfect cadence: Ib–V, Perfect cadence: V7–I, passing note, Interrupted cadence: V–VI, Perfect cadence: V7–I, Plagal cadence: IV–I]

There are many ways in which this piano arrangement could be strengthened and it may well be worthwhile to experiment with this a little.

Did you know ...

... that the nursery rhyme Pop Goes the Weasel is said to date back to the 1700s?

The words of the first verse are: *Half a pound of tuppeny rice, Half a pound of treacle, That's the way the money goes, Pop goes the weasel. Up and down the City Road, In and out of the Eagle, That's the way the money goes, Pop goes the weasel.*

The most common interpretation is that the word 'pop' is Cockney slang for 'pawn', so the rice and the treacle [seemingly unlikely purchases] and a visit to the *The Eagle* [a public house] have accounted for the expenditure. Consequently, the weasel [weasel and stoat – rhyming slang for coat] is taken to the pawnbrokers.

There is still a pub called *The Eagle* on the same site as the one referred to in the rhyme.

The Composer's Tool Kit

6.1 Introduction

Creating a piece of music might be compared to building a house or, perhaps, something slightly less ambitious to begin with, like a table.

You would need quite a number of specialist tools to complete such a project and this is equally the case when composing a piece. Of course, our house- or table-building analogy is only a rough and ready one: most of the composer's tool kit is stored in the memory and the so-called tools of the trade are acquired through gaining knowledge and experience. It has been suggested that, just as a builder acquires an ever-increasing collection of tools, so we all tend to build up a kind of mental musical 'sound bank' which will contain, amongst other things, recollections of melodies, harmonies, rhythms and tonal colours as well as many of the developmental devices which will be expanded upon later in this section.

To put it another way, just as it might be said that '... we are what we eat', musically speaking, '... we are what we listen to'.

In order to exploit these countless recollections and incorporate them into our own work, it helps to formalise our accrued knowledge and experience for easier access, and this aspect of the tool kit is addressed later in this section under the heading: *The mental tool kit*.

To begin with, however, some of the novice's [and, indeed, the professional's] problems are a good deal more practical and concern the whole process of recording [in a written sense – *i.e.* notating] and, indeed, constructing a musical composition.

Some of these problems can be, at the very least, eased a little by the use of a good software sequencing and score-printing programme.

6.2 The physical tool kit

It should be borne in mind that music software has only been with us for a relatively short time and that, until its invention, composers coped without the benefits which it can offer.

The Composer's Tool Kit

We would strongly recommend that all aspiring composers come to terms with the process of notating music by hand as well as grasping as much theoretical knowledge as possible. Then, and only then, can they make really effective use of software as a composing tool.

Continuing our analogy for the moment, music software might be described as the power tool for the composer of today.

Reference has been made throughout this book to the appropriate applications of music software. The following observations have been included specifically to examine its role in greater detail as well as considering some key technical aspects of setting up and using a music IT workstation.

The hardware set-up

A 'stand-alone' computer
Music software can be run on most modern computers and the files are relatively small. But processing speed and the type of soundcard in your computer may become an issue if you wish to play back your compositions. Time lags can occur which may have the effect of distorting rhythms, for instance, and it may be necessary to install a 'dedicated' soundcard.[1]

An IT music workstation
An alternative approach is to connect an external playback device such as a synthesizer which will also serve as your *MIDI*[2] keyboard and will allow you to 'play in' [input] your music. This may be done in *real time* [playing along with a *click track* as in a recording] or in *step time* where selected durations are input from the MIDI keyboard one at a time.

It may also prove useful to add some means of sound recording to your set-up such as a CD burner.

Ideally, the user of such a set-up needs easy access to both the computer keyboard and the music keyboard [sometimes simultaneously] and will probably favour an arrangement which is something like the one shown above. It is possible to purchase purpose-built furniture to house all the items in such a set-up.

---
[1] A reliable IT retailer should be able to supply such a soundcard, but we would suggest taking advice from the software manufacturer beforehand.
[2] A MIDI is an acronym for Musical Instrument Digital Interface.

What such a software programme may be able to do:

- It will allow you to correctly notate your music using all the relevant parameters, such as time signature, key signature, instrumental range and choice of clef, *etc*. A good notation programme, for example, will only permit you to write bars which add up to the correct number of beats and it will group those notes for you according to your chosen time signature.

- It will play back what you have composed and even, in some cases, observe expression marks, articulation, repeats, *etc.*

- Within limits [and these limits should not be underestimated] it will allow you to play your piece *into* the programme or, more realistically, parts of it using a click track to keep time.

- Like a word-processing programme, it will allow you to make changes and corrections to your compositions and to copy sections almost instantaneously.

- It will print out a professional-looking notated copy of your music with an intelligent page layout as well as extract and print out individual parts for players in correctly transposed keys.

- Some programmes will also allow you to run checks for various editorial purposes [adding cautionary accidentals, for instance] or will pick up certain kinds of errors.

- It will enable you to add lyrics to a vocal line, spacing the notes accordingly.

- It will allow you to save your music in different file formats which might be used to make a recording of your music.

- It will produce files which can then be emailed.

It is worth investigating different software programmes and taking advice on which is the most appropriate choice for you. Like most purchases in life, bear in mind that better programmes will usually be more expensive and this will reflect the development costs which have been invested in the programme.

Some programmes are very good at sequencing; *i.e.* ordering and layering the sequence of musical sounds in your piece and playing them back, but may not be such sophisticated score writers. More sophisticated software, however, should be able to offer the best of both worlds.

But, and this is very important, as frequently mentioned elsewhere in this book, there are many aspects of composition with which your software will not help you.

What software cannot do:

- Although some software can even arrange music for you, it cannot offer you good ideas or, with the possible exception of providing drum loops and the like, compose any part of the music for you.

- Neither is it a substitute for an understanding of a great deal of the theory and the development of music which is explained elsewhere in this book.

- Although it may tell you when you are writing outside the range of an instrument, it cannot judge the suitability of what you write for that instrument, either technically or aurally.

- Although it may be able to add chord symbols according to the harmony you write, it cannot tell you whether or not your harmony sounds good.

Another point worth remembering is that some music software programmes are extensive and very complex, that they will require considerable learning time in their own right and, very probably, some tutorial help. This is fine in a school, college or university environment where help may be at hand, but can be frustrating for the lone user.

If you are contemplating investing in the sort of set-up which we have described, it would certainly be worth seeing it in action first, and preferably trying to gain some 'hands-on' experience in order to discover if this is the way forward for you.

Demonstrations are often available at music fairs and, sometimes, in larger music retailers.

So, to sum up, the computer with its dedicated software may well be able to help us, but it is *not* a composer!

6.3 The mental tool kit

The following section outlines some of the compositional devices and strategies which composers have commonly used to extend or develop their musical ideas. Inevitably, there will be a degree of overlap with suggestions made elsewhere in this book.

As the composer becomes more experienced or, indeed, gains greater facility in their craft, the use of these so-called devices becomes an integral part of their thinking and the whole process of developing and structuring musical ideas becomes completely subsumed into the whole compositional process. Initially, however, it can be helpful to experiment quite consciously with some of the 'tricks of the trade'.

6.4 Some analogies

We began by comparing the process of composing a piece of music with building a house and most of us would concede that you would be unlikely to start such a project without a plan. The word *form* in music describes just such a plan and concerns the way in which a piece is structured, ordering its various sections and very often, their possible keys.

However, when using the building analogy, we are looking at a piece of music from the composer's point of view. But we should remember that the point of a piece of music is that it exists to be heard; the listener wants to make sense of the piece as it proceeds and to feel a sense of progression. From their point of view, the experience might, perhaps, better be compared to making a journey.

As the listener travels through the time-frame of a musical piece, its form might be more helpfully thought of as representing successive stages in that journey. And in making any journey, some familiarity with the plan helps us to know just where we are.

Unlike most of our journeys in real life, however, a musical excursion will often terminate where it began. We take a kind of circular route which is more like an afternoon stroll, or for the more energetic amongst us, a jog around the neighbourhood. Musically speaking, even on a small scale – perhaps in a 32-bar song, for instance – such an outing will usually end where it began, both in terms of repetition of the principal melody/theme [*recapitulation*] and by making a return to the *tonic* key. Departure from the home key creates a sense of tension in the listener which is resolved when we return to home base.

Having completed our stroll or jog, we return knowing a bit more about the neighbourhood and we might even have explored a little by taking in a few different streets. And the same might be true in reaching the end of a musical outing: hopefully, we know more about the subject matter of the piece than we did at the outset.

But, what we will probably very seldom do, when planning our outing, is to cover part of the same route more than once, except perhaps in the last leg as we return to home base. Here, perhaps, is where the analogy breaks down to some extent, since the form of most pieces of music includes repetition. In fact, repetition lies at the heart of musical form. Indeed, it might be said that without repetition, musical form can hardly exist. And, importantly, repetition in music allows the piece to 'teach itself' to the listener, even on the first hearing, and this is one factor which helps to leave the listener with a sense of satisfaction rather than frustration when they reach the conclusion of the piece.

6.5 Some common musical forms

As stated in *Section 2: Composition – Getting Started*, in order to simplify the description of different sections of a melody or an entire piece, these may be labelled with letter names: A, B, C *etc*.

It is also worth knowing that in larger-scale works, the melodic ideas upon which a piece or a movement may be based are often described as ***subjects***.

An understanding of the following structures may prove useful in planning your own pieces.

Form in shorter pieces

Strophic – verse-repeating as, for example, in songs, hymns or carols, and thus A A A *etc*.

e.g. – *While Shepherds Watched Their Flocks by Night* [Carol]
Scarborough Fair [Folk Song]

Verse and Chorus – A B A B *etc*., as in folk songs, for example, where both are likely to be in the same key. This form might also be described as strophic.

e.g. – *My Bonnie Lies Over the Ocean* [folk song]
What Shall We Do With the Drunken Sailor [sea shanty]

Binary – consisting of two components: thus A B.
This form has been explored in some detail in the context of the song *Rule Britannia* [again, see Section *2: Composition – Getting Started*].

Ternary – consisting of two components, arranged in three sections: thus A B A or, more often, arranged in four sections, A A B A. This form is used in a host of popular songs and, where each section is eight bars long, produces a 32-bar verse. In the popular song, the B section is sometimes referred to as the *middle eight* or the *bridge* and this is usually in a closely related key as follows:

e.g. – *Any Dream Will Do* from *Joseph and the Amazing Technicolour Dreamcoat* [Andrew Lloyd Webber] beginning in a major key. The middle eight begins in the subdominant key.

Who Will Buy? From *Oliver* [Lionel Bart]: beginning in a minor key. The middle eight is in the relative major

You might well apply any of the above structures to your own compositions and it would be a useful assignment to write a song which is structured in ternary form as outlined above. [see *Section 4: Understanding Key Signatures*]

Form in longer pieces

Rondo – where section A recurs, in alternation with new sections. Thus: A B A C A *etc.*

e.g. *Violin Concerto,* 3rd movement [Beethoven]
Horn Concerto No. 3 in E♭, 3rd movement [W. A. Mozart]
Blue Rondo a la Turk [Dave Brubeck from the album/CD *Time Further Out*]

Sonata/First Movement Form
Exposition: A [1st subject] B [2nd subject].
Sometimes repeated to complete the exposition.
Development: based upon subject A and/or subject B.
Recapitulation: A [1st subject] B [2nd subject but now in tonic key].
Coda: Tailpiece, sometimes containing new material and/or further development.

e.g. *40th Symphony in G minor,* 1st movement [W. A. Mozart]
5th Symphony in C minor, 1st movement [Beethoven]

Now, whilst we may not be concerned with the complexity of first movement form, we should certainly give the formal organisation of even quite short pieces some consideration.

6.6 Other approaches to form

Variation

Theme and Variations is a commonly used structure which explores a range of treatments, usually of an existing tune. In writing variations, it is worth exploring which aspects of a theme might be varied, and you may wish to experiment with this approach basing it on a simple well-known tune such as that of a nursery rhyme. You could vary:

- Tempo
- Key: major to minor or vice versa
- Time signature
- Harmony
- The note durations of your melody by shortening [*diminution*] or lengthening [*augmentation*]
- The orchestration [where relevant]

e.g. *Variations on the St. Anthony Chorale* [Brahms]
Variations [Andrew Lloyd Webber]
Goldberg Variations [J. S. Bach]

Programme Music

Another approach is to compose a piece which relates to a storyline or is descriptive of some other non-musical entity. This is described as ***programme music***.[1]

Often the programme is rather loosely applied to the music but it may well determine some of its elements.

e.g. *Fantasy Overture: Romeo and Juliet* [Tchaikovsky]
Night On a Bare Mountain [Mussorgsky]
The Sorcerer's Apprentice [Dukas]
The Planets – Suite [Holst]
Harlem [Duke Ellington]

Some suggested starting-points for your own programmatic compositions:

- A journey
- A disaster
- A story
- An event/festival or location

When using a storyline as a formal basis for a composition, composers have not always adhered slavishly to its sequence of events. Tchaikovsky, in his *Fantasy Overture: Romeo and Juliet* created themes or complete sections to describe characters/events in the storyline – a 'fight' sequence, for example – and the often heard 'love' theme. When these themes are transformed in the course of the composition, perhaps to adapt to the developing storyline, this gives rise to a developmental device which is described as ***thematic metamorphosis***. The final appearance of the 'love theme' in Tchaikovsky's *Romeo and Juliet* provides a good example of this.

Interestingly, it has been said that the 'love' theme from this overture is the longest melody ever composed. Whether or not this is the case, it does provide us with an excellent example of melody-building using sequence [see *Section 2: Getting Started*].

[1] Music which is not programmatic is known as absolute music.

Ground bass

Although not strictly a formal device, the *ground bass* can provide a structured approach to a composition.

A ground bass is a bass line which is repeated whilst the composition evolves above this unchanging foundation.

e.g. Dido's Lament [*When I Am Laid in Earth*] from Purcell's opera *Dido and Aeneas*.

Improvisation in jazz is also sometimes termed as '... a series of variations on a ground bass' which is a description which falls somewhat short of an adequate account of what takes place in this style of music. Nonetheless, there is an element of truth in such a description in as much that, very often, the harmonic progression of the piece is retained and repeated and this forms the basis for the improvised variations which follow [termed *solos* in jazz].

Ostinato

An *ostinato*, like a ground bass, is not a form but is another device which can provide structure and unity to a composition. An ostinato is a repeated figure, melodic or rhythmic, which proceeds, sometimes relentlessly, through a section of a piece or may pervade the entire composition. If the ostinato arises in the bass line, it may be described as a *basso ostinato*.

e.g. Ravel's *Bolero*

The pedal

The *pedal* in compositional terms, is a sustained or repeated note (usually in the bass) over which the harmony changes. It takes its name from the foot pedals of the organ which can be held down to produce a static bass note over which changing harmonies are played on the manuals. An example of the use of a pedal bass note is illustrated in Section 12.10 *Using Quartal Harmony*.

Pedal notes have been used in most types of music from pre-Baroque times and has been a particular favourite of progressive rock musicians. The pedal is an extremely simple but highly effective compositional device and can be used over several bars to create a sense of 'strengthening'. A *dominant* pedal (on the 5th degree of the tonic scale) is often used to prepare the listener for a return to the tonic or home key,

The pedal note can also be very powerful device when used as a high note under which the chords move in *parallel*. This works particularly well when approaching the end of a composition as in the final three bars of the *Toccata* from Widor's 5th Symphony for organ.

6.7 Development

One of the problems encountered by aspiring composers, having written a melody, for instance, is how to extend it into a more substantial piece.

Working within the context of one of the formal plans outlined above, there are a number of strategies which we can use to exploit the potential of our material. This exploitation is referred to as development.

Repetition with some variation

Even the smallest variation in repeating a section can transform it substantially. The following suggestions include some of the more obvious possibilities:

- Simply repeating a melodic idea an octave higher/lower or taking some notes up or down the octave can be effective.
- Ornamentation may not affect the melodic line substantially but can certainly enhance what has already been heard.
- Changing the dynamic on a repeat can also add interest and may reveal a very different character in your melody.

The real substance of extending a piece, however, lies in investigating the musical potential of your ideas, and this process is more applicable to extended compositions.

Fragmentation

This kind of development, as its name suggests, involves using a fragment of the melody and especially one which has a strong rhythmic element as a basis for a new section. Very often, a fragment may be used sequentially [*i.e.* repeated at different pitches] and, possibly passed from one voice/instrument or from one orchestral section to another. The following example from Mozart's *40th Symphony in G minor* illustrates this well:

Opening theme – first subject:

The Composer's Tool Kit

Development through fragmentation and sequence:

N.B.: All instruments notated in concert pitch.

Inversion and retrograde

Like intervals, melodic fragments or motifs can be turned upside down and this is known as an *inversion*.

For example:

The fragment could also be written/played backwards, known as ***retrograde***:

Or, these two devices can be successfully combined as a ***retrograde inversion***:

Contrapuntal treatment

Yet another approach to development is to investigate the **contrapuntal** potential of your melody/subject. The use of *fugato* or, indeed a full *fugal* treatment in the context of a substantially non-contrapuntal composition is a powerful developmental device and one which is used to great effect by many composers.

e.g. W. A. Mozart's *Symphony No. 41 in C [Mozart KV 551] 'The Jupiter'* 1st movement.

The subject of **counterpoint** is explored in some detail in *Section 7: Thinking Horizontally*.

6.8 Conclusion

Finally, although many of these procedures and devices may seem complex and very much part of the world of music theory and analysis, once they have found their way into our compositional repertoire they will greatly expand our potential.

Remember, it is perfectly possible to speak a language fluently while having no theoretical knowledge of its grammatical construction. But the truth is that the grammar of the language has been learned through listening and imitation, and this can be equally true in the case of the language of music.

Did you know ...

... that the Voyager unmanned space probes, launched in 1977 by the USA, carried the first recorded music to be sent into outer space? After 1986, they left the Solar System and Voyager 1 is now in excess of 9.4 billion miles from the sun.

Each Voyager space probe carried a gold-plated phonograph record which contained 90 minutes of music. The selection included excerpts from J.S. Bach, Mozart, Beethoven and Stravinsky as well examples from many different cultures including those of Japan, China, India, Peru, the Solomon Islands, the Australian Aborigines and the Navajo Indians. A blues from Louis Armstrong was included as well as the song *Johnny B. Goode* sung by Chuck Berry. A detailed account is provided in Murmurs of Earth by Carl Sagan. See Select Bibliography for details.

7 Thinking Horizontally

7.1 Introduction

In *Section 5: Understanding Harmony*, we dealt with the basics of adding harmony to a melodic line and in doing so, we were mainly thinking vertically; that is to say, we went through a process of deciding which chord would be appropriate for a particular note or group of notes in the melody. This way of thinking about harmony is well illustrated in hymns/chorales [or in basic academic harmony exercises] where the underlying harmony, whether sung or played, substantially moves rhythmically with the melody. This kind of harmonisation is described as *homophonic*:

St. George G. J. Elvery [1816–1893]; Words: H. Alford [1810–1871]

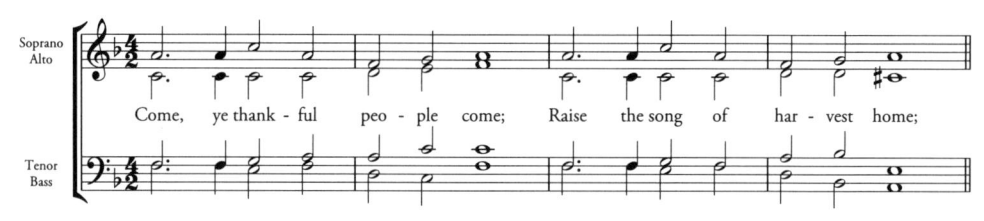

Track 38

Come, ye thank-ful peo-ple come; Raise the song of har-vest home;

Of course, there is a horizontal element to this thinking too, and that arises as we consider the successive effect of our chosen series of chords – the *harmonic* or *chord progression*. In tonal music, the sequence of chords has to be coherent and it is described as a progression because it must give a sense of forward movement towards the next *cadence* [see *Section 5: Understanding Harmony*].

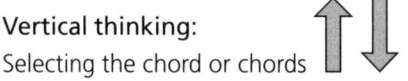

Vertical thinking:
Selecting the chord or chords

Horizontal thinking:
Considering the chord progression

This process of vertical thinking also substantially describes the way in which, say, a rhythm guitar accompaniment is added to the melodic line of a song although, of course, it can no longer strictly be described as homophonic. For example:

Rivers of Babylon Trad. Jamaican

Track 39

By the wa-ters of Ba-by-lon,____ Where we sat down,

And there we wept, When we re-mem-bered Zi - on.____

80

N.B. In the above example, no chords are used in the first [incomplete] bar and in order to show that this is intentional, the words 'no chord' or the abbreviation *N.C.* can be added where chord symbols would normally be placed. The remainder of this extract is harmonised entirely with *primary chords* which, in the key of **F** major, are **F**, **B♭** and **C** [I, IV and V]. [see *Section 5: Understanding Harmony*].

7.2 Towards a horizontal approach

In musical terms, thinking horizontally has its roots in vocal harmony [again, see *Section:5 Understanding Harmony*] and may seem to imply writing for voices. But, of course, the use of the word 'voices', in the present context, does not necessarily mean only vocal lines; the term can be applied to any line – instrumental or vocal – whether melodic or part of the harmony, and can even apply to independent lines in keyboard writing [see *Section 9: Writing for the Piano*].

Music which displays this kind of independent part-writing is described as *polyphonic* [polyphony: literally – many sounds] or *contrapuntal* [counterpoint: literally – note against note].

Thinking Horizontally

Most of us probably encountered very simple contrapuntal writing when singing *rounds* in primary school. In a round or *canon,* each successive voice enters in turn and sings or plays exactly the same tune. For example:

Frère Jacques Trad.

Track 40

And so, in a round or strict canon, each voice exactly imitates what is sung by the previous voice; not surprisingly, this is described as *imitation*. When a voice enters, it is, equally unsurprisingly, described as an *entry*. Perpetual rounds can be repeated endlessly, as anyone who has sung one in school can probably testify, and voices may enter at exactly the same pitch [unison] or at the octave.

There are many well-known rounds in existence including *Sumer is Icumen In* [Summer is Coming In], which is probably the earliest written example, as well as *London's Burning*, *Three Blind Mice*, and *Row, Row, Row Your Boat* to name just a few.

On the face of it, a round would appear to be a fairly easy kind of composition assignment, but it's not as easy as it might seem to write one which works really well.
The key to it lies in devising a very simple harmonic plan. In this example, notated in *short score*, the entire round is based on the tonic chord [**D** major]. Any notes which don't belong to the chord are *passing notes* – that is to say, they are *en route* to a note which does belong to the chord and passes between them:

Row, Row, Row Your Boat

This is quite a good way to start, but the effect of using only one chord [F in the following example] is to produce a sort of static aura of sound:

The One-Chord Canon

The following example illustrates a more complex canon, this time in a minor key. A bass line has been added to underline the tonic/dominant harmony:

Tonic and Dominant Round

Track 43

If you're interested in writing your own round, it might be a good idea to take an existing well-known example such as *London's Burning* and score it yourself – for four instruments or voices – to see and hear how it works. If you have access to a music software programme, then this should be a fairly straightforward exercise. Notice that this example begins with an **upbeat** [an ***anacrusis***] and so you will need to begin with an irregular [single-crotchet] bar. The numbers in boxed text show where each voice enters:

London´s Burning Trad.

[musical notation: London's Burning round in 4 parts]

Lon - don's burn - ing, Lon - don's burn - ing, Fetch the en - gines, fetch the en - gines, Fire! Fire! Fire! Fire! Pour on wa - ter, pour on wa - ter.

N.B. Appendix 4 [*Composing and Arranging Assignments*] contains a slightly easier 'way in' to scoring a round which is based on the short score of *Row, Row, Row Your Boat* which is notated in a previous example.

7.3 A two-part invention

You will probably already know from your own experience, or will have come to realise in the process of experimenting with the idea, that a ***perpetual canon*** where all the voices are in exact imitation of one another [either at the same pitch or at the octave] has some severe limitations.

During the ***Baroque*** period, the writing of contrapuntal music reached a level of perfection which many would say has never subsequently been surpassed.

In the following example, a two-part invention by J.S. Bach, the entire piece [from bar 3] is a ***development*** of the opening ***subject*** of the invention, stated in the first two bars, which is:

[musical notation: opening subject of Bach two-part invention]

Without attempting an academic analysis of this invention, it is worth looking at what follows in order to understand the differences between this piece and a round or canon.

Thinking Horizontally

Invention 1 BWV 772 J. S. Bach

♩ = 82

- In the first bar, the subject of the invention is first heard in the upper voice/part and then in the lower voice, an octave lower, with a modified ending to accommodate …

- … the re-statement of the subject in the upper voice in the second bar at the interval of a perfect 5th higher [see *Appendix 1: Intervals*]. N.B. this is not an exact [*real*] transposition – if it were, the **F** would be an **F♯**. This kind of transposition is referred to as *tonal*.

- The lower voice then imitates the first half of this re-statement, again with a modified ending, to accommodate …

- … the first developmental idea which consists of an *inversion* of the first half of the subject:

This is repeated and used *sequentially* through the next four bars – descending and then ascending – leading us to a *perfect cadence* in the *dominant* key of G major. It might be argued that the accompanying harmony, in quavers, derives from the second half of the subject. In academic analysis, this kind of sequential passage is sometimes referred to as an *episode*.

So, to summarise, the essential differences are:
- Imitation, from one voice to the next, is not exact. It may be tonally altered, or shortened, as required.

- The piece contains *development* [see *Section 6: The Composer's Tool Kit*] of the opening subject, which, in this case, consists of the inversion of part of the subject.

- The piece may change key [*i.e.* **modulate**] to another which is closely related.

Writing a two-part invention is, of course, a highly demanding assignment and one can only admire the technical and creative skill which is exhibited in such a piece. If we were to attempt this ourselves, then a Bach two-part invention might serve as a very good model, but leaving that prospect to one side for the moment, we can certainly learn a great deal from the compositional devices which they use.

The subject of compositional devices is more fully investigated in *The Composer's Tool Kit: Section 6*.

The ultimate in contrapuntal writing is to be found in the **fugue**. This type of composition for three voices/parts or more is a highly formulated type of piece, and further study of this subject would certainly be recommended for more advanced students.

Although fugal writing developed to a state of perfection at the end of the Baroque period, it has by no means been neglected by composers in the years which followed. Sometimes, only the opening [*exposition*] part of a fugue might be employed and this, together with any part of a piece which uses fugue-like writing, is termed **fugato**.

Suggested Listening:
J. S. Bach – *The Well-Tempered Clavier* [*The 48 Preludes and Fugues*] – any fugue, and Bach's most famous organ work: *Toccata and Fugue in D minor*
W. A. Mozart – No.10 [Sanctus] from *Requiem Mass* [KV 626]
Ludwig van Beethoven – Grosse Fuge [String Quartet, Op. 133]
Felix Mendelssohn – 4th Movement of the 4th Symphony
Frank Loesser – *Fugue for Tin Horns* from *Guys and Dolls*
Benjamin Britten – *The Young Person's Guide to the Orchestra*
Leonard Bernstein – *Fugue for Saxes* from *Prelude, Fugue and Riffs*
Ron Goodwin – Main theme from the film *Where Eagles Dare*

7.4 Descants and countermelodies

A descant [at least, in this context] is the addition of a melodic line above the original and is commonly encountered in hymn/carol-singing or in other songs which are **strophic** [verse-repeating]. A descant adds an extra dimension which can relieve the inevitable tedium of repetition and is often held in reserve for certain verses.
The decorative upper woodwind lines to be found in military marches are also a kind of descant which are designed to add excitement and brilliance to the overall effect of the piece. As such, the aim is one of enhancement rather than that of creating a coherent

alternate melody.

A countermelody, as its name suggests, is also an added melodic line [a melody which runs counter to an existing one] but is not necessarily added above the original melody. It may arise as a lower voice in the accompaniment, for instance.

On a good day, a countermelody might just occur to us while we are in the process of composing a piece, perhaps as a 'by-product' of the harmony. Equally, we might, quite deliberately, introduce the idea as we write or when we are in the process of reviewing a composition.

A few guidelines

- Rhythm: generally speaking, it's best to try to keep your added part moving when the given part is stationary. In broad and simple terms, in $\frac{4}{4}$ for example, write in crotchets when your given melody is moving in quavers, and vice versa.

- Pitch: contrary motion – moving in the opposite direction to the given melody – often adds strength.

- Harmony: the added part must agree with the harmony of the given part, whether actually stated or implied.

- Descants: try to save your highest-pitched phrase for the climax of the melody, which is often the last.

- And in general: try to create a countermelody or descant which is melodic in itself, although this is often easier said than done!

Two melodies to which parts may be added are given below.
Suggestions for the first few phrases of the added part have been given, which you may use, improve upon or adapt as you see fit:

Thinking Horizontally

Baa! Baa! Black Sheep Nursery rhyme – Trad.

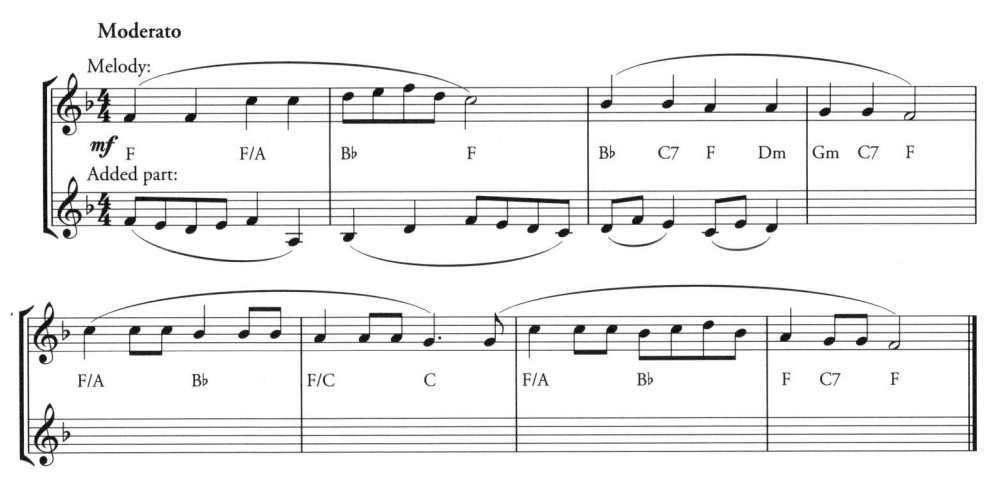

Moderato

[Melody with added part, chord symbols: F, F/A, B♭, F, B♭, C7, F, Dm, Gm, C7, F, F/A, B♭, F/C, C, F/A, B♭, F, C7, F]

Steal Away [excerpt] Afro-American Spiritual – Trad.

Larghetto ♩ = 60

[Chord symbols: D, Bm7, D/F♯, G, A7, D, D, F♯m, Bm7, G, Em7, A7, D]

In the following final example of countermelodies/descants, a harmonisation of *God Save the Queen* [UK] or *America / My Country, 'Tis of Thee* [USA] is given for piano with an added descant for flute which can be adapted or replaced by one of your own. Note the use of **sequence** in bars 7–8 and 9–10, and remember that if you use a different harmonisation, then there will be implications for the descant too.

God Save the Queen – My Country, 'Tis of Thee

Track 47

7.5 Counterpoint in jazz and jazzy styles

Interestingly, although the roots of jazz can hardly be said to lie in European music of the Baroque period or earlier [although there is some evidence to suggest that military marches from much later periods may well have been one important ingredient], examples of 'Traditional 'or 'New Orleans' jazz display a wealth of improvised counterpoint, often with **ad lib** melodic lines being added by many players simultaneously.

Sometimes, this profusion of counterpoint can be a little overwhelming and may account for the difficulty which some express in listening to this style of music. Others would undoubtedly say that it is precisely these spontaneous outbursts which give New Orleans jazz its energetic and instantly recognisable character.

Suggested Listening:
South Rampart Street Parade, At The Jazz Band Ball, 12th Street Rag, Tiger Rag

Counterpoint continues to be found at the heart of many of the subsequent developments in jazz as well as in jazz-styled compositions and the following notated examples have been included to suggest ways in which this might arise.

Both pieces are scored for two clarinets, the first for an unaccompanied duet whilst the second has a piano accompaniment.

Thinking Horizontally

Downtown Blues James Rae

from *Jazzy Clarinet Duets* [UE 19 430, © Copyright 1991 by Universal Edition (London) Ltd., London]

In *Downtown Blues*, the two clarinets are substantially playing in, what could loosely be described as, a homophonic manner. This changes, after the double barline, when the second clarinet begins playing in counterpoint with the first clarinet.

In the following example, *On a Roll*, the device of imitation is used with each clarinet playing in counterpoint with the other's imitative phrases, joining together at the ends of sections:

Thinking Horizontally

On a Roll — Mike Cornick
for 2 B♭ clarinets and piano

Track 49

At a lively swing tempo (♩ = 160, ♪♪ = ♩♪³)

Thinking Horizontally

© Copyright 2006 by Reedimensions (London) RD045

A fugato approach in a jazzy style can also be fun to write and play, partly because of the slight incongruity of using a blues-like fugue subject in a contrapuntal style which the listener would normally associate with a serious Baroque composition.

In the following example for three performers [six hands!] on one piano, notice how each entry is adapted to accommodate the progression of the piece:

Thinking Horizontally

Baroque to the Blues Mike Cornick

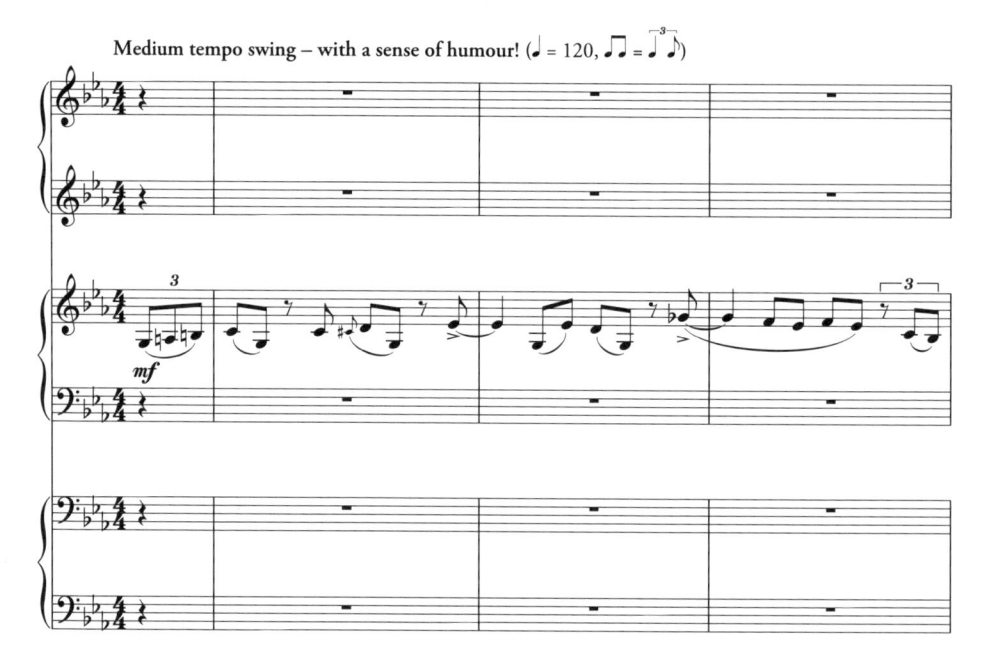

Track 50

Medium tempo swing – with a sense of humour! ($\quarter = 120$, $\eighth\eighth = \triplet{\quarter\eighth}$)

from *3 Pieces for 6 Hands at 1 Piano* [UE 21 123, © Copyright 2002 by Universal Edition (London) Ltd., London]

7.6 Conclusion

And so, finally, here are a few thoughts which may be worth considering in your own writing:

- Contrapuntal writing may have a place in pieces in a range of styles.

- Contrapuntal sections may make an interesting and effective contrast to homophonic writing within the same piece.

- Your use of counterpoint might consist simply of a descant or countermelody, or arise in the opening of a piece.

- Counterpoint can be an effective device within a piano accompaniment, too.

- Experiment with simple two-part counterpoint at first and develop your own skills by studying notated and recorded examples of contrapuntal writing by such composers as J. S. Bach, Handel, Mozart and Mendelssohn and, perhaps, broaden your scope to include other contexts where the counterpoint is improvised – in the jazz recordings of Gerry Mulligan's *Pianoless Quartet*, for example.

- Sometimes an added countermelody may be an intrinsic part of the style, as in the previously mentioned upper woodwind parts which decorate some sections of marches.

- And, if you maintain an analytical approach to listening, you may find instances of counterpoint where you might least expect to find them.

- Contrapuntal writing is possibly one of the most difficult aspects of composition to master. However, perseverance, and a willingness to modify and improve will pay dividends in the long run.

> *Did you know ...*
>
> ... that the soprano saxophone was the first musical instrument to be played in space? The event occurred on the space shuttle *Challenger* in February 1984.
>
> The player was a physicist, Dr. Ronald E. McNair, who subsequently died in the *Challenger* disaster on 28th January, 1986.
>
> from *Saxophone* by Paul Harvey ISBN 1-871082-53-6

8

Instruments and their Characteristics

8.1 Introduction

In this section of the book we discuss what instruments can, and equally importantly, what they *can't* do well. It is vital to have a working understanding of whatever musical forces for which you choose to write. For example, don't expect a trumpet player to be able to play a whole page of music comfortably without leaving adequate rests, whereas a violinist or pianist could do this without any difficulty.

It is well worth spending time listening to recordings of instruments playing in a wide variety of styles. This will give you a good idea of their capabilities and also how they sound. Each description in this section contains suggested listening. It also shows the full range of notes playable by each instrument. A good music software programme will give visual warning of writing outside of the comfortable range of any instrument, but …

Beware! When using music software, always bear in mind that computers can perform the technically impossible, so ensure that you take note of the specific limitations of each instrument outlined in this section.

Transposing instruments

All instruments can be divided into two fundamental groups with regard to how they are pitched. They are said to be either **concert pitched** or **transposing**. The verb *to transpose* in music means to raise or lower the pitch of the original written notes. A concert pitched instrument, when reading the note **C**, will produce a **C**. However, a transposing instrument, when reading the note **C**, will produce a different note. This means that the notes which the player reads, when played, will sound at a different pitch. *e.g.* **C**, when played on a **B♭** clarinet will sound as a **B♭**.

Transposing instruments usually have the key in which they are pitched written before or after their names. *e.g.* Horn in **F** or **E♭** alto saxophone. Here is an example of how transposition works, in this case, for the **B♭** clarinet:

Clarinet in B♭

written:

sounding:

N.B. The ranges of instruments shown in each of the following sections are based on practical usage and may not necessarily include the highest or lowest attainable notes.

8.2 The woodwind family

Track 51
flute
oboe
clarinet
bassoon

The woodwind family is divided into six subfamilies, primarily according to the method of sound production:

- The recorder family
- The flute family
- The oboe family
- The clarinet family
- The bassoon family
- The saxophone family

It may seem obvious, but woodwind players need to breathe! Avoid writing unduly long notes and allow adequate time for breathing between phrases. Of course, when a number of players are playing the same part, as is the case in a band or orchestral situation, the breathing can be staggered.

Also, equally obvious, but worth mentioning, is the fact that these are all melodic instruments which can only play one note at a time. If you want the flute sound in harmony, for instance, you will need as many flutes as there are notes in your chord.

Try to avoid writing too many large, slurred, downward intervals as these are generally difficult to execute. Many composers tend to work from the keyboard where this type of

Instruments and their Characteristics

writing works well, but remember, what may work well on a keyboard instrument or sound effective when played back through music software, may not be successful or playable in practice.

All woodwind instruments, apart from the bassoon, bass recorder and, occasionally, the bass clarinet read from the treble clef.

The recorder family

The recorder, although no longer a member of the orchestral woodwind section, is very much a woodwind instrument. There are five recorders in common use. A group of recorders, when played together, is described as a consort. They are:

- The sopranino recorder
- The descant recorder
- The treble recorder
- The tenor recorder
- The bass recorder

The recorder is a relatively quiet instrument and has a limited dynamic range. Changes in breath pressure can affect the pitch! For these reasons, great care should be taken when combining recorders with other instruments in ensembles. However, recorders sound well when accompanied by strings or an acoustic guitar. Smaller members of the family are extremely agile; however, the larger instruments are not capable of such a degree of agility, so avoid writing too many rapid passages for them.

All recorders read from the treble clef with the exception of the bass.

Ranges:

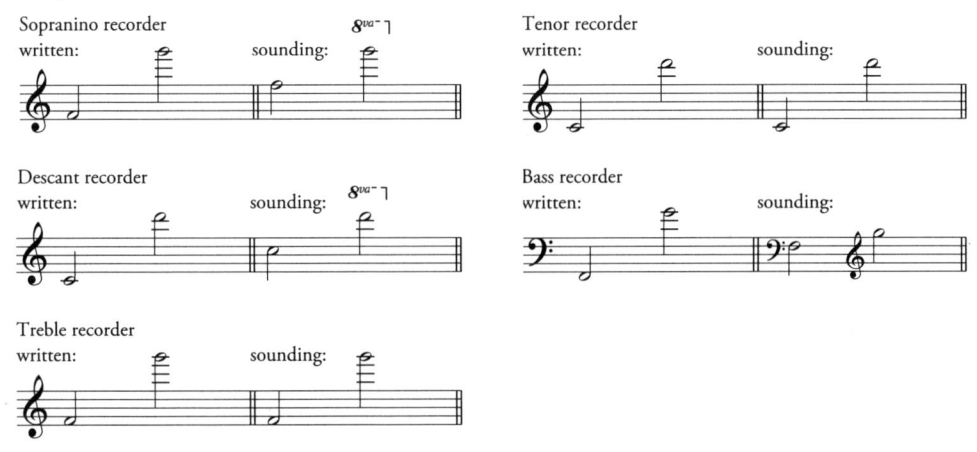

Sopranino recorder — written / sounding (8va)

Descant recorder — written / sounding (8va)

Treble recorder — written / sounding

Tenor recorder — written / sounding

Bass recorder — written / sounding

Suggested Listening:
J.S. Bach – *Brandenburg Concerto No.4 in G*
Lennox Berkeley – *Sonatina for Treble Recorder*
Hans Martin Linde – *Music for a Bird*

The flute family

There are four principal members of the flute family:

- The piccolo
- The flute
- The alto flute
- The bass flute

The piccolo

The piccolo is a half-sized flute which sounds one octave higher; however, it should be noted that its lowest note is **D** rather than **C**. Although it is the highest pitched instrument, its sound can cut through an entire symphony orchestra. A rapid staccato effect is attainable through single, double and triple *tonguing*.

Range:

The flute

The flute is an extremely agile instrument, capable [within the limitations of the player] of playing rapid passages. Like the piccolo, the flute has of the same staccato facility. Flute writing often looks very 'busy' although the instrument's expressive qualities also lend themselves to slower and more lyrical passages too.

Range:

The alto flute

The alto flute is less commonly encountered, is less agile, but produces a warm sound in its lower register. This is a transposing instrument which is pitched in **G** [*i.e* sounding a perfect 4th lower than concert pitch].

Range: Alto Flute in G
written: sounding:

The bass flute

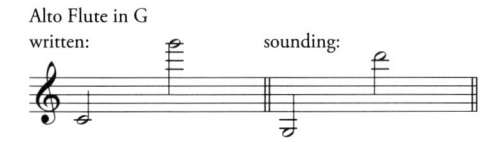

The bass flute sounds one octave lower than a standard flute, is considerably less agile, and is very rarely met. It may be used for special purposes, as in a film score for example, and is capable of creating an atmosphere of suspense or drama. Like the alto flute, it is the lower register which is often exploited.

Range: Bass Flute
written: sounding:

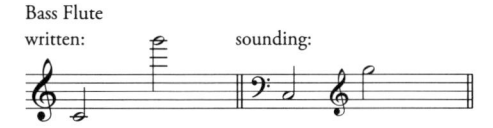

Suggested Listening:

The piccolo
Solo:
John Phillip Sousa – *The Stars and Stripes Forever*
Maurice Ravel – *Empress of the Pagodas [Mother Goose Suite]*

Ensemble:
Pyotr Il'yich Tchaikovsky – *Chinese Dance [The Nutcracker]*
Quincy Jones – *Soul Bossa Nova*

The flute
Solo:
J.S. Bach – *B minor Suite for Flute & Orchestra*
W. A. Mozart – *Concerto in G for Flute & Orchestra*
Claude Debussy – *Syrinx*
Ian Anderson – *Locomotive Breath [rock]*

Ensemble:
Pyotr Il'yich Tchaikovsky – *Dance of the Flutes [The Nutcracker]*

The oboe family

The only two instruments in common use in this double-reed family are:

- The oboe
- The cor anglais [or English horn]

The oboe
The oboe is less agile than the flute and has a more limited range. However, it is at its most effective when given lyrical passages. It is well worth avoiding writing quiet low notes as these are difficult to produce securely and can sound 'honky'.

Range:

The cor anglais
The cor anglais is a transposing instrument and is pitched in F, a perfect 5th below the oboe. Because of its larger size, it has a deeper, more melancholic sound and can produce very rich low notes.

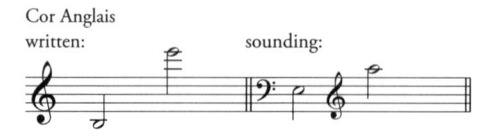

Range:

Suggested Listening:

The oboe
Solo:
Tomaso Giovanni Albinoni – *Concerto in D*
Richard Strauss – *Oboe Concerto*
Benjamin Britten – *Six Metamorphoses after Ovid*
Ralph Vaughan Williams – *Oboe Concerto*

Ensemble:
Pyotr Il'yich Tchaikovsky – *Dance of the Cygnets [Swan Lake]*
G. F. Handel – *The Arrival of the Queen of Sheba*

The cor anglais

Jean Sibelius – *The Swan of Tuonela*
Antonín Dvořák – *Largo ["From The New World" Symphony No.9]*
Alexander Borodin – *In the Steppes of Central Asia*

The clarinet family

There are four principal members of the clarinet family. They are:

- The E♭ clarinet
- The B♭ clarinet
- The A clarinet
- The B♭ bass clarinet

The clarinet family are single reed instruments and, unlike the oboe, can produce soft lower notes with great ease and effect. All clarinets in common use are transposing instruments and all read from the treble clef. However, some composers write for bass clarinet in bass clef in order to avoid excessive use of ledger lines.

The E♭ clarinet

The E♭ clarinet is the smallest member in current use and produces the highest notes. It is highly agile and full of character. However, overuse of this instrument should be avoided as its tone can be strident under certain circumstances. The E♭ clarinet can be found in wind bands, clarinet choirs and, occasionally, in the symphony orchestra.

Range:

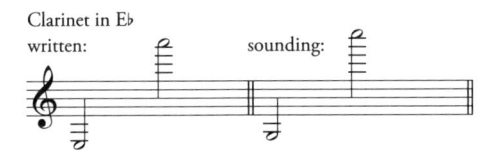

The B♭ clarinet

The B♭ clarinet is the most commonly used member of the family and is encountered in many different settings and styles of music. It has a much larger range than the oboe and is as agile as the flute, except in its highest register. The low, or chalumeau register, has a rich dark sound which is capable of an expressive quality and this has been exploited by many composers.

Range:

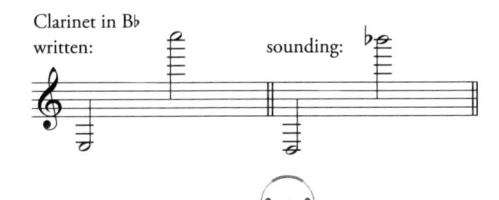

The A clarinet

The A clarinet is slightly larger than the B♭ clarinet and produces a darker sound, much favoured by orchestral composers for long, lyrical solos. It also has all the facility of the B♭ clarinet.

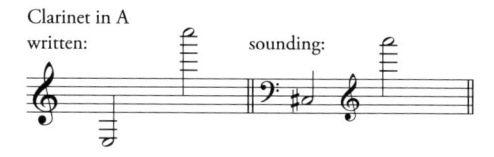

Range:

The B♭ bass clarinet

The B♭ Bass Clarinet is pitched one octave lower than the B♭ clarinet and is often used for its sonorous sound quality in the low register. Bass clarinets are found in all the same musical situations as the E♭ clarinet.

Range:

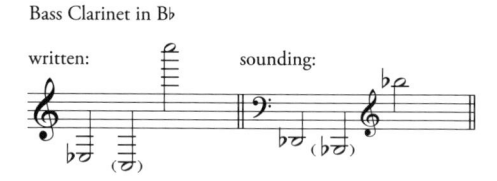

Other instruments in the clarinet family include the basset horn in F, the E♭ alto clarinet and the B♭ and E♭ contrabass clarinets.

All clarinets, with the exceptions of the A clarinet and the basset horn, are often combined to form the clarinet choir.

The basset horn was favoured by W. A. Mozart for certain works because of its dark sound quality. It is very similar to the alto clarinet but pitched one tone higher.

Suggested Listening:

The E♭ clarinet
Solo:
Hector Berlioz – *The Witches' Sabbath [Symphonie Fantastique]*
Henry Mancini – *Baby Elephant Walk*

The B♭ clarinet
Solo:
Carl Maria von Weber – *Concertino*

Aaron Copland – *Clarinet Concerto*
Artie Shaw – *Clarinet Concerto*
George Gershwin – *Rhapsody in Blue* [opening]

Ensemble:
Alec Templeton – *Bach Goes to Town*
Elmer Bernstein – The main theme from *The Great Escape* [film]

The A clarinet
Solo:
W. A. Mozart – *Clarinet Concerto*
Sergei Rachmaninov – Slow movement of the *Second Symphony*
Carl Neilsen – *Clarinet Concerto*

The B♭ bass clarinet:
Pyotr Il'yich Tchaikovsky – featured in *Dance of the Sugar Plum Fairy* [The Nutcracker]
Don Warren – The theme from *Mr. Ben*

The bassoon family

There are only two principal members of this family:

- The bassoon
- The contrabassoon (or the double bassoon)

The bassoon

The bassoon is essentially a bass instrument although it is capable of producing a singing quality in its tenor register. It can provide an effective bass to a group of woodwind instruments or, indeed, to the entire orchestra. It is capable of considerable agility despite its size and is sometimes used to great effect when given bouncy staccato lines to play. It reads principally from **bass clef** but often ventures into **tenor clef** for prolonged higher passages, thus reducing the need for *ledger lines*.

Range:

Bassoon
written & sounding:

The contrabassoon

The contrabassoon is pitched an octave lower than the bassoon, and reads an octave higher than it actually sounds. It is often used to great effect to portray 'the monster' in film scores.

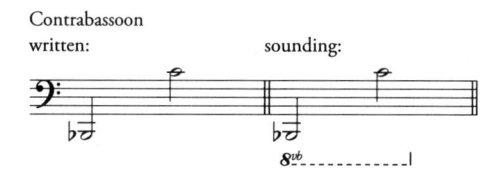

Range:

Suggested Listening:

The bassoon

Solo:
Igor Stravinsky – *The Rite of Spring* [opening]
W. A. Mozart – *Bassoon Concerto*
Sergei Prokofiev – *Peter and the Wolf* [representing the Grandfather]
Franz Schubert – *5th Symphony* [3rd movement – trio]
Vernon Elliot – *Ivor the Engine*

Ensemble:
Paul Dukas – *The Sorcerer's Apprentice*
W. A. Mozart – *Wind Serenades*

The contrabassoon
Maurice Ravel – *Beauty and the Beast* [The Mother Goose Suite]

The saxophone family

There are four principal instruments in this family. They are:

Track 53
B♭ soprano
E♭ alto
B♭ tenor
E♭ baritone

- The B♭ soprano saxophone
- The E♭ alto saxophone
- The B♭ tenor saxophone
- The E♭ baritone saxophone

As you can see, these are all transposing instruments. However, they all read from the treble clef irrespective of their size and pitch. Each is a different sized version of the same instrument but each has its own distinctive character. Although the saxophone is a single-reed instrument, it has very little in common with the clarinet. Technically, it is more akin to the oboe with regard to its written range and character but, unlike the clarinet, it finds the production of quiet, lower passages difficult.

All saxophones, regardless of size, are capable of great agility. Notes above the standard range, called *harmonics*, are highly effective when played by an accomplished performer. When writing in this register, avoid rapid, flute-like, scalic passages as these notes are more difficult to produce. Harmonics are used by saxophonists in all styles of music.

The B♭ soprano saxophone
The B♭ soprano saxophone is the most oboe-like of the family as it is pitched just one tone lower and is capable of all that the oboe can achieve but with a wider dynamic range. Because of its small size, it is one of the most difficult saxophones to play in tune.

Range:

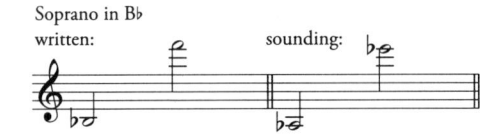

E♭ alto saxophone
The E♭ alto saxophone is the most commonly used member of the family and is found in wind bands, rock and pop bands, jazz ensembles and even, occasionally, in the symphony orchestra. The instrument is pitched in roughly the same-sounding range as the B♭ clarinet but shares few of its characteristics.

Range:

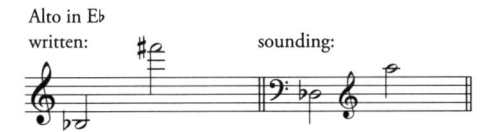

B♭ tenor saxophone
The B♭ tenor saxophone is used in similar situations to the alto and is the favoured instrument of most of the great jazz saxophonists. It is pitched one octave lower than the soprano and is capable of a wide expressive range from soulful to raucous and edgy.

N.B. The tenor does not make a suitable bass-line instrument because of the timbre of its lower notes.

Range: Tenor in B♭ written: / sounding:

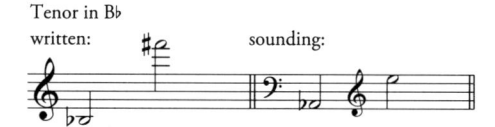

E♭ baritone saxophone

The E♭ baritone saxophone is the lowest commonly used member of the saxophone family. Unlike the tenor, it is an excellent bass instrument. In spite of its size, it is capable of considerable agility in all registers.

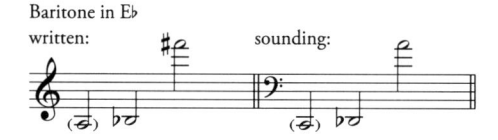

Range: Baritone in E♭ written: / sounding:

The four instruments listed above form the standard saxophone quartet which is the nearest wind equivalent to the string quartet. Many eminent composers have written effectively for this ensemble. The other, and more common standard saxophone grouping, is the section found in a big band. This consists of two altos, two tenors and a baritone.

Other members of the family include the B♭ sopranissimo saxophone or soprillo [pitched one octave higher than the soprano], the E♭ sopranino saxophone [pitched one octave higher than the soprano] and the B♭ bass saxophone [which is pitched one octave below the tenor]. There is also a B♭ sub-contrabass saxophone called a tubax, pitched one octave below the bass sax, but they are very rare!

The only instance where most of these saxophones are found playing together is in the saxophone choir which normally consists of 1 Sopranino, 2 Sopranos, 3 Altos, 3 Tenors, 2 Baritones and 1 Bass.

Suggested Listening:

The B♭ soprano saxophone
Maurice Ravel – *Bolero*
Hector Villa-Lobos – *Fantasia for Soprano Saxophone*
Kenny G – *Songbird*

The E♭ alto saxophone
Modest Musorgsky/Maurice Ravel – *The Old Castle [Pictures at an Exhibition]*
Alexander Glazunov – *Concerto for Saxophone*

Paul Desmond – *Take Five* [recorded by The Dave Brubeck Quartet]
Gerry Rafferty – *Baker Street*
Any recordings by Charlie Parker, David Sanborn or Johnny Hodges.

The B♭ tenor saxophone
Maurice Ravel – *Bolero*
Henri Mancini – *The Pink Panther*
Any recordings by Coleman Hawkins, Ben Webster, Michael Brecker or John Coltrane.

The E♭ baritone saxophone
Any recordings by Gerry Mulligan [in his Pianoless Quartet]

The saxophone quartet
Alexander Glazunov – *Quartet for Saxophones*
Gordon Jacob – *Quartet for Saxophones*

The big band sax section
The Duke Ellington Orchestra – *April in Paris* or any other recording.
The Count Basie Orchestra – any recording
The Glenn Miller Orchestra – *In the Mood*, or any recording.
The Ted Heath Orchestra – any recording

8.3 The brass family

Track 54
trumpet
french horn
trombone
tuba

The following information relates to the use of brass instruments in a solo, orchestral or big band context. There are many other brass instruments which have more specialist applications as, for instance, in a brass band and information concerning these should be sought elsewhere.

The most commonly used brass instruments are:

- The trumpet
- The french horn
- The trombone
- The tuba

The brass section is the loudest section of the orchestra or band and, as such, should be used sparingly. Playing a brass instrument calls for a great deal of stamina and when writing for these instruments care should be taken to provide sufficient rests.

Producing notes at the extremities of the ranges of these instruments is very much dependent on the skill of the player. This applies to brass players to a greater extent than for any other family of instrumentalists and should be kept in mind when writing for particular musicians.

The quality of tone produced by all brass instruments can be softened and modified by the use of **mutes**. These are devices inserted into the bell of the instrument and come in a variety of shapes depending on the desired effect. The Italian term **con sordino** is used in classical music to denote the use of the mute. Senza sordino means without the mute. In jazz music the direction is usually written in English e.g *'with straight mute'* or *'open'* to indicate no mute.

Like the woodwind family, brass instruments can only play one note at a time. If you want the trumpet sound in harmony, for instance, you will need as many trumpets as there are notes in your chord.

The trumpet

The trumpet is usually a transposing instrument and comes in a variety of keys but the most common is the trumpet in B♭. Trumpet players read from the treble clef. The trumpet is capable of producing a very bright and powerful sound and is a very articulate instrument.

Range: Trumpet in B♭

written: sounding:

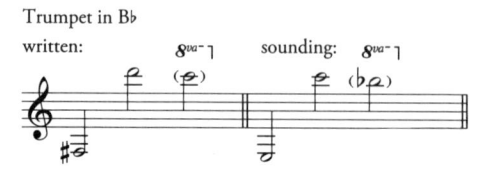

N.B. *Notes from high D and above can be produced by experienced trumpet players.*

Suggested Listening:

Solo:
Josef Haydn – *Trumpet Concerto*
Antonio Vivaldi – *Double Trumpet Concerto*
Miles Davis – *Kind of Blue*

Ensemble:
Aaron Copland – *Fanfare for the Common Man*
Bill Conti – *Gonna Fly Now* [Theme from the film *Rocky*]
John Williams – Theme from the film *Superman*

The french horn

The french horn, like the trumpet, can be pitched in a number of keys but the most commonly used is the horn in F. Although it is a valved instrument, it cannot achieve the same degree of agility as the trumpet. When used orchestrally as a section, horns can provide effective and powerful harmonic support as well as being superb solo instruments.

Range:

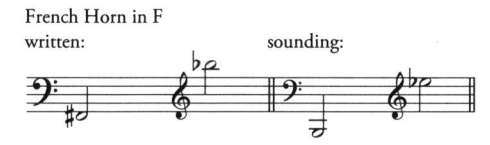

Suggested Listening:

Solo:
W.A. Mozart – any horn concerto
Benjamin Britten – *Serenade for Tenor, Horn and Strings*
Gilbert Vinter – *Hunter's Moon*

Ensemble:
Jean Sibelius – *Karelia Suite* [Intermezzo]
Pyotr Il'yich Tchaikovsky – *Waltz of the Flowers* [*The Nutcracker*]
Richard Strauss – *Don Juan*
Ron Goodwin – the main theme from the film *633 Squadron*

The tenor trombone

The most commonly encountered trombone is the tenor trombone which is used in most musical instrumental settings. Trombones differ from all other members of the brass family as they have a slide which allows the instrument to play an effect called a ***glissando***. There is also the valve trombone but it is very rarely used.

The trombone generally reads from bass clef and is not a transposing instrument except in a brass band context where it reads from treble clef and is treated as a **B♭** transposing instrument. Occasionally, orchestral trombone parts are written in tenor clef when the writing is high but in big band and wind band scores it is always written in bass clef no matter how high the part goes!

Range:

The bass trombone

The bass trombone is a larger instrument and is also used in bands and orchestras. It produces a bigger, fatter and of course, lower sound than the tenor.

Range:

Trombones can offer a wide dynamic range and their expressive qualities can be successfully exploited in a number of diverse musical styles.

Suggested Listening:

Solo:
John Greenwood – *The Acrobat*
Bassman and Washington – *I'm Getting Sentimental Over You* – as recorded by Tommy Dorsey
Noel Coward – *Mad About the Boy* [intro] as recorded by Dinah Washington

Ensemble:
Gustav Holst – *The Perfect Fool*
Louis Prima – *Sing, Sing, Sing* as recorded by The Benny Goodman Orchestra
Erskine Hawkins – *Tuxedo Junction* as recorded by The Glenn Miller Orchestra
Quincy Jones – *Soul Bossa Nova* [intro]

The tuba

The tuba, like the trombone, reads from bass clef in an orchestral context and is pitched in C. In a brass band context, it reads from treble clef in either E♭ or B♭ depending on which tuba is used.

It is the lowest pitched instrument of the brass family and can provide an extremely powerful bass line. In contrast, it is also capable of producing a beautiful singing quality in its high register. The tuba's agility depends greatly on the skill of the player and this should be taken into account when writing for the instrument.

Range:

Suggested Listening:
Ralph Vaughan Williams – *Tuba Concerto*
John Greenwood – *Tubby the Tuba*

The brass quintet
The standard brass quintet consists of two trumpets, a french horn, a trombone and a tuba. This is a highly effective ensemble capable of producing a huge range of dynamics and colour. Many composers and arrangers have written successfully for this medium.

8.4 The string family

Track 55
violin
viola
cello
double bass

The strings are the busiest orchestral section and provide the basis of orchestral sound. In an orchestra, the violins are the only stringed instruments to be scored as two sections: 'firsts' and 'seconds' and these can play parts which are further subdivided. Violas, cellos and double basses can also be divided and this is indicated on the score or part by the word *divisi*. When these instruments are bowed the term commonly used is *arco*. The indication for plucking the strings is *pizzicato*. Where there is no such indication, then the player will assume that the passage is to be bowed.

Unlike woodwind and brass, each string instrument is capable of playing more than one note at once and this is termed *double stopping*. Care needs to be taken to ensure that what is written is actually playable and non-string players would be well-advised to consult a string player as to the feasibility of the writing.
All stringed instruments are in concert pitch.

- The violin
- The viola
- The cello
- The double bass

The violin
The violin is the highest pitched string instrument and reads from the treble clef. Like most other members of the family, it has four strings tuned in perfect 5ths. It can be used equally effectively as a solo instrument or in sections and the quality of the upper range of the instrument, like those in the brass family, is greatly dependent upon the skill of the player. It is the most agile of the family and is often called upon to play virtuoso passages. Although primarily a 'classical' instrument, violins are often heard in popular music and even occasionally, in jazz. The instrument is also strongly associated with folk music from many different cultures.

Range:

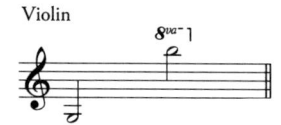

Violin range notation

Suggested Listening:
Antonio Vivaldi – *The Four Seasons* [Concerti]
Felix Mendelssohn – *Violin Concerto*
Alban Berg – *Violin Concerto*
Stefan Grappelli – any recording
John Williams – *Schindler's List* [main theme from the film]

The viola

The viola is the alto member of the family and generally reads from the **alto clef**. Because of its larger size, it has a darker and deeper sound and is usually heard in the inner parts of sectional string harmony. However, its solo sound has been exploited by many composers.

Range:

Viola range notation

Suggested Listening:
W.A. Mozart – *Sinfonia Concertante for Violin and Viola in E♭, KV 364.*
Hector Berlioz – *Harold in Italy*
William Walton – *Viola Concerto*

The cello

The cello is the second lowest member of the family. It can be used as the bass or tenor part in the orchestral string section and also in the **string quartet**. Its immensely expressive powers as a solo instrument have been widely exploited by many composers in a range of genres. It reads principally from the **bass clef** although **tenor clef** and treble clef may be used for prolonged higher passages.

Range:

Cello range notation

Suggested Listening:
J.S. Bach – *Suites for Unaccompanied Cello*
Antonín Dvořák – *Cello Concerto*
Camille Saint-Saëns – *The Swan* [*The Carnival of the Animals*]
Edward Elgar – *Cello Concerto*
Andrew Lloyd Webber – *Variations*

The double bass
The double bass is the lowest pitched instrument of the family and its strings are tuned in perfect 4ths. It generally reads from the bass clef and is called the double bass because it sounds an octave lower than its written pitch. Its pizzicato (plucked) qualities have been thoroughly exploited in jazz giving the instrument a rhythmic function and its lack of agility has, on occasion, been used to produce comic or special effects.

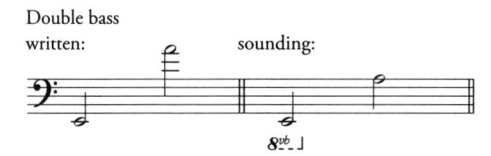

Range:

Suggested Listening:
Camille Saint-Saëns – *The Elephant* [*The Carnival of the Animals*]
Ray Brown – recordings of The Oscar Peterson Trio
Benjamin Britten – *The Young Person's Guide to the Orchestra*

8.5 Plucked stringed instruments

There are many other instruments which fall into this category, particularly in the world of folk and ethnic music, but for the purposes of this book we will deal with the four most commonly used.

- The harp
- The acoustic guitar
- The electric guitar
- The electric bass guitar

This family is unique as it includes the softest and the loudest of all musical instruments. It might sound obvious but it is well worth noting that, balance-wise, an electric guitar is much louder than an acoustic guitar. Do not be fooled by how music software programmes can play both of these at the same level. All plucked stringed instruments can be used to accompany vocal music whether amplified or acoustic, hence their popularity in pop and folk music.

When writing for these instruments please remember that their notes 'decay'. *i.e.* they can't hold long notes or chords at the same volume without dying away.

The harp

The harp comes in many forms, the most common being the concert harp. It reads from a double stave just like the piano and shares many of its characteristics. Harps can be used effectively in a variety of musical settings from symphony orchestras to chamber music. They are also used as unaccompanied solo instruments.

Writing for the harp requires very specialist knowledge of the capabilities of the instrument and the novice would be well advised to consult an experienced player.

Range: Harp written & sounding:

Suggested Listening:
Pyotr Il'yich Tchaikovsky – *Waltz of the Flowers [The Nutcracker]*
Benjamin Britten – *A Ceremony of Carols*
Paul Reade – *Suite [The Victorian Kitchen Garden]*

The acoustic guitar

Track 56
Four acoustic guitars

The acoustic guitar exists in many forms and is a specialist study in its own right. It is an ideal instrument for the accompaniment of vocals and softer instruments such as recorders. It is also an excellent solo instrument when used in classical music.

Music for guitars can be written in treble clef [sounding an octave lower than written], in chord symbols (**Cm**, **G7** etc.) or in TAB (tablature). All good music software programmes cater for these.

Suggested Listening:
Joaquin Rodrigo – *Concierto de Aranjuez*
Francisco Tárrega – *Memories of La Alhambra*
Django Reinhardt – Any recordings [jazz]
Heitor Villa-Lobos – *5 Preludes*

Oasis – *Wonderwall* [strumming]
The Beatles – *Blackbird* [picking]

The electric guitar

The invention of the electric guitar was one of the most significant musical instrument developments of the 20th century. By the addition of amplification, the guitar went from being the softest instrument in the band to the loudest. Further enhancements to its sound can be made by the use of a range of electronic effects such as overdrive, distortion and digital delay which are often controlled by pedals and the mechanical pitch-bending *whammy bar*. These are used extensively in rock music.

A close relative of the electric guitar is the semi-acoustic guitar which has a shallow, hollow body but also uses electronic amplification. This is the favoured instrument of jazz guitarists.

Range:

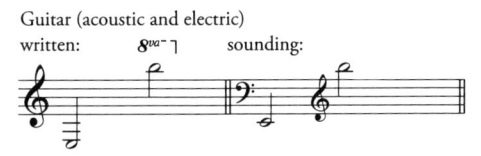

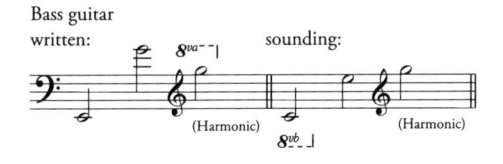

Suggested Listening:

The electric guitar
Any recording by Jimi Hendrix, Brian May or Eric Clapton

The semi-acoustic guitar
Any recording by Jim Hall or George Benson

The bass guitar

The bass guitar produces notes at the same pitch as the double bass. Its music is either written in bass clef or in TAB (tablature) but an experienced player can work out an effective bass line from reading chord symbols. The bass guitar is found in all rock bands and many jazz ensembles and big bands. Because it is amplified, it is capable of sustaining longer notes than double bass [pizzicato] where the sound 'decays' more rapidly.

Range:

Suggested Listening:
Any recording by Jaco Pastorius with *Weather Report* or Mark King with *Level 42*

8.6 The percussion family

The percussion family includes all instruments where the sound is generally produced by striking.

This family is divided into two major groups: pitched/tuned, where the instrument is capable of producing sounds of definable pitch, and unpitched/untuned where this is not the case.

There are differing approaches to the notation of percussion parts, sometimes on a single line, sometimes with cross noteheads and sometimes with solid noteheads. The appropriate form of notation will depend on circumstance or convention and this will need to be investigated beforehand.

Pitched percussion

Track 58
glockenspiel
xylophone
vibraphone
marimba

The timpani / kettledrums

The pitch of these instruments is prepared beforehand according to the key requirements of the piece. They are notated on bass clef. Most modern timpani have pedals which facilitate a rapid change of pitch from one note to another. Timpani are used in groups of two, three or four.

Ranges:

Timpani: 32" written & sounding: Timpani: 30"   Timpani: 28"   Timpani: 25"

Suggested Listening:
Hector Berlioz – *March to the Scaffold [Symphonie Fantastique]*
Benjamin Britten – *A Young Person's Guide to the Orchestra*

The xylophone

The xylophone is a wooden-barred instrument which is laid out like a keyboard. It is notated in treble clef and skilled players are able to play chords by holding a number of beaters in each hand. The xylophone is often used to great effect in music for cartoons to accompany fast chase sequences.

Range:

    Xylophone
    written & sounding:

Suggested Listening:
Camille Saint-Saëns – *Danse Macabre* or *Fossils [The Carnival of the Animals]*
Dmitry Kabalevsky – *The Comedian's Gallop*

The glockenspiel
The glockenspiel, like the xylophone, is laid out like a keyboard but has metal bars. Its music is written in treble clef, two octaves lower than it sounds. Because of its high pitched, bell-like quality it is often used to create a magical atmosphere and to add sparkle to the overall orchestral sound. In a marching band, glockenspiels [called bells or bell-lyra, mainly in the USA] also add brightness to the body of sound.

Range:

    Glockenspiel
    written: sounding:

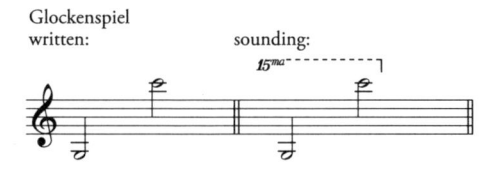

Suggested Listening:
Sergei Rachmaninov – *Scherzo [2nd Symphony]*
John Philip Sousa – *The Thunderer* [March]

The marimba
The marimba is a wooden-barred instrument similar to the xylophone but pitched one octave lower. It is often used to great effect in music for films set in Africa as the modern marimba is a development of its African forefather.

Range:

    Marimba
    written & sounding:

Instruments and their Characteristics

Suggested Listening:
Steve Reich – *Music for Mallet Instruments, Voices and Organ*

The vibraphone
The vibraphone [or 'vibes'] is a metal-barred instrument with the added facility of having a damper bar to stop the notes from sustaining. It is also unique as it can produce a vibrato effect by the use of rotating discs below the bars operated by a variable speed electric motor. It has been widely used in jazz music of all types.

Range: Vibraphone written & sounding:

Suggested Listening:
Any recording by Lionel Hampton
Wayne Hill – *Left Bank Two* [*The Gallery Theme* from the televison programme *Vision On*]

The celeste
The celeste has a piano-type keyboard and although technically a percussion instrument, it is generally played by a pianist. Its 'music-box' sound is a cross between a glockenspiel and a vibraphone. It is mainly used in orchestral music.

Range: Celeste written: sounding:

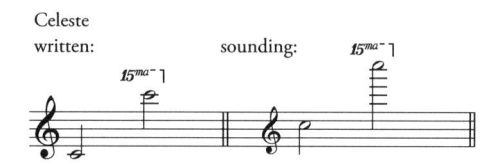

Suggested Listening:
Pyotr Il'yich Tchaikovsky – *Dance of the Sugar Plum Fairy* [*The Nutcracker*]
Béla Bartók – *Music for Strings, Percussion and Celesta*
John Williams – *Hedwig's Theme* from Harry Potter [the films]

Tubular bells
Tubular bells or 'chimes' sound very similar to church bells but are more convenient to play! They are arranged chromatically over one-and-a-half octaves and like the vibraphone they also have a damper pedal. They are sounded by being struck with a mallet.

Range: Tubular bells
written & sounding:

Suggested Listening:
Hector Berlioz – *A Witches' Sabbath [Symphonie Fantastique]*

Steel pans

Pans are manufactured from sawn-off fifty-five gallon oil drums, the end of which is beaten into a concave surface and then further tuned to provide a range of different pitches.

Pans are produced in bass, 'guitar' and tenor pitches with the tenor instrument holding the melody. The instruments are played with pairs of sticks with rubber heads and longer notes are sustained by a continuous tremolo action, rather like a drum roll.

The instrument is Afro-Caribbean in origin and its repertoire, although based in this culture, has been extended to include transcriptions of pieces from a range of popular genre.

Unpitched percussion

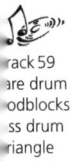

There are countless unpitched percussion instruments in existence from every culture and, certainly, from every civilisation, and cannot possibly be fully listed.

The following is a small representative selection which we have categorised under the headings Metal, Wood and Skin:

Metal
Cymbals
Tambourine [skin with metal jingles]
Pop tambourine [metal jingles but no skin]
Triangle
Cow bell
Mark tree
Bell tree
Cabasa
Agogo bells
Castanets
Tam-Tam

Wood
Claves
Maracas
Wood block
Chinese temple blocks
Whip
Guiro

Skin
Tom-toms
Snare drum
Bass drum
Conga drums
Bongo drums
Tambour

The drum kit
The drum kit is used in most band situations and occasionally in orchestras. It mainly consists of:

Bass drum
Snare drum
Tom-toms [two or more]
Hi-hat [pair of cymbals operated by a pedal]
Crash cymbal
Ride cymbal

Additional instruments are often added to this such as the cowbell, woodblock, extra cymbals, *etc*.

There is no standard notation for drum kit music and many good drummers don't 'read'. However, nowadays, when notated, the clef used is usually just two short vertical lines ||. The bass drum part is written in the bottom space, the snare drum in the third space and the hi-hat in the top space with cross-head notes. Other cymbals are notated with cross-heads, either on top of the stave or in the top space. Tom-toms are generally notated in the spaces with solid noteheads. Often the drum kit part is simply a guide and it is left up to the player to do the rest. This is mainly because the part would look very complicated if every note was written down.

The following is an example of a commonly used style of drum kit notation:

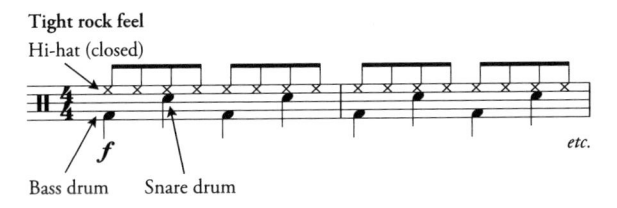

Tight rock feel
Hi-hat (closed)

Bass drum   Snare drum   etc.

Suggested Listening:
Any recording by Gene Krupa, Buddy Rich, Steve Gadd or Billy Cobham

8.7 Keyboard instruments

Like the guitar family, keyboard instruments can be divided into two basic categories, acoustic and electric. There are many keyboard instruments but for the purpose of this book we will just deal with the most common.

Acoustic
- The acoustic piano
- The harpsichord
- The pipe organ
- The accordion

Electric
- The electric piano
- The electronic keyboard
- The synthesizer
- The electronic organ

Acoustic

The acoustic piano
The acoustic piano in one of the most versatile of all musical instruments and can be used in many musical settings. It is equally effective as both a solo and an accompaniment instrument. There are just two basic types of piano, the upright and the grand [see also Section 9: *Writing for the Piano*].

Suggested Listening:
W. A. Mozart – *Rondo a la Turca*
Edvard Grieg – *Piano Concerto*
Frederic Chopin – virtually his entire output
Sergei Rachmaninov – the piano concertos
Any recording by Oscar Peterson (Jazz)

The harpsichord

The harpsichord was the main keyboard instrument in the **Baroque** period but has also been used to great effect in more recent times because of its distinctive plucked attack. Its two main limitations are that it cannot sustain notes for very long and that it can only play at one dynamic level. Both of these problems were addressed and rectified with the invention of the piano.

Suggested Listening:
J.S. Bach – *Goldberg Variations*
Vic Mizzy – The *Addams Family* Theme

The pipe organ

The pipe organ, like the harpsichord, was widely used in the Baroque era and has been popular ever since. The advantage which the organ has over most other keyboard instruments is that it can hold notes indefinitely without 'decaying'. It also has a huge dynamic range controlled by the number of **stops** deployed and the use of the swell pedal. Organ music is usually written on three staves, one for each hand and the third for the pedals.

Suggested Listening:
J.S. Bach – *Toccata and Fugue in D Minor*
Charles Marie Widor – *Toccata [Organ Symphony No.5]*
Olivier Messiaen – *La Nativité du Seigneur*

The accordion

Accordions come in various shapes and sizes. Some have a piano-type keyboard (piano accordion) and others just buttons. They are capable of great expression due to the nature of how the airflow is controlled by the bellows. The French and Italian accordions have been used to great effect in film scores to accompany Parisian or Neapolitan scenes.

Suggested Listening:
The theme tune from the TV series *'Allo 'Allo* written by David Croft and Roy Moore and orchestrated by Ronnie Hazlehurst.

Electric

The electric piano
The electric piano works in the same way as the acoustic piano but its hammers strike metal bars [called tine bars] instead of strings and these are electrically amplified. It is mainly used in jazz and rock settings and hardly ever in classical music.

Suggested Listening:
Any recordings on this instrument by Chick Corea or George Duke

The electronic keyboard
The electronic keyboard can produce a huge variety of sounds [voices] as well as many pre-set rhythm-section accompaniments. It is also a good compositional tool as many have built-in sequencing [recording] devices. Better instruments have 'touch sensitivity' and some are pre-programmed with intros, endings and drum breaks in each pre-set style.

These instruments are capable of producing a range of chords using so-called 'single-finger' chording – a facility which should not be taken too literally since more than one key needs to be depressed to produce anything other than a major chord.

The synthesizer
The synthesizer is capable of recreating the sound of any band or orchestral instrument with varying degrees of authenticity. The sounds of certain instruments are difficult to synthesize and this would include most of the woodwind family and solo stringed instruments. Brass, keyboard and percussion sounds are generally much more convincing. Synthesizers also have their own special sounds and effects that can be edited by the user. Music for synthesizer can be written on one or two staves.

Suggested Listening:
Any recording by Jean Michel Jarre

The electronic organ
The electronic organ is based on the pipe organ, having usually two manuals [keyboards] and a pedal board. Many of these instruments have or are connected to a *Leslie Speaker* which can give a tremolo and slow chorus effect. This effect is very popular with jazz and rock organists.

Suggested Listening:
Any recording by Jimmy Smith [jazz] or Keith Emmerson [rock]

8.8 The Scottish Highland bagpipes

These instruments are a law unto themselves! They can only produce nine melody notes, they have their own scale [which is roughly *mixolydian* – see Section 4.7] and they can only play at one dynamic level – extremely loud!

All of the articulation on the pipes has to be done by using a wide variety of specialised *grace notes* as, unlike all other wind instruments, they cannot be *tongued*.

They are generally for outdoor use because of their high volume level [120 decibels on a good day!] and can only be successfully combined with other loud instruments such as drums.

In more recent times, pipes have also been used on some rock albums as they can compete on an equal footing with amplified electric instruments.

Range:

Scottish Highland bagpipes
written: sounding:

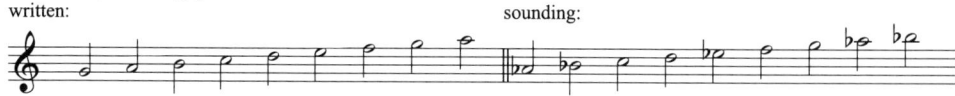

N.B. *In bagpipe music, the written notes are not an exact transposition of the sounding notes.*

Suggested Listening:

Traditional – *Amazing Grace*
Gioachino Rossini [melody] – *The Green Hills of Tyrol*
Traditional – *Flowers of the Forest*
Hamish MacCunn – *Highland Laddie*

Did you know …

… that the world's largest pipe organ is to be found in Convention Hall in Atlantic City, USA?

Statistics:
- in excess of 33,000 pipes
- 7 manuals
- louder than 25 brass bands
- loudest organ stop – *Grand Ophicleide* which is six times louder than a locomotive whistle
- designed by Emmerson Lewis Richards [1884–1963]

9

Writing for the Piano

9.1 Introduction

Although an outline guide to the characteristics of the piano is given in *Section 8: Instruments and Their Characteristics*, there are a number of reasons for examining the instrument and its repertoire in greater detail:

- Because of its self-sufficient capability, the piano has, almost certainly, the most extensive solo repertoire of any instrument.

- It has become the most commonly used instrument by composers [as have other keyboard instruments at different times] in the planning stages of composition.

- It is widely used as an accompaniment instrument.

- A survey of the piano repertoire alone gives us an opportunity to sketch an overview of the development of Western music from the mid-18th century.

The invention of the piano is usually accredited to the Italian instrument builder Bartolomeo Cristofori [1655–1731] in about 1700 [different sources suggest varying dates] who described his instrument as *gravicembalo col piano e forte* [*i.e.* harpsichord with loudness and softness].

The harpsichord, which, apart from the church organ, was the predominant keyboard instrument in its day, was limited in its expressive qualities since no variation of attack and/or loudness could be achieved by the player from the keyboard. And so this description of the early piano as a kind of harpsichord was partly a misnomer. The major breakthrough was to create a mechanism whereby the strings could be struck with hammers rather than plucked.

The piano is, therefore, a pitched percussion instrument.

Such a seemingly simple concept, however, called for a very complex mechanism and it is worth considering this briefly. Besides developing the means by which the hammer could strike the strings, the following attributes, at the very least, were also required:

- An escapement mechanism, whereby the hammer becomes freed from the key which has launched its forward motion. The operation of this can easily be demonstrated on a modern instrument by depressing a key slowly. With insufficient impetus, the hammer never reaches the strings and the point of escapement can usually be felt. It is, therefore, the speed or velocity with which the keys of the piano are struck which produces variations in volume.

- A system of dampers to stop the strings from vibrating once the key is released.

- A system of pedals [or, in early instruments, other devices], one of which would lift all of the dampers from the strings, so allowing them to continue sounding.

An account of the subsequent development and refinement of this mechanism [usually referred to as the 'action' of the piano] and of the piano's increasing compass [range], power and tonal richness, is beyond the scope of this book. However, it is worth bearing in mind, when examining piano writing, especially of the Classical period, that the piano of the 18th century had a limited compass [five octaves or fewer] and that its tone and power would not begin to compare with that of the modern instrument.

Mozart's first encounters with the piano, together with his detailed description of Stein's early instruments in a letter to his Father, are thoroughly researched and described by H. C. Robbins Landon in his book *Mozart: The Golden Years* [see Bibliography for details] and this gives a very clear picture of one piano maker's progress in the development of the instrument.

It is probably self-evident that the way in which composers have subsequently written for the piano reflects, to a greater or lesser extent, the developing capabilities and range of the instrument. The remainder of this section includes a limited number of 'snapshots' of the piano music of selected composers and improvisers whose approach to piano writing might very well serve as models to be copied and adapted in our own writing.

Consequently, the examples which have been chosen are not, for the most part, those which demand the technique of the virtuoso. Before this, however, a brief explanation of a few of the technicalities of piano notation is given, and this is followed by a description of the modern piano.

9.2 Piano notation

- Piano music is almost always written on two staves [although in exceptional circumstances, three staves might be used] bracketed together to show that they are to be read simultaneously. Notice that barlines are carried through from the upper to the lower stave.

Writing for the Piano

It will be seen in this example that the upper stave is given a treble clef and the lower stave a bass clef.

- As a general rule, the upper stave is used to notate what the right hand plays and the lower stave is used for the left hand, but exceptions to this are often found.

- But, if we follow this general rule, then changes of clef will sometimes be necessary. If what the left hand plays is more easily notated in treble clef or, conversely, if the right hand descends into the realm of the bass clef, then we keep to the same stave and simply change the clef. The main point to bear in mind is that we are aiming for clarity and ease of reading and trying to avoid the excessive use of ledger lines.

- A good example of alternative approaches to this problem arises in the opening bars of Scott Joplin's piano rag *The Entertainer*. Here, the left hand is playing in octaves with the right hand, beginning on 4th line **D** in the treble clef. Following the general guidelines given above, this would be notated as follows:

The Entertainer Scott Joplin [ca. 1867–1917]

What is commonly seen, however is:

In this notation, we realise that the left hand is intended to play the lower line because the stems of the notes *descend* from the **noteheads** and no rest is inserted in the bass clef empty bar. There are arguments in favour of both notations. For instance, in our second example, a change of clef is avoided.

And so, although we have a general rule, there may often be alternatives and personal preferences and, to reiterate, the best advice is always to make your intentions clear and to avoid a cluttered score.

9.3 Dealing with more than one part/voice

Another issue which arises in piano writing is that each hand may be playing more than one voice or part, as in the following example:

Little Siciliana Mike Cornick

from *30 Easy Piano Studies* [UE 21 298, © Copyright 2005 by Universal Edition (London) Ltd., London]

In this example, each hand is being called upon to play two parts/voices. If we notated the example with one voice to a stave, it would look like this:

In order to rationalise this in piano writing, we notate the upper voice with stems upwards and the lower voice with stems down on each stave, respectively. If both voices coincide on the same note [as arises on the first beat of the first complete bar in this example] then their noteheads are either superimposed on one another [which is possible if both have the same type of notehead] or placed alongside one another if they differ.

Strictly speaking, each voice or part should be complete with its own rests, although this sometimes makes the notation difficult to read and they are sometimes omitted if they duplicate those of another voice or if the rhythm is clear without them.

The independent writing of voices can be disregarded when upper and lower voices move together in the same rhythm as is the case in the left-hand part of the first complete bar of Little Siciliana. Here, they are simply notated as chords.

9.4 A few other issues

Problems can arise when notating more than two voices on each stave, and these are usually solved by displacing the notes of a third part so that they are as close to their appropriate position as possible whilst still remaining legible. The stems of such a part will coincide in direction with an existing part and so the choice of stem direction becomes a matter of judgement.

When a voice or part crosses from one stave to another, then a dotted or solid line indicating the direction of this move is sometimes added to make the continuity clear:

Another way of showing this [as was shown in the Scott Joplin example] is to allow notes in beamed groups to cross from one stave to another:

9.5 Indicating use of the pedals

Although notation for the piano may give rise to many more questions beyond the basics outlined above, one more essential needs to be considered and that is the means by which we indicate the use of the pedals.

The use of the sustaining/damper pedal is essential to some styles of piano writing and notation of its precise application may well be included by composers and/or editors.

If you, as many before you, are happy to entrust pedalling to the pianist, then the general instruction:

con 𝓟𝑒𝒹. may be given at the beginning of the piece.

Precise pedalling can be indicated [among other symbols] by:

𝓟𝑒𝒹.　　　　✶　　[where the asterisk indicates release of the pedal]
or:
𝓟𝑒𝒹. ⎯⎯⎯⎯⎯⎯⌋

So-called half-pedalling, which implies lifting the pedal half way, is indicated by:

𝓟𝑒𝒹. ⎯⋀⎯⋀⎯⋀⎯⌋

The instruction: *senza ped.* means without sustain pedal.
When use of the left [soft] pedal is to be indicated, the instruction: *una corda* [one string] is the most commonly used.
The instruction SP indicates use of the middle [or *sostenuto*] pedal on grand pianos [see below] but it is seldom seen because this facility generally does not exist on upright pianos.

9.6 The modern piano

The grand piano
This instrument, which retains the original concept of the horizontal soundboard, frame and strings, is available in a range of sizes and with some variation in compass. Physically longer instruments allow for a longer string-run [the pitch of each string being determined by a combination of the factors: length, tension, diameter and the density of the material from which they are made] together with a bigger soundboard and this offers tonal superiority as well as greater power. The instrument can, of course, be played with its lid open or closed, so to some extent affecting its loudness, and the lid also serves the function of directing the sound towards the audience.

The number of strings allotted to each note varies across the range of the instrument with more strings being used to compensate for the lack of resonance in the shorter strings employed at higher pitches. Some pianos have also been provided with additional strings which are not struck by the hammers but which vibrate with sympathetic resonance, so enhancing the tone.

In general, we see three pedals which function as follows:

- The right pedal is the sustain pedal [damper pedal in the USA] and lifts all the dampers from the strings as long as it is depressed.

- The middle pedal allows the pianist to selectively sustain those notes being played at the moment when the pedal is depressed.

- The left pedal is usually called the soft pedal and has the effect of reducing the loudness of the instrument by moving the entire action of the piano so that hammers strike one less of the multiple strings provided throughout most of the range of the instrument.

The upright piano
With the growth of the popularity of the piano came a demand for more compact instruments for domestic use and this led to various attempts to reduce the size of the instrument without overly compromising its sound.

Real progress was made in this regard by placing the soundboard, frame and strings in a vertical position, shortening the length of the bass strings and by arranging the strings so that their string-runs overlapped diagonally. This arrangement is described as ***overstrung***.

Of course, the upright piano is a compromise, although a very good one in the case of most modern instruments, but there are differences in the function of the middle pedal and the way in which the soft pedal achieves its effect. Notably:

- The left pedal reduces the loudness of the instrument by moving all of the hammers closer to the strings and not by moving the action. The shorter 'throw' of the hammers results in reduced velocity and, consequently, a lower volume.

- The function of the middle pedal is commonly to drastically reduce the loudness of the instrument by dropping a felt 'curtain' between the hammers and the strings. This can result in a rather strange muffled effect and is probably included for the benefit of next-door neighbours in adjoining houses who will probably appreciate its inclusion rather more than the performer.

9.7 Some stylistic 'snapshots'

The 'Classical' period:
Many examples of piano writing from these early days of the piano display a lightness of texture which may reflect the contemporary instrument's lack of sonority. Equally, accompaniment figures to a single-note melodic line could not be allowed to overpower, whilst some measure to sustain the continuity of the underlying harmony was required.

The following example from a Mozart piano sonata illustrates a commonly encountered left-hand accompaniment style of the late Baroque/Rococo and Classical periods which we often describe as the **Alberti bass** [named after the composer Domenico Alberti 1710–1740]:

Sonata in C [KV 545] Wolfgang Amadeus Mozart [1756–1791]

Rather than playing block chords to accompany the melodic line, the notes of the chord are played in an arpeggio fashion [strictly speaking as broken chords] moving, in this example, in quavers. This has the combined effect of sustaining the harmony, lightening the texture and maintaining momentum.

So commonplace was this style in the latter half of the 18th century that Mozart [and probably others], if pressed for time, did not always fully notate the left-hand part if he was going to perform the piece himself, indicating only the harmony for an extemporised realisation when required.

A variation of this means of sustaining both harmony and momentum is well illustrated in the slow movement of Beethoven's *Pathetique* Sonata, Op. 13, where initially, the lower voice in the right-hand part maintains semiquaver movement in accompaniment of the 'singing' melodic line:

Sonate Pathetique Op. 13 Ludwig van Beethoven [1779–1827]

Interestingly, this style of piano writing can work equally effectively in the accompaniment to a contemporary pop-styled ballad where quaver movement in $\frac{4}{4}$ is sometimes [possibly misleadingly] referred to as 'an eight-beat' feel.

Romanticism and the piano

The 19th century saw the development of the piano and its repertoire bloom and the names of a number of composers come to mind: Chopin, Schumann, Mendelssohn and Liszt, among others, all emerge as great exponents and are clearly deserving of specialist study.

In terms of popular appeal, we can, perhaps, single out Chopin for his distinctive and individualistic approach in the writing of his nocturnes, preludes, waltzes, mazurkas, études and the piano concertos.

The hallmark of much of Chopin's writing, perhaps especially in the nocturnes, is the so-called *bel canto* [meaning beautiful song] melodic line, together with the increasing chromaticism of the accompanying harmony.

The following example is included to illustrate the simple device of placing a bass note followed by the chord beneath a decorated melodic line.

Nocturne Op. 55 No. 1 Frédéric Chopin [1810–1849]

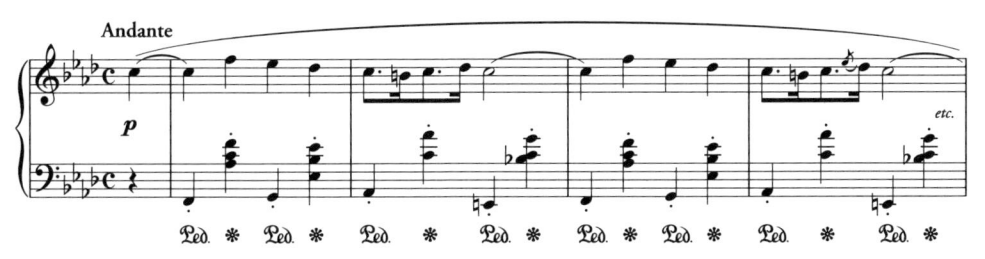

By way of contrast, Chopin can also fully exploit the increasing sonority of the developing piano and in this example, using full chords moving in a chromatic progression, we find him in a much darker mood:

Prelude Op. 28 No. 20 Frédéric Chopin

And, in yet another prelude, Chopin provides us with a further model, once again employing the singing melodic line, but here accompanying that line with repeated chords which display a haunting chromatic metamorphosis:

Prelude Op. 28 No. 4 Frédéric Chopin

Briefly looking back, stylistically, Mendelssohn provides us with a good example of the persistence of the Alberti-styled bass figure seen in the Mozartian example above, but here integrated into his own style, and accommodating more frequent changes of harmony:

Andante Sostenuto [from Christmas Pieces] Felix Mendelssohn Bartholdy [1809–1847]

Late Romanticism

Here we see the continuing development of the piano writing which has its roots in the music of Tchaikovsky, Chopin, Brahms, Liszt and others and which exploits the power, expressive range and the compass of the piano and displays, especially in the show-piece piano concertos, the virtuosic technique of the soloist. Perhaps some of the best examples of this last flowering of romanticism are to be found in the works of Sergei Rachmaninov [1873–1943]. In his technically demanding piano writing, we encounter vast sweeping melodies, bravura passages and a luxuriant chromatic harmonic vocabulary.

Although it might justifiably be suggested that the novice composer is unlikely to attempt to imitate such a style, this argument is to some extent countered by the realisation that the hugely popular 1975 Eric Carmen song *All By Myself* borrowed substantially from the melodic theme of the 2nd movement of Rachmaninov's *2nd Piano Concerto* in C minor, Opus 18. This song has been 'covered' by many other artists, not least Celine Dion [1996] and has undoubtedly yielded some revenue to the Rachmaninov estate.

Similarly, the works of Chopin and other Romantic composers have provided rich pickings for some song writers and it would be an interesting exercise to draw up a list of such songs.

On a more serious note, the following example is a brief excerpt from Rachmaninov's *Prelude in C♯ minor* [transposed into **D** minor for ease of reading] which displays a cascade of chromatic writing:

Prelude in C♯ Minor [transposed] Op. 3 No. 2 Sergei Rachmaninov [1873–1943]

© Copyright by Universal Edition A.G., Wien

Diversity in the reaction against romanticism and the movement away from tonality

In the latter half of the 19th and the early years of the 20th century, we see the emergence of a number of new styles, partly as a result of the reaction against German Romanticism [which, in itself, contained the seeds of the increasing breakdown of tonality through increasing *chromaticism*] and partly as a consequence of the conviction that tonal music had reached the 'end of the line'. Some of these emerging styles represent quite deliberate attempts to create a new music which was divorced from tonality completely.

Music which has no key is described as *atonal*.

Amongst the most significant new departures are:

- Nationalism – an attempt to give music a national or cultural identity by returning to the scales and the idioms of the folk music of the composer's country and culture.

- Experiments with the scales and other aspects of the music of other cultures and a movement away from functional harmony.

- The invention of systems of composition which would create music which was truly atonal.

Nationalism

The music of Béla Bartók [1881–1945] is steeped in the folk tradition of his native Hungary and led to experiments with bitonality [music in two different keys, simultaneously], atonality, and with powerful rhythmic patterns. This example is drawn from Volume VI of *Mikrokosmos* and has provided a stimulus to many composers:

Mikrokosmos Vol. VI – No. 6 Béla Bartók [1881–1945]

© Copyright by Boosey & Hawkes Music Publishers Ltd.

Experiments …

Among those whose writing involved experiments with scales and modes, and whose influence has proved seminal in the evolution of 20th-century music, is the French composer Claude Debussy [1862–1918].

Examples appear elsewhere in this book of his often quoted use of parallelism and whole-tone scales, and many composers continue to find inspiration in his work.

Of interest, too, is another resident of Paris, Erik Satie [1866–1925], a close associate of Debussy, who worked as a café pianist, and is remembered, not only for some of his more outlandish musical experiments and the bizarre titles of some of his pieces, but particularly for his simple but evocative *Gymnopédies*.

The extract below relies on the slow, repeated rocking movement between just two major chords, each with the added major seventh. The absence of any real sense of harmonic progression, combined with the slow tempo in the opening section of the piece effectively produces a sense of calm and simplicity which has brought this piece to prominence.

Gymnopédie No. 1 Erik Satie [1866–1925]

It is worth remembering, too, that Satie was very much an 'outsider' as seen from the standpoint of the academically trained musicians of the time. Although he attended the Paris Conservatoire, it has been said that he was not very successful in his studies there, and yet his motivation to compose, although largely in a miniaturist fashion, has given us a number of piano pieces which are both memorable and inspirational.

The invention of new systems

Probably the best known of those who experimented with devising new music systems was Arnold Schönberg [1874–1951].

After early years of composing pieces which exhibit the extremes of chromaticism and which were most certainly romantic in intention and style [*Verklärte Nacht* for String Sextet and later arranged for String Orchestra is probably the best-known example], Schönberg began experimenting with atonality and this culminated, ultimately, in a thoroughly rationalised new approach to composition which is described as *serialism* or *dodecaphony.*

The basis of this system was to treat all twelve pitches equally and to avoid the repetition of pitches which tends to give a particular note a degree of prominence. He began by creating a *tone row* which contained all twelve tones in a given order and then devised a matrix in which the row was reversed, inverted and then reversed and inverted. The matrix then formed the basis for his composition.

It is beyond the scope of this book to examine this process any further, but readers may very well wish to study *serialism* and the continuing inspiration that it has subsequently given to composers in finding new directions.

The serial music of Schönberg and his immediate followers including Berg and Webern is sometimes referred to as *The Second Viennese School.*

9.8 The roots of jazz piano

The roots of jazz are to be found in a number of diverse musical influences of which the most important are certainly those of Afro-American origin and include spirituals, work songs and the blues.

The origin of the blues is a complex subject and those who wish to pursue this further would do well to consult a specialist volume such as *The Rough Guide to the Blues* by Nigel Williamson – ISBN 1-84353-519-X.

A number of significant piano styles emerged in the evolution of Afro-American musical culture and their influence in the Western world would be difficult to overstate. They include:

- **Barrelhouse** – a style of piano blues which originated in the saloons of the lumber camps in the Southern USA.

- **Boogie-woogie** – another style of blues-based piano playing which may, perhaps, share its origins with barrelhouse and which reached a popular audience in the 1930s through exponents such as Meade Lux Lewis, Albert Ammons and Pete Johnson.

- **Ragtime** – a style of piano playing which, in the more 'manicured' compositions of composers such as Scott Joplin [1868–1917], is firmly based in 'two-step' dance metre with stylised syncopations.

The main point to grasp about each of these styles [and this includes the original exponents of ragtime] is that they were all substantially improvised, almost certainly highly idiosyncratic and, unless recorded, are substantially a lost art.

Fortunately, some early recordings of barrelhouse and boogie piano players do exist and are now obtainable on CD compilations.

Barrelhouse and boogie

Both of these piano styles are firmly rooted in the blues and tend to follow the established 12-bar chord pattern using primary chords [tonic, subdominant and dominant] with added minor [flattened] 7ths:

C^7 / / / | F^7 / / / | C^7 / / / | C^7 / / / |

F^7 / / / | F^7 / / / | C^7 / / / | C^7 / / / |

G^7 / / / | F^7 / / / | C^7 / / / | C^7 / / / |

The technical prowess of pianists in these styles is prodigious, as anyone who has tried to imitate them will soon discover, and involve the use of relentless, driving left-hand figures such as:

or:

These sorts of bass figures have to be sustained while complex riff-like figurations are added in the right hand.

Barrelhouse players may drive the harmony and rhythm on with figurations like:

Ragtime

In the case of the notated and composed examples of ragtime, we enter a world of more stylised and polished piano composition, formally organised with main theme and trio sections, and with a pattern of right-hand syncopations played over a steady two-in-a-bar left-hand accompaniment. The following example, from Scott Joplin, typifies this approach, which can be simplified and imitated:

Rag-time Dance Scott Joplin

It is worth noting that ragtime, at least in notated examples, does not swing. The jazzy effect of the music results substantially from the right-hand syncopations.

Ragtime underwent a wave of popularity which, like most fashions, reached a peak and then faded away. However, authentic jazz came to be increasingly accepted and its influence through the 1930s and 1940s spread to the world of popular music to the point where certain jazz styles, like swing, became the popular music of the day.

Evidence of this powerful influence can be clearly seen in the songs of Broadway musicals and especially in the compositions of Irving Berlin, Jerome Kern and George Gershwin. Their music frequently displays a harmonic, rhythmic and melodic sophistication borrowed from jazz which has, in turn, further inspired later jazz musicians who continue to use many of these songs [now termed *standards*] as a vehicle for improvisation.

George Gershwin [1898–1937], however, emerges as the composer who brought many of the stylistic mannerisms and the harmonic and melodic vocabulary of jazz out of 'Tin Pan Alley' and the musical theatre and elevated his writing to the level of the concert hall. Students of the piano may wish to investigate Gershwin's *Rhapsody in Blue* – 1924 [which puts the piano in a concerto-like context], the *Concerto in F* [1925] and his *Preludes for Piano* [1926]

The evolution of jazz piano

The development of jazz and, in particular, of jazz piano styles through the 20th century could certainly fill many volumes and those who have an interest in this subject may well wish to consider the following suggestions for further listening which include a small selection of jazz pianists who offer a huge diversity of style:

Count Basie, Duke Ellington, Art Tatum, Teddy Wilson, Erroll Garner, Bud Powell, Thelonious Monk, George Shearing, Oscar Peterson, John Lewis, Bill Evans, Keith Jarrett.

Although notated transcriptions of the work of some of these pianists is available, including their improvised solos in some instances, much of the learning about these pianistic styles will have to be undertaken 'through the ear'.

9.9 Modernism: an experiment with the piano

The second half of the 20th century gave rise to many experimental approaches to music which have included:

- The exploitation of electronics and the combining of 'live' and recorded sound.
- The use of non-musical sounds in a musical context – musical collage.
- The employment of chance procedures in determining musical outcomes – *aleatory* music.
- The use of graphic scores employing symbols which offer performers a wide range of interpretative freedom.

The work of the American composer, John Cage [1912–1992] has included experiments with what he describes as the ***prepared piano***. In this approach items, such as bolts and screws, are placed on the strings of the grand piano in specific positions so as to substantially affect the sound of the instrument.

For further study: John Cage – *Sonatas and Interludes*

You may wish to replicate this experimental approach yourself if you have access to a grand piano. More detailed information on *The Prepared Piano* can be found in specialist publications or at reliable websites.

9.10 Piano duet and piano for six hands

As we all know, the wide compass of the modern piano allows for more than one player to perform on the instrument and there is a huge repertoire for piano duet which is worth exploring and, perhaps adding to.

Many piano duets are arrangements of orchestral pieces and provide an opportunity for two players to explore repertoire as performers. Interestingly, too, some orchestral works [e.g. Peter Warlock's *Capriol Suite, 1926*] began life as duets and were subsequently orchestrated.

What may be less well-known is that there is a growing repertoire of original pieces and arrangements for six hands at one piano as well as many pieces for multiple pianos.

9.11 A few starting points

The following examples are offered as starting points, to be continued as improvisations or in writing.

The chosen melody is *Twinkle, Twinkle Little Star* [in the key of C major] and each 'starter' relates very loosely to one of the more easily illustrated styles referred to above. It will be seen at once that the simple melodic line passes through many metamorphoses in order to accommodate the differing styles and these include quite fundamental rhythmic changes as well as stylistic decoration in some instances. As such, they also represent a series of *variations on a theme* [see Section 6: The Composer's Tool Kit]

Clearly, the technical difficulty encountered in playing these examples varies considerably and the more advanced selections are included for those with a good measure of keyboard facility.

Writing for the Piano

The Alberti bass

Track 63

Moderato

Single-note bass line

Track 64

with quaver movement in the lower voice/part of the right hand:

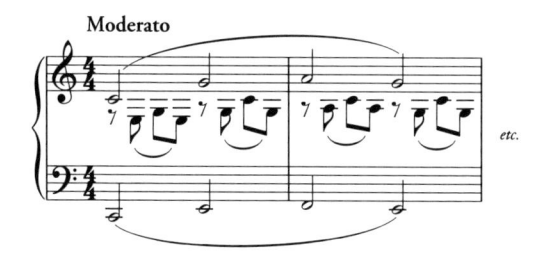

Moderato

As a waltz

Track 65

Using the pattern of a bass note followed by left-hand chords:

Andante

p *mp* etc.

con Ped.

In the tonic minor

Track 66

A darker mood results from the change to a minor key. Initially, a single-note bass line, moving by step, is harmonised in tenths by the lower voice of the right hand. In bars 3 and 4, we begin on a *cycle-of-fifths* harmonisation which could be continued:

Adagio

Parallelism

Parallel movement in the introductory bars is followed by the use of some chromaticism in the harmonisation which follows:

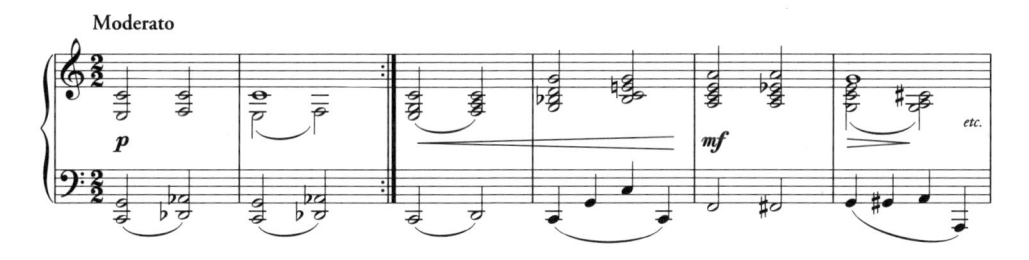

Blues

Repeated left-hand chords with added [minor] 7ths form the steady rhythmic and harmonic accompaniment to a melodic transformation which makes use of some typical blues-styled mannerisms [Note the *swing-quaver* symbol]:

Boogie

Here, a characteristic 'boogie-woogie' left-hand figuration maintains the forward momentum of the style while the melodic line is reduced to punctuating chordal figures [once again, note the 'swing-quaver' symbol]:

Ragtime

Track 70

A steady two-in-a-bar left-hand '*stride*' style consisting of a bass note followed by a chord provides the accompaniment to a transformed and highly elaborated melodic line with characteristic *syncopations*:

Swing

Track 71

A bass line 'lead-in' provides the introduction to a more 'punchy' arrangement which makes use of a wider harmonic vocabulary.

9.12 The electronic keyboard

Although these instruments, in their early days, earned a rather poor reputation as a result of their basic auto-accompaniments and unconvincing voices, the modern instrument, as has been mentioned elsewhere in this book, can prove to be a very useful tool for the composer. More 'up-market' models offer very sophisticated accompaniments together with a range of 'voices' which are, for the most part, convincing enough to be used in the planning stages of a composition at the very least.

Selecting different accompaniment 'styles' on the instrument may very well suggest a range of compositional approaches and the so-called 'single-finger' chording option will allow the player with a more limited keyboard facility the opportunity to experiment harmonically. And so, as an alternative …

... those who have access to an electronic keyboard might like to take the *Twinkle, Twinkle Little Star* theme through a stylistic journey which might include the *Bossa Nova*, a *March*, *Big-Band Swing*, or *Piano Ballad*.

> ## *Did you know ...*
>
> ... that the song *White Christmas*, by Irving Berlin, composed for the film *Holiday Inn* [1942] and sung by Bing Crosby is the best selling record in any music category?
>
> Recordings of the song in all permutations [singles and as part of album collections] have sold in excess of 400,000,000 copies.
>
> Incidentally, Irving Berlin could only play the piano in a very limited range of keys. He used a specially constructed instrument which allowed him to change key mechanically.

Writing for Voices

10.1 Introduction

The voice is the only musical 'instrument' which is given to all, free of charge and, although few of us would claim to be pleased with the quality of that gift and an even smaller number ever develop its full potential, singing is a form of music making with which we all become involved at one time or another.

This section of the book is concerned mainly with songwriting and, in particular, with the relationship between lyrics and the rhythm of the melodic line in the popular song.

Songs, in one form or another, continue to make up by far the vast majority of popular music and the ambition of many a composer is to write a great song – one that stays with us throughout the day or even for weeks on end – the song which we sing in the shower or, maybe, even have the courage to perform in a Karaoke bar.

10.2 Which comes first? The melody or the lyrics?

The answer to this most frequently-asked question is far from 'cut-and-dried', but some clues can be found by briefly examining the ways in which the professionals have worked.

The show tune

The so-called 'Broadway' or 'West End Musical' show [and its offshoot: the musical film] has been the spawning ground for thousands of songs, many of which have long outlived the show for which they were originally written.

As is the case in opera, such songs might be composed as 'solos' [the modern counterpart of the operatic *aria*], or as duets, trios, *etc.* and some as chorus numbers. Every single one of these songs was probably written with the hope that it might become a 'hit' but, more to the point, they all had to function within a storyline [no matter how tenuously] and strike the right mood at the right time.

This question of the mood of the song and, consequently, a suitable choice of tempo, key and style, should really be considered right from the outset. Whether or not it has to function within a storyline, the song may still be telling a story or, at the very least, be sending a message and we should ask ourselves, as composers, what we are trying to convey. A very good start is to study existing songs in a chosen genre and, possibly, to select one as a model. There is nothing wrong with doing this – we all learn from the work of our predecessors – as long as we don't borrow the specific ideas of others and pass them off as our own.

The very best songs exhibit lyrics and melody which fit together perfectly and would seem to have been conceived together, although there is plenty of evidence that, often, this is not the case, especially where composers are working in a long-standing partnership with a *lyricist*.

Those who are interested in researching the way in which some of these partnerships actually worked might choose to read about:

- George Gershwin [1898–1937] – composer, and his lyricist brother – Ira Gershwin [1896–1983], whose partnership produced such songs as: *I Got Rhythm, Embraceable You, The Man I Love, Someone to Watch Over Me*.
- Alan Jay Lerner [1918–1983] – lyricist, and Frederick [Fritz] Loewe [1901–1988] – composer, who collaborated on the musicals: *My Fair Lady, Gigi* and *Camelot*.
- Andrew Lloyd Webber [b.1948] – composer, and Tim Rice [b.1944] – lyricist.

The precise way in which these collaborations have worked is not always easy to discover and, in any case, may have varied from one song to another. In the case of the Gershwins, some insight may be gained by reading Rodney Greenberg's book *George Gershwin*.

Lerner and Loewe's partnership comes under the full glare of the spotlight in Alan Jay Lerner's book *The Street Where I Live* [see the *Select Bibliography* for full details of these publications].

In both the Gershwin/Gershwin and Lerner/Loewe collaborations, it seems to have been the case that the writing of the melody preceded the lyrics, although changes may have been made in some cases to accommodate 'second thoughts' about a particular song.[1]

Not all collaborations have worked like this and in some instances [Rodgers and Hammerstein, for example] the lyric has been the inspiration for the melodic line – a process which is described as 'word-setting'.[2]

---

[1] George Gershwin – Rodney Greenberg [see Select Bibliography for details of this publication]
[2] as above

Andrew Lloyd Webber has worked with and without a collaborating lyricist. When writing the musicals *Joseph and the Amazing Technicolour Dreamcoat* [1968], *Jesus Christ – Superstar* [1971] and *Evita* [1976], he collaborated with the lyricist Tim Rice. However, for his 1981 musical *Cats*, he based his songs on a collection of poems by T.S. Eliot published under the title of *Old Possum's Book of Practical Cats* [Faber and Faber] and was able to dispense with the services of a lyricist completely.

In his autobiography *Oh, What A Circus*, Tim Rice writes extensively about working with Andrew Lloyd Webber and states that the music always came first although he makes the point that the significance of each song with reference to the storyline and the message which it delivers were always decided before the song-writing began[1].

This suggests a possible starting point for the 'would-be' song writer and that is to set an existing favourite poem or other text to music. Remember, though, that your chosen text may be in copyright [*i.e.* where the legal right to use it belongs to the author or to a publisher] and you cannot publish such a word-setting without obtaining permission.

So, the answer to our question 'Which Comes First ...' in the case of songs for musicals is: it might be either, but in our brief survey it seems that the melody is more frequently composed first!

Singer/Songwriters

There are many singers who compose their own songs – or, to put it another way, composers who are also the performers of their songs – in the world of popular music. Once again, a great deal of research would be required before making generalisations about how this approach to songwriting may work in practice. One interesting example, which may not be entirely typical, is the song *Yesterday* [1968] by Paul McCartney.

Reputedly, this song has been the subject of more 'cover' versions than any other and is, without doubt, a song which most composers would dearly love to have written, and not just for financial reasons.

Anecdotal accounts of how this song came into existence vary to some extent but it does seem that it is an example of a melody [and, in this case, potentially, a song] arriving in the composer's consciousness virtually complete. Apparently however, the original rather improvised lyrics, were fairly mundane and the words with which we are now so familiar were composed subsequently.

So, is this an example of 'word-setting' – music and then the lyrics? It would seem so. What seems more probable in the case of most singer/songwriters is that they improvise

---

[1] See Select Bibliography for details of this publication.

their way into a new song, possibly stimulated by a particular chord sequence, a melodic 'hook', or perhaps by the sound and rhythm of particular words or phrases. In these circumstances, it may very well be the case that the melody and the words are conceived together, a process which might call for a kind of constant updating as the work progresses.

Undoubtedly, each reader will have their own favourite singer/songwriter who will probably have exerted a strong influence on their chosen song-writing direction. In the absence of such a favourite, the songs of Paul Simon [b. 1941] would make a very suitable subject for study.

It's a guess, and you may know otherwise, but the 'stream of consciousness' or loose association to be found in the lyrics of some of Paul Simon's songs suggests that they may well begin life in this way. Many of his songs would certainly reward further study, not only for their innate quality and obvious attractiveness, but because Paul Simon has drawn inspiration from a very wide multicultural range of sources including classical, folk, rock, blues, jazz, gospel, Afro-Caribbean, the rhythms of Brazilian music and the bands of the South African townships.

Once again, a range of starting-points for the songwriter are suggested by this all-encompassing approach: why not set out to write a song which draws on a particular genre – a *blues*, a *calypso* or a *bossa nova*, maybe – and this will help by setting many of the parameters right from the start.

So, the answer to our question "Which Comes First …" in the case of songs by singer/songwriters is: it still might be either, or the words and music may even be composed simultaneously.

The best advice is really to follow your own intuition. If you've written or found a good lyric or text, then try improvising until you find a way in. Or if you have a strong melody, sing it over and over and see if it suggests certain words or phrases. Or, if you're working in a partnership, maybe hand your melody over to a would-be lyricist and see what they come up with.

10.3 Word-setting

Whichever way you choose to proceed, you must give attention to making an appropriate match between the stresses or accentuated syllables in the lyrics and those in the rhythm of the melodic line.

If you're beginning with the words – yours or somebody else's – then say them out loud, and decide where the stresses fall. Try not to distort the lyrics but, rather, come as close to the natural rhythms of speech as possible.

It may be a good idea to write down the lyrics and to mark the stressed words or syllables, perhaps by underlining them. It's probable that you may then feel that a pattern of accents begins to suggest itself which will imply a time signature – simple or compound – of two, three or four beats to the bar. And remember that the first word or words in your lyrics may well be unstressed suggesting an 'upbeat' or *anacrusis*.

If you want to end up with a written copy of your song and find the notation of rhythm difficult, you might start by playing that rhythm into a music software programme which offers that facility, but it would be a good idea to establish the time signature first. As has been pointed out repeatedly in this book, however, you will need to play your rhythm very accurately against a *click track* to avoid a nonsensical result!

If you're working in an educational establishment – a school or college, maybe – where some professional help is available, you may be able to persuade someone else to get you started by writing the rhythm for you. We tend to assume that all professional songwriters have been sufficiently musically literate to do this for themselves but it has not always been the case. Lionel Bart [1930–1999] – who composed the songs for the hugely successful and recently revived musical *Oliver* [1960] – worked with a tape recorder and left the notation to somebody else. Irving Berlin [1888–1989] who wrote many phenomenally successful popular songs, including, *White Christmas*, never properly came to terms with musical notation. He would learn to play/sing his own song and dictate it to an *amanuensis*.

Some simple illustrations of word-settings

The following examples are taken from folk songs and exhibit a reasonable fit of the natural stresses of the lyrics to the rhythm of the melody. The stressed syllables or words have been underlined:

Widdecombe Fair

Tom |Pearse, Tom Pearse, lend |me your grey mare|

This suggests a steady two beats in a bar in compound time:

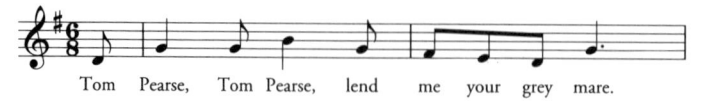

or, maybe:

Tom |Pearse, Tom |Pearse, lend |me your grey |mare|

Possibly, a faster three beats in a bar [in simple time]:

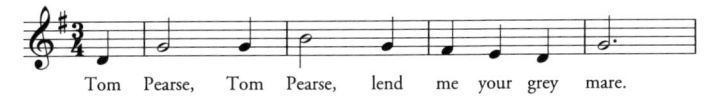

[musical notation: 3/4 time, one sharp]

Tom   Pearse,   Tom   Pearse,   lend   me   your   grey   mare.

Either of these is acceptable, but the first example in **compound time** [$^6_8$ – two beats in a bar – see *Section 3: Understanding Pulse, Time Signatures and Rhythm*] seems to move along more naturally. Although we are mainly concerned with rhythm here, note that the unstressed first word [the anacrusis] on the note **D** provides a step up to the tonic [**G**] on the first stressed word, and in doing so firmly establishes the key [**G** major in this case].

An anacrusis may frequently consist of a number of words as is illustrated by the following example:

The Water Is Wide

The water is |wide, I cannot cross |o'er,

And neither |have I the wings to |fly.

[musical notation in 4/4 with one flat]

The   wa - ter   is   wide,_____   I   can - not   cross   o'er,_____

___   And   neith - er   have_____   I   the wings   to   fly._____

This example contains a couple of other features, too. The words *wide* and *o'er* are tied over into the following bars so that the opening words of each successive phrase also form an anacrusis. The contraction of the word *over* to *o'er* is a kind of **elision** – a device which allows a two-syllable word to be reduced to one.

A couple of examples to try

The following lyrics have been chosen because they belong to songs which you probably already know and this will give you a very good start. Try marking the accented words or syllables and, having decided on a time signature, add barlines to the text and then notate the rhythm [which can be added above the words]:

Writing for Voices

Three Blind Mice

Three blind mice,
Three blind mice.
See how they run,
See how they run.
They all ran after the farmer's wife,
Who cut off their tails with a carving knife,
Did you ever see such a sight in your life,
As three blind mice?

Here's a possible answer:
<u>Three</u> blind	<u>mice</u>,
<u>Three</u> blind	<u>mice</u>.
<u>See</u> how they	<u>run</u>,
<u>See</u> how they	<u>run</u>.
They |<u>all</u> ran after the |<u>farm</u>er's wife,
Who |<u>cut</u> off their tails with a |<u>carv</u>ing knife,
Did you |<u>ev</u>er see such a |<u>sight</u> in your life,
As |<u>three</u> blind |<u>mice</u>?|

And here's a possible notation [which includes melody as well] – in compound two-in-a-bar – $\frac{6}{8}$.

Compound time has been chosen because of the frequency with which we need to fit three words or syllables to one beat [see *Section 3: Understanding Pulse, Time Signatures and Rhythm*]

[musical notation: Three blind mice, Three blind mice. See how they run, See how they run. They all ran after the farmer's wife, Who cut off their tails with a carving knife, Did you ever see such a sight in your life, As three blind mice?]

If the stresses which you marked on the text came twice as frequently, then you might have notated the rhythm in simple triple time [$\frac{3}{4}$] in which case, your answer might look like this:

Writing for Voices

Three blind mice, Three blind mice. See how they run, See how they run. They all ran after the farmer's wife, Who cut off their tails with a carving knife, Did you ever see such a sight in your life, As three blind mice?

But, of the two alternatives, the first answer is certainly the better choice.

Clementine

Verse:
    In a cavern, by a canyon,
    Excavating for a mine.
    Dwelt a miner, forty-niner,
    And his daughter, Clementine.

Chorus:
    Oh my darling, oh, my darling,
    Oh, my darling Clementine.
    Though art lost and gone forever,
    Dreadful sorry, Clementine.

N.B. Both verse and chorus use the same melody and rhythm.

Here's a possible answer:

Verse:
    In a |cavern, by a |canyon,
    Exca-|vating for a |mine.
    Dwelt a |miner, forty-|niner,
    And his |daughter, Clemen-|tine.

Chorus:
    Oh my |darling, oh, my |darling,
    Oh, my |darling Clemen-|tine.
    Though art |lost and gone for-|ever,
    Dreadful |sorry, Clemen-|tine.

Here's a possible notation [which includes melody as well] – in simple three-in-a-bar – $\frac{3}{4}$.
N.B. Because this is a folk song, various versions of the musical setting of this song exist.

[Musical notation: "Clementine" song with lyrics]

In a ca-vern, by a can-yon, Ex-ca-va-ting for a mine, Dwelt a
dar-ling, oh, my dar-ling, Oh, my dar-ling Clem-en-tine, Though art

mi-ner, for-ty ni-ner, and his daugh-ter Clem-en-tine. Oh, my
lost and gone for-ev-er, Dread-ful sor-ry Clem-en- tine.

10.4 Vocal ranges

In the world of popular music, the classification of voices is not really very significant. A vocalist will naturally sing within the range that they find the most comfortable and that is really all there is to it. This is really a consequence of the fact that initially, at least, songs for the pop/rock market are usually produced as studio recordings by a specific singer or group of singers. It is only when that song is 'covered' by another singer or singers that vocal range may become an issue and a change of key [*transposition*] might be needed.

In the realm of 'classical' music [for want of a better term], adult voices tend to be classified, firstly as male or female voices and then further subdivided, primarily according to their range, but also taking into account the quality of the voice. Suggested ranges vary from one source to another and alternative suggestions are given using bracketed notes. The following is offered as a rough guide:

[Musical notation showing Female voices: Soprano, Mezzo-Soprano, Contralto [alto]]

[Musical notation showing Male voices (for treble, see soprano): Tenor, Baritone, Bass]

Other voices

The countertenor/male alto

This is a term used in classical music to describe a male adult voice in the range of the soprano or contralto. Nowadays, it is attained by the use of falsetto.

Falsetto

A method of voice production used by adult males to attain notes in the treble register, effectively exploited by some exponents in the pop/rock genre [*e.g.* The Bee Gees – *Night Fever*, 1977 and, more recently, Mika's song *Grace Kelly*, 2007] and also heard in 'Barbershop' Quartets and other 'close harmony' male vocal ensembles. Interestingly, in the 'Barbershop' Quartet, the melodic line is usually taken by the tenor with harmony above in the countertenor and below in the baritone and bass.

Coloratura

This term is usually used to describe a soprano who has an extended upper range and who can sing with great agility at a high *tessitura*. In 18th century classical opera, it also suggests the highly ornamented style of performance associated with this voice. Probably the best-known coloratura soprano operatic role is that of the *Queen of the Night* in Mozart's *The Magic Flute*.

Writing sympathetically for singers

What is, perhaps, a more important consideration when writing a vocal line is to ensure that we do not demand that the performer is constantly required to sing close to the limits of their vocal range. We must also, of course, allow adequate opportunities for breathing, avoid awkward leaps to the highest and lowest notes of a vocal range and think carefully about melodic intervals which are difficult to pitch.

When writing vocal harmony, we must also give some thought to how the harmony voices will find the pitch of the first notes of phrases. If we provide them with a frame of reference in the accompaniment or, if they can make a connection with the pitch of notes in other parts, this can alleviate many difficulties.

Children's voices

The following ranges are suggested for Primary school mixed voices [in the U.K. – Keystage 2] *i.e.* boys and girls. Two ranges are given, the first being appropriate for general ensemble singing and the second for a choral setting where the children will have greater experience:

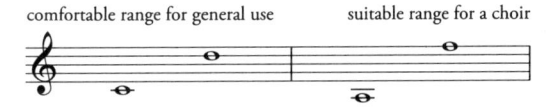

10.5 Scoring

As long as none of the voices divide, four-part vocal writing [*e.g.* SATB – Soprano/Treble, Alto, Tenor and Bass] can be comfortably accommodated in so-called **short score** [*i.e.* a treble and a bass stave, bracketed together] as the following example illustrates.

This could be sung by four individual voices or by a choir:

Heinrich Isaak [ca. 1450–1517]; Adapted and harmonised by J. S. Bach

If all of the voices in a chorus are singing in the same register, as may be the case when writing for a mixed-voice children's choir, for instance, it may be convenient to use just one vocal stave on which divided voices are indicated by the stem direction of the notes for each part. The following is an excerpt from a comic song taken from the children's musical *Ali Baba* [UE 14 068] by James Rae and Mike Cornick, and begins at the point where the chorus joins a solo singer.

from The Pizza Song Words & Music: James Rae

When notating a vocal setting of greater complexity or, indeed, any vocal piece where independent vocal lines for different voices are involved, a vocal score should be produced.

This simplifies and clarifies, for each vocal line, differences in articulation, phrasing, dynamics and words and should result in an easy-to-read score for both performers and conductor. A short score can be added below which may provide a piano accompaniment [or a piano reduction of an orchestral score] or, in the case of *a cappella* settings, a short score version of the vocal parts for rehearsal purposes as in the following example.

Sweet Was the Song by Richard Rodney Bennett is scored for Soprano, Alto, Tenor and Bass, to be performed either with one voice to each part or by a choir.

Five Carols [for choir SATB a cappella]
4. Sweet Was the Song Richard Rodney Bennet [* 1936]; Words by William Ballett (17th century)

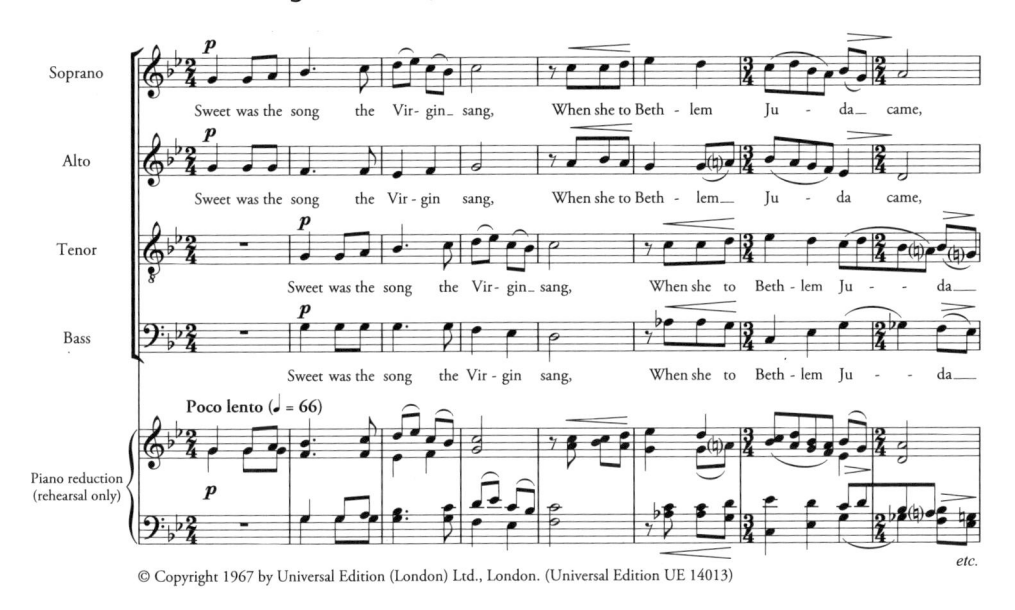

© Copyright 1967 by Universal Edition (London) Ltd., London. (Universal Edition UE 14013)

When this type of vocal score is intended for choral performance, each vocal line may also be divided, since there is more than one performer singing each line.

In a vocal score, all voices are notated at their actual pitch with the exception of the tenor which is written one octave higher and in the treble clef. Sometimes, a treble clef with an added figure *8* below is used – as in this example from Handel's [1685–1759] *Messiah* [1741] – and this signifies that the actual pitch is one octave lower. Sometimes, a normal treble clef is used and the transposition is taken for granted:

from **Messiah – Chorus: And the Glory of the Lord** George Frideric Handel [1685–1759]

[Handel's score shows the word 'glory' in bar 3 of this excerpt as sung to a single crotchet]

10.6 Interpreting the lyrics

Finally, although it may seem obvious, we should give some thought to achieving a suitable musical interpretation of a lyric. A complete mismatch of the meaning and mood of words and the musical setting – including tempo, choice of major/minor key, *etc.* – can produce a comic effect which has been used deliberately on occasion, but we wouldn't want this to arise inadvertently.

An extremely literal interpretation of the meaning of the words is described as **word painting** and there are countless examples to be found in the madrigals of the 16th and 17th centuries. Here, for instance, the use of rising and falling scalic passages in the setting of words such as 'running up and down' or the choice of a suddenly dissonant harmony in the setting of words such as 'death' might well have been expected and was frequently employed. Word painting is not restricted to the madrigalists. The quotation below, once again from Handel's oratorio *Messiah,* is one of many possible illustrations from that work:

No. 48 Air – The Trumpet Shall Sound

Such obvious linking of the words and music may not always appeal to us as a device in our own songwriting, but we should not treat the idea too dismissively. For instance, a lyric which in any way describes the idea of 'descent' – say, 'down, down he fell …' might seem ludicrous if set to a rising sequence of notes. Turning to existing songs, the opening melodic phrase of the Afro-American Spiritual *Swing Low, Sweet Chariot,* would be hard to imagine with anything other than a falling melodic phrase:

[musical notation: "Swing low, sweet char-i-ot."]

Consider, too, the melodic rise and fall in the opening bars of the chorus of the Scottish folk song *Loch Lomond* :

[musical notation: "Oh, ye'll take the high road, an' I'll take the low road," etc.]

You can probably think of dozens more examples which seem perfectly acceptable. It's all a matter of judgement in the final analysis and a subtle relationship between the meaning of the words and the vocal line can work very well.

Suggested Listening:

Here's the beginning of a list to which you could certainly add many more titles:

- The seemingly inseparable match of the **syncopated** rhythms of the melodic line in Gershwin's songs: *I Got Rhythm* and *Fascinatin' Rhythm.*

- And in a similar vein, Ellington's *It Don't Mean a Thing [If It Ain't Got That Swing]* which is an uptempo big band swing number which makes use of syncopated ['Do-wah'] **scat** singing.

- Although not strictly ragtime in style, but displaying some jaunty syncopations, Irving Berlin's *Alexander's Ragtime Band* uses bugle-call melodic figures in the setting of the line which specifically refers to them.

- *One Note Samba [Samba De Uma Nota So]* by Antonio Carlos Jobim – English lyrics by Jon Hendricks – uses a melodic line [in the key of B♭] with bar after bar of repeated Fs and then B♭s. This is relieved and contrasted in the **middle-eight** of the song by a beautiful **sequential** melody.

10.7 And so, in conclusion …

It has been said that music is the most abstract of the arts because it can connect more directly with our emotions than any other form of expression. Whilst we could discuss this assertion at length – and some may disagree, after all – it is certainly true that the great strength of vocal music is that it combines that abstract expressive power with words which can convey a precise meaning.

Perhaps it was such a thought as this which motivated Beethoven to use voices for the first time in a symphonic context in his 9th Symphony [in D minor Op. 125, 1824] which contains a choral setting of part of Friedrich Schiller's poem: *An die Freude*.

> ## *Did you know ...*
>
> ... it has been suggested that the hugely popular song *Over the Rainbow* nearly didn't make it into the final cut of the 1939 film *The Wizard of Oz?* MGM executive, Louis B. Mayer wanted it deleted from the film but fortunately the composer, Harold Arlen, successfully argued for its retention.
>
> However, a reprise of the song elsewhere in the film did end up on the cutting room floor.
>
> The American Fim Institute subsequently voted *Over the Rainbow* "... the greatest movie song of all time".

Adding Important Instructions to Your Score

11.1 Introduction

When we examine any musical score, including the notated examples in this book, we will see that composers [or, sometimes, editors] have added words and symbols to the notation in an effort to make their intentions clearer to the performer.

Players and singers will be familiar with many of these, although we have included some specific applications which may not be considered common musical knowledge.

Many of the words/phrases which appear on musical scores are written in a foreign language [from the English reader's point of view] and, if it can be said that there is an international language for musical instructions, then Italian has become, for historical reasons, the first choice. But for every rule, there seems to be an exception and it has become commonplace, in more recent times, for composers to use their own language [Debussy, for example, often uses a mix of French and Italian terms – see 11.7] and some instances can be quite idiosyncratic and entertaining – those of the Australian composer Percy Grainger [1882–1961] for example.

More commonly used Italian terms are also frequently reduced to abbreviations and this may sometimes lead to confusion. Consequently, commonly seen abbreviations have been included where appropriate.

11.2 Where words or symbols may be needed

To simplify matters, we can divide the use of added words and symbols into five important types of instruction:

- Tempo and changes of tempo
- Dynamics – [*i.e.* loudness] and changes of dynamic
- Articulation [the way in which a specific note/chord or a sequence of notes is to be played, and other effects
- Indicating repeats and other 'shorthand' notation
- Words which convey a sense of mood or style

11.3 Tempo and changes of tempo

Following the invention of the metronome [see *Section 3: Understanding Pulse, Time Signatures and Rhythm*] it has become usual to give a specific value in beats per minute at the head of a musical score to indicate the tempo.

e.g. ♩ = 120

Prior to the invention of the metronome and also, frequently since, in addition to this mark, a suitable speed/tempo term might be added.

e.g. *Allegro* – meaning fast

The problem with using words such as *Allegro* to describe a tempo is that they are open to a fairly wide range of interpretation and this can be well illustrated by comparing a range of recordings of, say, a Mozart or Haydn symphony.

Nevertheless, a selection of commonly used speed/tempo Italian terms is given below [ranging from the slowest to the fastest], bearing in mind that a performer may not always have a metronome to hand in order to determine the tempo exactly, and that many of these terms imply a particular mood or 'feel' as well as tempo:

Grave – very slow but also implying 'solemn'

Largo – slow and broad

Larghetto – a little faster than *Largo*

Lento – slow

Adagio – slow but not as slow as *Largo*

Adagietto – slow but not as slow as *Adagio*

Andante – 'walking'

Andantino – slightly faster than *Andante*

Moderato – at a moderate tempo

Allegretto – quite fast, but not as fast as …

Allegro – fast

Vivace – lively

Presto – very fast

Prestissimo – as fast as possible

Of course, you may well want to suggest changes of tempo within your piece or to indicate that there could be a degree of 'give-and-take' in the tempo, for which the following commonly used terms may be useful:

Accelerando [abbreviated to *accel.*] – becoming gradually faster

Più mosso – more movement *i.e.* faster [*più* means more]

Rallentando [abbreviated to *rall.*] or *Ritardando* [abbreviated to *ritard.*] – becoming gradually slower

Ritenuto [abbreviated to *rit.*] – held back

Meno mosso – less movement *i.e.* slower [*meno* means less]

Allargando – becoming gradually slower and louder

Rubato or *Tempo Rubato* – literally, 'robbed time' which allows the performer the freedom to speed up or slow down slightly within each phrase.

11.4 A few other useful tempo-related words and symbols

Tempo primo – return to the first tempo

The *fermata*:

... or 'pause' which allows the performer to lengthen or hold a note or chord at their own or the conductor's judgement.

The addition of the words *lunga pausa* indicates a long pause.

ad libitum [abbreviated to *ad lib.*] – literally, *at will* – may be used to indicate freedom in the interpretation of the tempo or the rhythm of a passage, although it has other applications, too.

a tempo – [literally 'in time'] which means a return to playing in time.

Colla parte/colla voce – is a direction to an accompanist instructing them to follow the changing tempo of the solo instrumentalist / singer.

Generally speaking, tempo indications are given in italic script over the staff/stave.

Although not a tempo direction, but rather one concerning rhythmic execution, we also include here two jazz–related 'swing-quaver' symbols. These symbols direct the performer to play all quaver movement, also taking account of rests, with a swing 'feel':

(♩♩ = ♩♪) ³ or (♩.♩ = ♩♪) ³

Occasionally, a similar symbol is used which indicates that both even quavers and the dotted quaver rhythm are to be swung.

Playing with a swing 'feel' is always a matter of interpretation but, roughly speaking, the symbol above suggests the playing of pairs of quavers with a two-thirds to one-third division of the beat. Commonly, the word *swing* is added to the score, either in the direction at the head of the piece or at the relevant point if a change from even quavers to swing quavers is required. A return to even quavers after a swing passage can be indicated by the word *straight*.

11.5 Dynamics

Dynamic markings are usually given as abbreviations of Italian terms, as follows:

pp or even *ppp* – *pianissimo,* meaning very soft or quiet

p – *piano,* meaning soft or quiet

mp – *mezzo piano,* meaning moderately soft or quiet

mf – *mezzo forte,* meaning moderately loud

f – *forte,* meaning loud

ff or even *fff* – *fortissimo,* meaning very loud

Other more specialist dynamic markings include:

fp – *forte piano,* meaning loud and then immediately soft or quiet

sf or *sfz* – *sforzando,* meaning accented, suddenly loud

Accentuation may also be marked with the use of symbols.
e.g. in this excerpt to be played in swing quavers:

The horizontal accent [>] is appropriate for the longer note and the vertical accent [ʌ] for the note of shorter duration.

Accents of this type are usually placed at the notehead.

The term:
marcato [abbreviated to *marc.*] – meaning *marked* or *accentuated* can be used as a general indication to play a passage with accentuation.

11.6 Changes of dynamic

Indications of a change in dynamic are also usually given as abbreviations of Italian terms, for example, as follows:

- *cresc.* – *crescendo*, meaning becoming gradually louder
- *dim.* – *diminuendo*, meaning becoming gradually softer or quieter
- *decrescendo* – also means becoming gradually quieter

As long as the crescendo or diminuendo does not extend over too many bars, the so-called 'hairpin' symbol offers a good alternative, in this example illustrating a crescendo followed by a diminuendo:

As a general rule, the final dynamic of each *diminuendo* or *crescendo* should always be indicated.

When adding crescendo or diminuendo words or symbols to a score, we should certainly consider whether the instrument in question is capable of achieving what has been written. Some instruments can crescendo through long notes, for example, and others – like the piano or most pitched percussion instruments – certainly cannot. Some instrumental sounds have a natural **decay** [which means that their sound dies away] – again, like the piano or the acoustic guitar, for instance – and we should consider how long their sound will sustain given a particular dynamic marking.

Of equal importance, when combining acoustic instruments, we should consider the relative power/loudness of each and to add our dynamic markings accordingly [see *Section 8: Instruments and Their Characteristics*].

11.7 Articulation

The general term *articulation* describes the way in which a performer plays a particular note or series of notes and this can be indicated by a range of words and/or symbols. The way in which articulation is achieved depends entirely on the specific family of instruments for which we are writing and, once again, we should always consider what is actually possible. Probably the most important distinction which composers might want to indicate is whether a note or succession of notes is to be played *legato* or *staccato*.

Legato – means playing successive notes so that no break is heard between one note and the next. Sometimes, the term *legatissimo* is used to indicate the maximum degree of legato, although it is questionable whether, in reality, a player or listener could distinguish between *legato* and *legatissimo*. Sometimes, the term *legato* may be qualified by the addition of other words. e.g. *sempre legato* – means always *legato*. The simplest way of indicating legato movement from one note to the next, or through a succession of notes is to use the *slur* – shown as a curved line usually from notehead to notehead [see musical example below].

Staccato – means short and detached. Depending on the tempo, notes are shortened to approximately half of their written value with the remaining duration becoming a rest. It may also imply a lighter attack. Where extremely short notes are required, the term *Staccatissimo* may be used; if the intention is to moderate the staccato effect, the term *mezzo staccato* is used. *Staccato* is indicated by the use of dots *above/below* the notehead, as distinct from the meaning of adding a dot *following* a notehead which extends its value by 50%.

The opening bars of Beethoven's *Piano Sonata* [Op. 2, No. 1] provides us with examples of *staccato* and a *slur* [as well as the tempo indication *Allegro*, a metronome mark and the dynamic indication *p* – piano]:

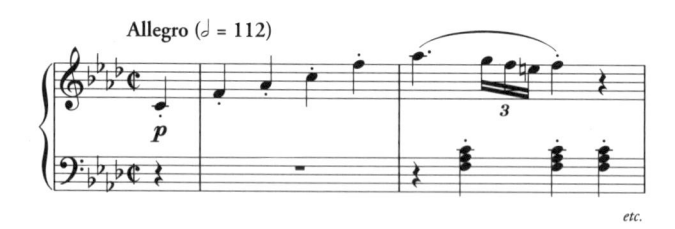

Mezzo staccato can be indicated by including notes marked with *staccato* dots within a *slur* or by the addition of a *tenuto* mark, the short horizontal line [see below] added to each *staccato* dot:

Adding Important Instructions to Your Score

Staccatissimo is indicated by small wedge-shaped symbols to the notehead:

It is worth reiterating here that the *tie* is really just a rather specialised use of the *slur*. If we slur two notes of the same pitch, then the 'join' is not heard and the effect is of one note lasting for the value of the two tied notes. [see *Section 1: Notation – the Basics*]

The *phrase mark*, like the slur, is indicated by a curved line but conveys a different meaning. Generally speaking, phrasing marks out sections of music which have a sense of completeness [perhaps rather in the way that a phrase within a sentence may be marked out by commas] and so it is perfectly possible for a phrase to contain notes with other articulation marks too, as this example from a Debussy *Prelude* [Book 2: VIII] illustrates, using both slurs and phrase marks simultaneously:

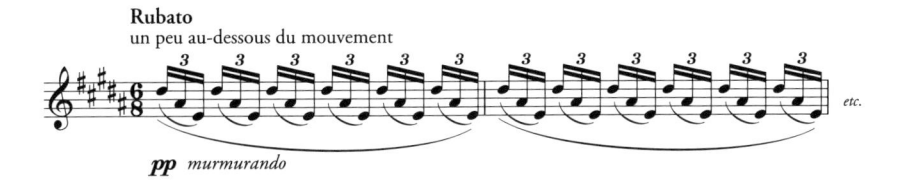

N.B. also, in this example, the use of:

pp – *very soft*

murmurando – *murmuring*

rubato – *'robbed time'*

un peu au-dessons du movement – *a little less movement.*

The word *tenuto* means 'held' and, in a musical context, it indicates that a note is to be held for its full value, and sometimes for longer. The symbol for *tenuto* is a short horizontal line to the notehead:

By implication, the *tenuto* sign may also imply a sense of 'leaning' on the note.

11.8 How *legato* and *staccato* is achieved on different instruments

The piano

Legato is achieved by not releasing one note until the next begins to sound and/or by use of the sustaining pedal. Without use of the pedal, *legato* can only be achieved if the fingering of the passage allows for the holding or slight overlapping of consecutive notes.

Staccato is achieved when the key is released and the damper stops the sound.
[see *Section 9: Writing for the Piano*]

Brass and woodwind instruments

Legato on wind instruments is achieved by only tonguing the first note of a slur and not the successive notes.

Staccato is achieved by lightly tonguing each note.

Bowed strings

Legato is generally achieved by playing the succession of slurred notes in one bow.

Staccato is achieved by short detached bowing. Pizzicato, which means plucking the strings, can be classed as a staccato effect because the sound decays rapidly.

11.9 Further effects possible on some instruments

Arpeggiation

Arpeggiare – is an instruction to 'spread the chord'. The example below, as applied to a piano score, uses the wavy-line symbol in two ways: in the first three bars, the **arpeggiation** applies only to the right-hand chords. In the fourth bar, the line extends through both staves, indicating that the arpeggiation should begin with the left hand and continue upwards through the right-hand chord. The direction of the arpeggiation is always upwards unless indicated by an arrow head at the bottom of the wavy line. The arpeggiation may be executed beginning on the beat or, in some circumstances, played so that the top note of the arpeggio arrives on the beat.

For further information on the subject of *arpeggios*, see *Appendix 3: Understanding Arpeggios*.

The glissando

The word *glissando* means, literally, 'a slide' and a perfect *glissando* is achievable on the trombone, on stringed instruments, the clarinet and, to some extent, the saxophone.
An approximation to a *glissando* can be played on the piano [and other keyboard instruments] and on 'barred' pitched percussion instruments [e.g. the vibraphone or the glockenspiel] but cannot, of course, include the black keys or their equivalents.
The *glissando* can be indicated as follows:

Tremolo / Tremolando

Tremolo [literally, *shaking/trembling*] means the rapid repetition of a note which is achievable on bowed stringed instruments or, on other instruments, the rapid alternation of two notes. On keyboard instruments, *tremolando* will often involve alternation of a chord with another note or even two chords [within the compass of one hand], and is written:

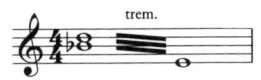

When *tremolando* is required on single notes played by stringed instruments, it is written as follows:

Con sordino / sordini

Con sordino [singular] sordini [plural] means with mute(s)

For the violin, viola, cello and double bass, the mute consists of a device which fits onto the bridge of the instrument and this has the effect of damping the transmission of vibrations from the strings to the body of the instrument, so making it quieter.

Brass instruments employ a variety of mutes which fit into the bell of the instrument.

Special effects for bowed strings

Col legno – with the wood – is an instruction to tap the strings with the wood of the bow which produces an eerie effect.
Spiccato – is a technique of playing a staccato effect on stringed instruments by bouncing the bow.
Sul ponticello – is an instruction to play close to the bridge, a technique which reduces the tone.

Symbols which are specific to bowed strings

The direction of bowing may be indicated by the following symbols:

Down-bow ⊓   Up-bow V

The following example [J. S. Bach – *Chorale Prelude* arranged for cello and piano by Kodály – 1882–1967] illustrates the indication of bowing:

I. Ach was ist doch unser Leben   J. S. Bach / Z. Kodály

from *Drei Choralvorspiele* [UE 7756, © Copyright 1924 by Zoltán Kodály, Budapest; Copyright renewed 1951; Copyright assigned 1952 to Universal Edition (London) Ltd., London]

N.B. The use of the term *simile* [cello – bar 2]. *Simile* means that the player should continue to play in the same way and use of this term avoids the necessity of adding the same articulation [*tenuto* or *staccato* indications, for example] throughout a passage.

11.10 Repeats and 'shorthand' signs and symbols

Repeats:

Words and Symbols:
We can save ourselves a great deal of time, effort and paper [as well as avoiding unnecessary page turns for the performer] by using the accepted signs and symbols which instruct the player to repeat one or more bars or, indeed complete sections of our pieces.

Da Capo – abbreviated to *D.C.* – [literally: *the head*] instructs the performer to repeat from the beginning to the word *fine* [meaning *end*] appears, usually above a double barline.

Dal segno – abbreviated to *D.S.* – [literally: *from the sign*] instructs the performer to repeat, not from the beginning of the piece, but from the sign: 𝄋

When a different ending to a piece is to be played [*i.e.* a *coda*] to conclude the repeated section, we may use:

D.C. [or *D.S.*] *al Segno e poi la Coda* – [literally: *from the head – or, when D.S. is used from the sign* 𝄋 *to the coda sign and then play the coda*], or more often: *D.C.*[or *D.S.*] *al Coda*.

The sign indicating the point where the coda replaces the first ending is:
to Coda
⊕

whilst this version of the sign indicates the start of the Coda:

⊕ **Coda**

Barlines and symbols
Shorter repeated sections can be indicated by the use of modified barlines, as follows:

‖: To begin the repeated section, and :‖ to indicate the end.

When a modified ending to a repeated section occurs, then so-called *first-* and *second-time* endings are indicated. *e.g.*

|1.　　　　　　　　　　|2.　　　　　　　　　　　　　　|

The use of repeat barlines and first- and second-time endings is illustrated in the following Irish air *The Minstrel Boy:*

The Minstrel Boy Thomas Moore [1779–1852]

The Min-strel Boy____ to the war has gone, In the
fath-er's sword____ he has gird-ed on, And his

ranks of death____ you'll____ find   him: His
wild harp slung____ be - -   hind   him;

When the player reaches an end-of-repeat bar-line, he/she will return to a start-repeat bar-line or, if none is shown, from the beginning.

[*N.B.* the use of the slur when syllables are sung over one or more notes]

Multiple endings can be added in this way [by numbering them accordingly] or even shared [*e.g.* 1 and 2 or even, perhaps: 2, 3 and 4]. However, some discretion should be exercised in the overuse of such multiple endings; we should always ensure that the score doesn't become so complex that it cannot be understood at first sight.

Repeat barlines can also be used 'back to back' when one repeated section follows another:

Generally speaking, the use of repeats is only appropriate when a section of the music is to be repeated exactly, although exceptions are made. In **strophic** [verse-repeating] songs, for example, changes of slurring, tying of notes, and additional notes for specific verses may be indicated using some method of showing that they do not apply to every verse: *e.g.* slurs and ties in broken lines. Once again, it should be said that such devices can be confusing and should only be employed when absolutely necessary.

Repeating a bar one or more times
More than one bar's rest [i.e. *multi-rest*]:
There are a number of symbols which indicate consecutive bars of rest. The following example is most commonly seen. The number above the stave indicates the number of bars involved:

Adding Important Instructions to Your Score

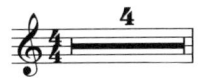

Repeating a bar containing notation:

Or, in the case of two bars:

Repeating chords or chord symbols:

When exact repetition of a chord [notes and rhythm] or chord symbols is to be indicated:

Other 'shorthand' methods exist for repeating individual notes [of the same value and pitch] and groups of notes within the bar and details of these can easily be found in dedicated theory books.

11.11 Some Italian terms which indicate style or mood

Useful prefixes: *con* – meaning with; *senza* meaning without, *molto* meaning much, *meno* meaning less, *quasi* meaning in the style of, and *senza* meaning without.
The following is a small selection of, literally, hundreds of terms:

appassionata – with passion

brillante – brilliantly

cantabile – in a singing style

con bravura – boldly

dolce/dolcissimo – sweetly/very sweetly

doloroso – sadly

espressivo [abbr. *espress.* or *espr.*] – expressively

175

Adding Important Instructions to Your Score

giocoso – playfully/jokingly

grandioso – grandly

grazioso – gracefully

lacrimoso – [lit. tearfully] sadly

maestoso – majestically

scherzando – jokingly

semplice – simply

triste – sadly

vigoroso – vigorously

Many of these are used in conjunction with tempo marks [*e.g. Andante semplice* or *Allegro appassionata*].

Did you know ...

... that the American composer John Milton Cage [1912–1992] composed a piece entitled *Imaginary Landscapes No.4* [1951] – for twelve short-wave radios? Each radio requires two operators/performers – one to control the tuning of the radio and the other to control its volume.

Instructions for the operation of the radios are scored but the sound content also depends on the radio programmes being broadcast at the time.

Breaking the Rules

12.1 Introduction

Many significant developments in compositional style have come from composers who have deliberately flouted the rules of convention and ploughed their own musical furrows. However, it is worth noting that the majority of these composers such as Igor Stravinsky, Arnold Shönberg and John Williams for example, have all had a firm grounding in the harmonic, melodic and rhythmic fundamentals of music. In order to break the rules successfully, it is a good idea to understand them in the first place.

In this section of the book we deal with some of the 'legal' and effective methods of breaking the rules.

- Changing time signatures during the course of a melody.
- Including 'rogue' notes into a melody.
- Introducing sudden dynamic changes.
- Incorporating large interval leaps.
- Ending on a note other than the tonic.
- Using chord substitutions.
- Using parallel intervals.
- Using chords with no 3rds.
- Using quartal harmony.
- Using unprepared and unresolved suspensions.
- Doubling 3rds in major chords.

12.2 Changing time signatures during the course of a melody

This is an effective way of throwing a 'rhythmic spanner' into the works. For example, if we have a simple melody, which moves along in $\frac{4}{4}$ time, we could insert a bar of $\frac{3}{8}$. This will throw the listener off balance as the pulse does not do what they expect it to; however, it can add character to the piece.

Many eminent musicians from the classical, jazz and rock worlds have made great use of this type of compositional device including Igor Stravinsky, Leonard Bernstein, Aaron Copland, Dave Brubeck and Pink Floyd. The following examples will illustrate how this works:

Trumpet

Track 76

Allegro

f

etc.

Flute

Track 76

Moderato

mp

etc.

12.3 Introducing 'rogue' notes into a melody

Introducing the 'unexpected' during a melody can also add to the originality of the piece. A good example of this is *Hedwig's Theme* from 'Harry Potter' (John Williams) where there is an unexpected melodic 'twist' giving the melody a sense of mystery.

If all music did what we expected it to, it would all sound the same!

Don't be afraid to experiment. It is also a good idea to play your melody several times over. Even if it sounds odd at first, it might start to grow on you. If it doesn't, then it must be weak. However, if it does have something about it then make sure that you notate it, otherwise you could forget it.

N.B. All notes can relate to all keys and can be successfully harmonised, so what might look odd could sound quite effective. Always remember, if it sounds good, then it is good! For example:

Oboe

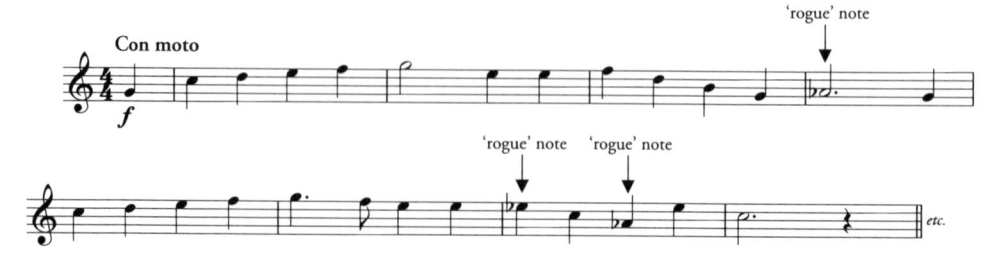

Track 77

Con moto

f

'rogue' note

'rogue' note   'rogue' note

etc.

Bassoon

'rogue' note   *'rogue' note*

Andante

mp

etc.

12.4 Sudden dynamic changes

Dynamics are a hugely important ingredient in music. By suddenly changing the level of sound, we can create a very dramatic effect. This was greatly exploited in the 20th century by composers such as Alban Berg, Luciano Berio and Harrison Birtwistle. A sudden change in dynamic is often difficult to achieve due to the technical limitations of the particular instruments involved. However, players of a high standard are very adept at this. The following examples simply illustrate this device:

French Horn [written pitch]

Vivace

ff   *pp*

ff   *pp*   *ff*   etc.

Clarinet [written pitch]

Presto

pp   *ff*

pp   *ff*   etc.

12.5 Incorporating large interval leaps

Many older textbooks on the subject of composition state that when composing a melody it is *'good practice to keep its range within an octave and only to use fairly modest intervals not exceeding a major 6th'*. However, many great composers have successfully broken this rule over the years including the great J. S. Bach himself! His suites for solo cello are full of large leaps.

Another good example of this type of writing can be found in one of the most famous melodies of all time, *Somewhere Over the Rainbow* (Harold Arlen) which begins with an octave leap. *N.B.* Intervals greater than an octave can be very effective in instrumental music but should be avoided in vocal music as they are difficult to sing. In general, instrumental ranges are much greater than vocal ranges; therefore large interval leaps are more practical.

Here are two examples of instrumental melodies using large intervals:

Violin

Clarinet [written pitch]

12.6 Ending on a note other than the tonic

The compositional rule that states that *'melodies must end on the tonic'* (the key note) has also been broken many times. As we all know, melodies such as *Happy Birthday to You* and *God Save the Queen* obey this rule and do end on the tonic. However, in the original versions of the famous songs *Speak Low* and *Mack the Knife* by Kurt Weill, the melody ends on the 6th degree of the scale. In the key of **C** this would be an **A** which is not even part of the tonic triad! Here are two examples of melodies which do not end on the tonic:

Cello

ending on the 3rd

Breaking the Rules

Vibraphone

Bright jazz waltz tempo

mf

ending on the 5th

12.7 Using chord substitutions

A chord substitution is the harmonisation of a melody note by a chord not governed by the conventional rules of harmony. One of the most effective substitutions is what is called *Tritone Substitution*. Here the chord used is a tritone (an interval of three whole tones) away from the expected harmonisation.

e.g. The chord of **C** in a piece in **C** major could be substituted with a chord of **F♯** half-diminished. (**F♯**, **A**, **C** and **E**.)

Similarly, in a perfect cadence [V-I] in **C** major, the dominant chord **G** [V] could be replaced by a chord of **D♭7** which is a tritone away.

181

The use of substitutions increases your harmonic vocabulary and can really enhance the musical integrity of the piece. Try to experiment by substituting chords in a simple tune like *Jingle Bells*. This is an interesting exercise and you will be pleased and surprised by the results!

12.8 Using parallel intervals

For many years, the use of parallel 5ths and octaves in classical music was a harmonic 'no-no' and was classed as weak in terms of chord progression. However, many great composers, classical and jazz alike, have ignored this rule and have created their own individual musical 'fingerprints' by incorporating parallel movement in their writing.

Piano

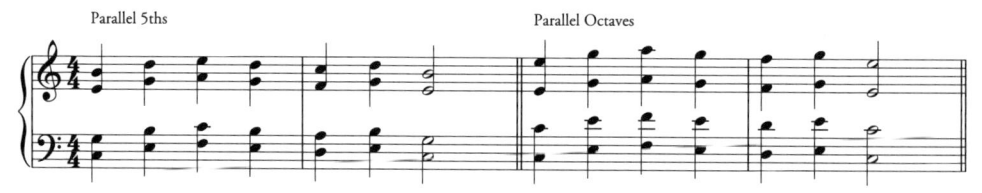

Track 82

The following example is taken from *La Cathédrale engloutie (The Submerged Cathedral)*, one of the *Preludes for Piano* by the French Impressionist composer, Claude Debussy. It appears in the original key and is also transposed for ease of reading:

La Cathédral engloutie Claude Debussy

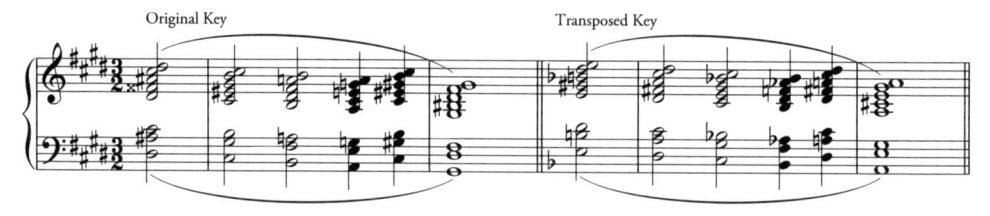

Track 83

12.9 Using chords without 3rds

This type of writing in parallel 'bare' fourths and fifths was extensively used in medieval music in a style called *organum*. This became a harmonic taboo from the Baroque to the Romantic period but became popular again with Impressionist and modern composers in the twentieth century because of the 'openness' of the sound it produced. In the rock world, chords without a 3rd (bare 5ths) are known as 'power chords' and are very popular with electric guitarists as they have a very earthy quality and are relatively easy to play.

A good example of the use of bare 5ths in the 20th century can be heard in the famous introduction and accompaniment to the *Pink Panther* theme by Henry Mancini.

A very effective and atmospheric way of ending a piece can be achieved by omitting the 3rd from the final chord, as the following examples show.

Bare 4ths

Bare 5ths

12.10 Using quartal harmony

Quartal harmony is produced by superimposing intervals of perfect 4ths. It has a very pleasant sonority and is particularly effective when used in parallel motion over a sustained pedal note. Be careful not to overuse this type of writing as, like eating chocolate, too much of it is not a good thing!

Organ

If you keep on superimposing fourths you end up forming what is called a 'total chromatic' chord where every note of the chromatic scale is present. This is a very powerful sound and highly effective when used in orchestral and band writing.

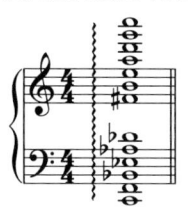

12.11 Using unprepared and unresolved suspensions

In music, the word suspended means 'hung'. This originally referred to a 'dissonant' note in a chord that appeared as a 'consonant' note in the previous chord, thus being 'hung over' or suspended. This note would then have to be 'resolved' onto a consonant note. (*i.e.* the tonic, the 3rd or the 5th note of the chord.)

In the Baroque and Classical periods of music, all suspensions had to be prepared and resolved. However, it is now acceptable and highly effective to write chords which include suspended notes without preparing or resolving them. The most common suspended notes are the 2nd and the 4th of the scale. Chords containing suspended notes are highly effective when used in introductions and accompaniments as they add 'bite' to the flavour of the music.

Unresolved suspended 2nd chords

Unresolved suspended 4nd chords

12.12 Doubling 3rds in major chords

When you first study the art of writing four-part harmony, one of the most important things you are told *not* to do is to double the third in a major chord [see *Section 5: Understanding Harmony*]. This means that in a four-part chord of **C** major, you must never use the note **E** twice. However, if you write a five-part chord of **Cma7** in open position *i.e.* **C, G, E, B,** and **E**, this doubling can be done successfully and gives a warm colour. This is particularly effective when used in parallel motion.

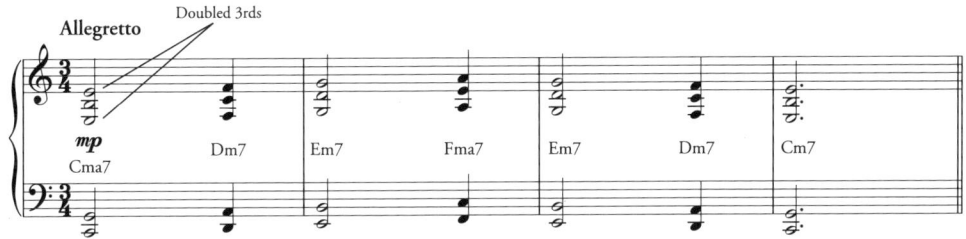

12.13 Conclusion

There are many ways of finding new methods of successfully breaking compositional conventions. Those listed above are just a few examples. Experiment with combining several of the techniques mentioned in this section to enhance your compositional skills. For example, the combination of rogue melodic notes and changing time signatures works particularly well. Also experiment with new *chord voicings* by adding unusual notes to conventional harmonies.

You never know, you could stumble across something that could entirely change the course of musical development!

Did you know ...

... that King Henry VIII [1491–1547] supposedly composed the song *Greensleeves*, although this has been often disputed?

... that Don Carlo Gesualdo [1560–1613], Prince of Venosa, was a composer, lutenist and murderer?

... that King Frederick the Great of Prussia [1712–1786] was a flautist, composer and patron of music?

... that Ignacy Jan Paderewski, who became Prime Minister of Poland in 1919, was a composer and pianist?

... that Edward Heath, British Prime Minister from 1970–1974, was a conductor and organist?

... that His Majesty King Bhumibol Adulyadej of Thailand played the saxophone and led his own Dixieland band whilst studying in Switzerland?

Do politics and music make a good mix? What do you think?

Appendix 1

Understanding Intervals

An *interval* in music can be described as the distance in pitch between two notes. It can be either a melodic interval where the notes are played consecutively or an harmonic interval when the notes are sounded together.

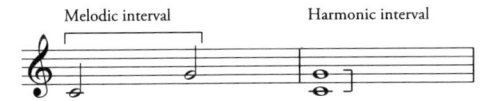

Intervals are indicated by ordinal numbers *i.e.* 2nds, 3rds, 4ths, 5ths, *etc.* [not to be confused with fractions]. Unlike numbering floors in a building, where the 2nd level is called the 1st floor, levels of musical intervals are measured with the 'ground floor' being 'level 1'. The term 2nd in music, therefore, refers to the note on the next line or space above or below that main note.

As well as being numbered, intervals are also described as being **perfect, major, minor, augmented** or **diminished.** For example, the interval from **C** to **E** is called a *major 3rd* as E is the third note of the scale of **C** *major*.

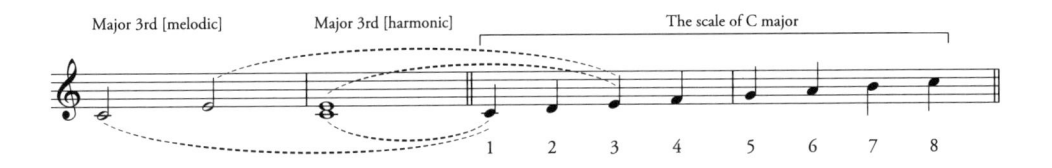

The interval from **C** to **E♭** is called a *minor 3rd* as E♭ is the third note of the scale of **C** *minor*.

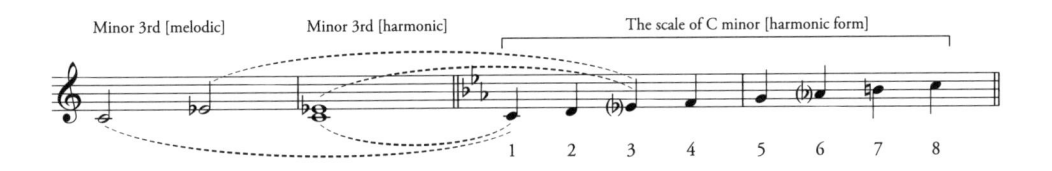

Major intervals

Major intervals can all be related to the key note or *tonic* of the major scale. However, the 4th, 5th and 8th or *octave* are called **perfect intervals** and are common to both major and minor scales. Nowadays, the **perfect octave** is simply called the octave.

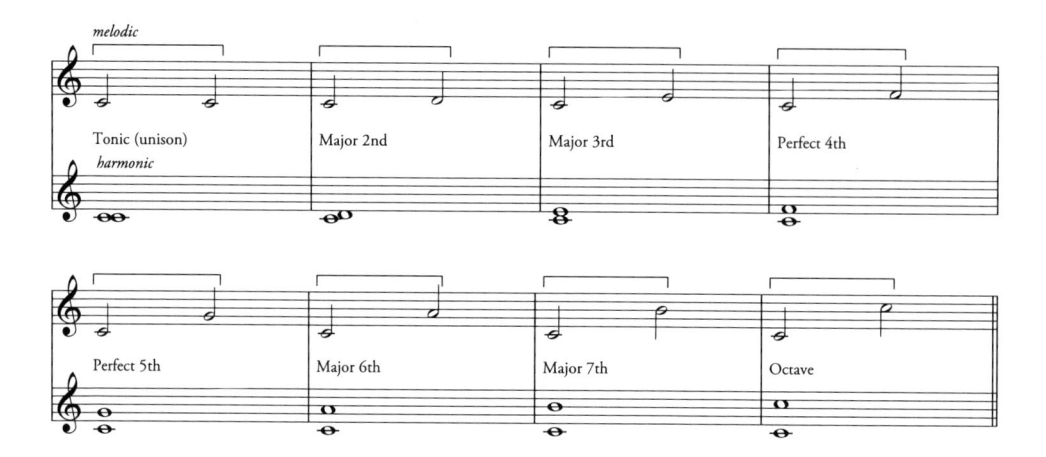

Minor intervals

Minor intervals are *not* necessarily related to the *tonic* of the minor scale. For example the interval between the first and second notes of a minor scale is a *major* second. Minor intervals can be best described as simply one semitone less than their major counterparts.

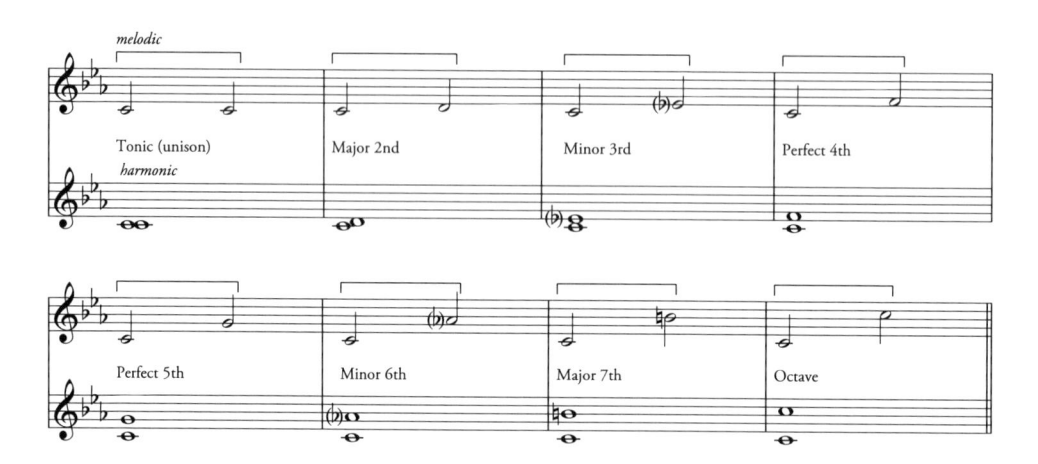

Diminished intervals

Diminished intervals are either one semitone less than a perfect or minor interval or a whole-tone less than a major interval. The word 'diminished' means reduced.

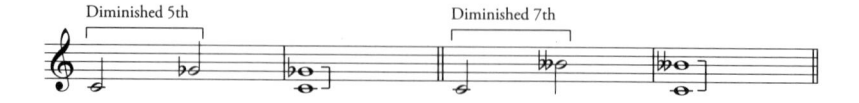

Augmented intervals

Augmented intervals are always one semitone greater than their perfect or major counterparts. The word *augmented* means enlarged.

The following shows all the permutations of intervals in **C** major.

Tonic [unison]

2nds: Diminished 2nd, Minor 2nd [semitone], Major 2nd [tone], Augmented 2nd

3rds: Diminished 3rd, Minor 3rd, Major 3rd, Augmented 3rd

4ths: Diminished 4th, Perfect 4th, Augmented 4th [tritone]

5ths: Diminished 5th [tritone], Perfect 5th, Augmented 5th

6ths: Diminished 6th, Minor 6th, Major 6th, Augmented 6th

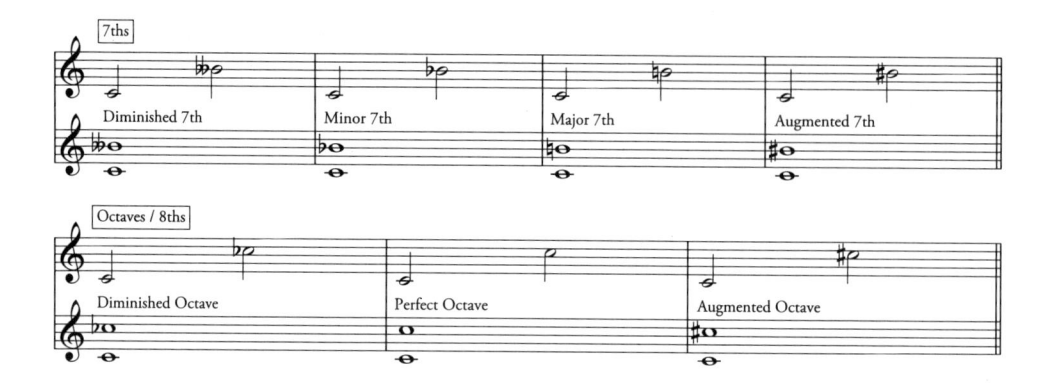

Enharmonic intervals

As you can see from the given examples, there are many intervals such as **C** to **F♯** [an augmented 4th] and **C** to **G♭** (a diminished 5th) which, although written or 'spelt' differently, actually sound the same. These are known as *enharmonic intervals*. By the same token, the melodic interval of **F♯** to **G♭** can also be described as enharmonic.

There are specific rules in 'traditional' harmonic and melodic writing which dictate which is the 'correct' one to use in certain cases. However, nowadays it is often clearer and quite acceptable to write the notation which looks the least confusing, without entering the world of double sharps and flats!

Inversions of intervals

To invert an interval, simply means to turn it upside down. For example, if we take a *major 3rd* in the key of *C major*, [**C** and **E**], we would invert it by placing the **C** one octave higher.

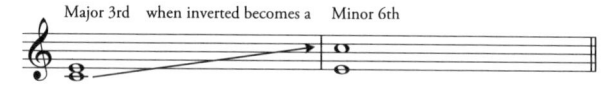

This forms a new interval of a *minor 6th* [**E** and **C**].

Similarly:

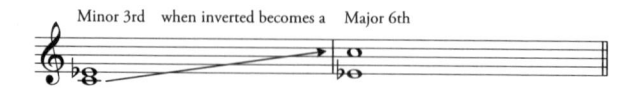

This forms a new interval of a *major 6th* [**E♭** and **C**]

All *major* intervals when inverted become *minor* and all *minor* intervals when inverted become *major*.

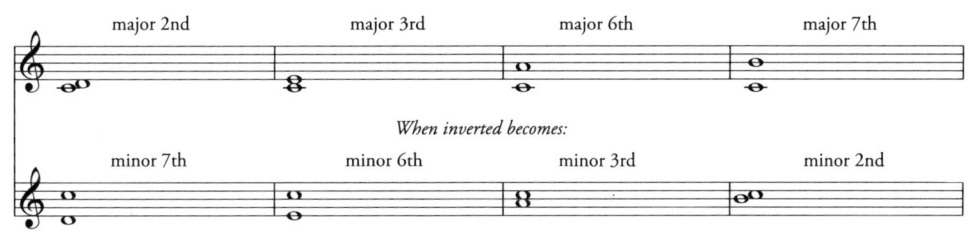

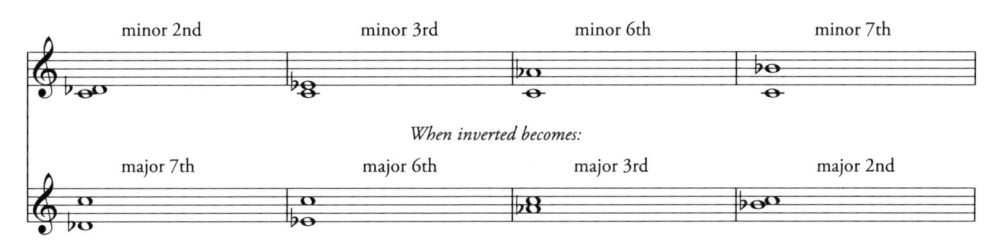

N.B. All intervals are measured from the bottom note up.

Likewise, all *augmented* intervals when inverted become *diminished* and all *diminished* intervals when inverted become *augmented*.

However, all *perfect* intervals when inverted remain *perfect*.

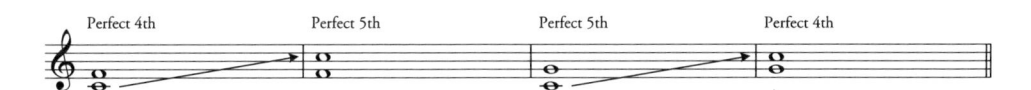

Intervals greater than an octave

Intervals greater than an octave are known as **compound intervals**. For example, an interval of a 10th is also called a *compound 3rd* as the upper note is still the 3rd but written one octave higher.

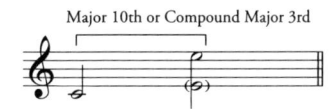

Intervals normally don't exceed a 13th or compound 6th but if desired they can go on to infinity! Many composers, particularly in the twentieth century, have utilised the entire compass of the piano keyboard in their works thus throwing up intervals in excess of seven octaves!

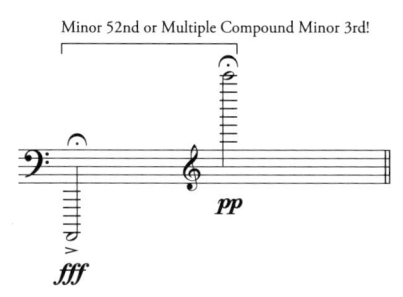

Minor 52nd or Multiple Compound Minor 3rd!

pp

fff

Conclusion

Understanding intervals does not necessarily make you a better composer, any more than the understanding of car mechanics makes you a better driver. However, it does give you an insight into, and an appreciation of, the vital role that these components have to play in the construction of a piece of music.

Appendix 2

Commonly Used Chords & Chord Symbols

The following chords are all shown with the root note as **C** and in root position. Each has been given, where relevant, two frequently used styles of chord symbol [descriptor] although other variations may be seen.

When the root of the chord is not played as the lowest note [*i.e.* the bass] the chord is said to be in inversion [see *Section 5: Understanding Harmony*] and the alternate bass note is shown following a forward slash [*e.g.* **C7/E**].
The number which appears in the chord descriptor is referred to as an **added note** since it has been added to one of the four types of triad: *major, minor, diminished* or *augmented*.

Chord symbols of greater complexity are used – including those which use added notes which form a compound interval above the root of the chord – especially in jazz notation. Information on these should be obtained from specialist reference sources.

N.B. Commonly, any diminished chord would be played to include the diminished 7th. *dim* is the abbreviation for *diminished* and *aug* is the abbreviation for *augmented*.
sus is an abbreviation for *suspended*.

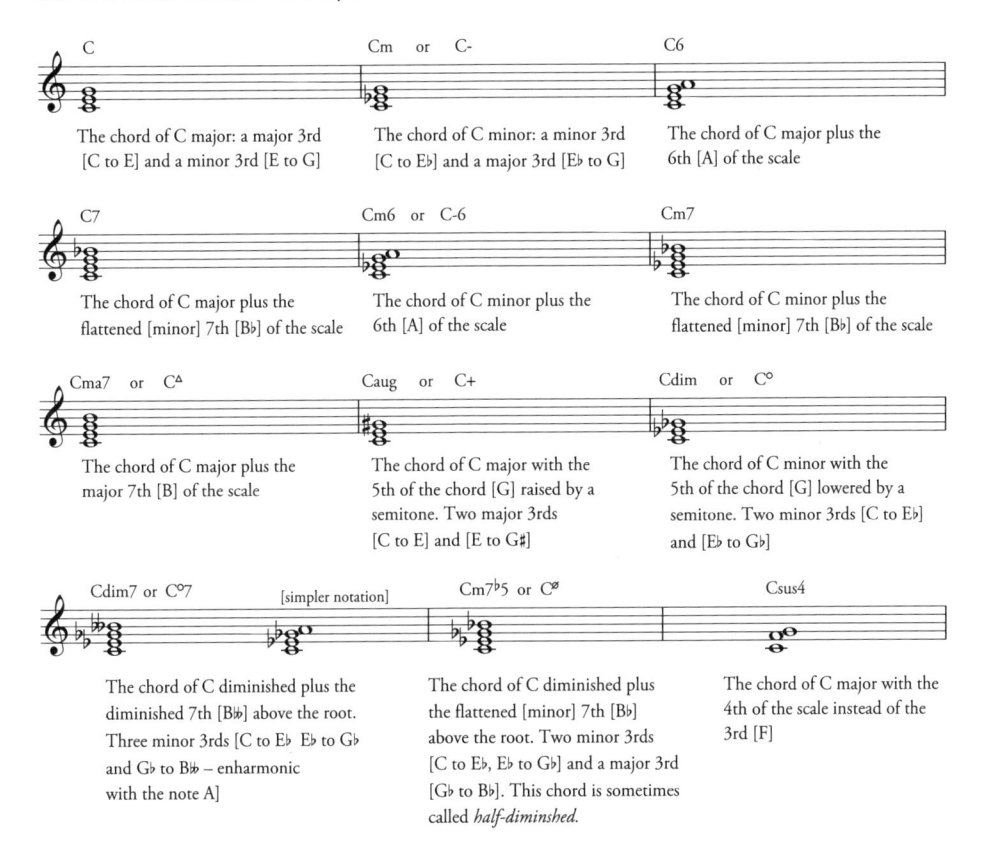

C
The chord of C major: a major 3rd [C to E] and a minor 3rd [E to G]

Cm or **C-**
The chord of C minor: a minor 3rd [C to E♭] and a major 3rd [E♭ to G]

C6
The chord of C major plus the 6th [A] of the scale

C7
The chord of C major plus the flattened [minor] 7th [B♭] of the scale

Cm6 or **C-6**
The chord of C minor plus the 6th [A] of the scale

Cm7
The chord of C minor plus the flattened [minor] 7th [B♭] of the scale

Cma7 or **C△**
The chord of C major plus the major 7th [B] of the scale

Caug or **C+**
The chord of C major with the 5th of the chord [G] raised by a semitone. Two major 3rds [C to E] and [E to G♯]

Cdim or **C°**
The chord of C minor with the 5th of the chord [G] lowered by a semitone. Two minor 3rds [C to E♭] and [E♭ to G♭]

Cdim7 or **C°7** [simpler notation]
The chord of C diminished plus the diminished 7th [B♭♭] above the root. Three minor 3rds [C to E♭, E♭ to G♭ and G♭ to B♭♭ – enharmonic with the note A]

Cm7♭5 or **C⌀**
The chord of C diminished plus the flattened [minor] 7th [B♭] above the root. Two minor 3rds [C to E♭, E♭ to G♭] and a major 3rd [G♭ to B♭]. This chord is sometimes called *half-diminshed*.

Csus4
The chord of C major with the 4th of the scale instead of the 3rd [F]

193

Appendix 3

Understanding Arpeggios

The word arpeggio comes from the Italian word for harp: *arpa*. In music, we use the word arpeggiated [harp-like] when we refer to the notes of a chord being 'spread'. Therefore, an arpeggio can be best described as the notes of a chord played individually.

Arpeggios can ascend and descend:

Simple major and minor arpeggios use the 1st, the 3rd, the 5th and the 8th [octave] notes of the scale to which they relate. The 8th, of course, is really the same note as the 1st but written an octave higher.

So, in practice, a standard major or minor arpeggio contains only three *different* notes. These happen to be the first three odd-numbered notes of the scale. *i.e.* 1, 3 and 5.
Most melodic instruments cannot play chords as they can only produce a single note at a time but they can play arpeggios very effectively.

Arpeggios, like chords, have inversions. This is where the lowest note is other than the *tonic* or *root*.

Understanding Arpeggios

Arpeggio of C major in:
Root position — First inversion — Second inversion

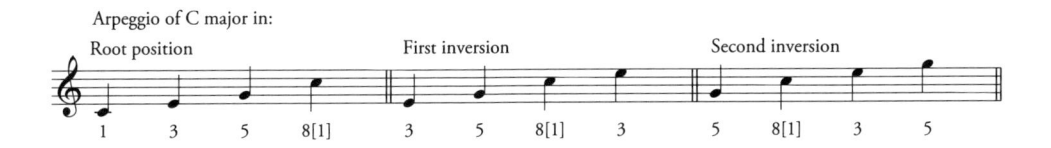

Arpeggios can be extended over several octaves. The extent to which this can be done of course naturally depends on the compass of the instrument.

A two-octave arpeggio of C major

A three-octave arpeggio of G major

Any chord can be played as an arpeggio. Here are some examples of other common chords in arpeggio form:

C7 — Arpeggio of C7 [dominant 7th in the Key of F]

Cma7 — Arpeggio of Cma7

Cm7 — Arpeggio of Cm7

Cdim7 — Arpeggio of Cdim7

Caug — Arpeggio of Caug

Understanding Arpeggios

The arpeggio is commonly encountered in both melodic writing and accompaniments. It is an effective melodic motif since it defines key or chord as the following examples illustrate:

Example 1 beginning with an ascending **C** major arpeggio:

Track 88

Morning Has Broken Trad: Gaelic

Example 2 beginning with a descending **C** minor arpeggio:

Track 89

Fantasia in C Minor J. S. Bach

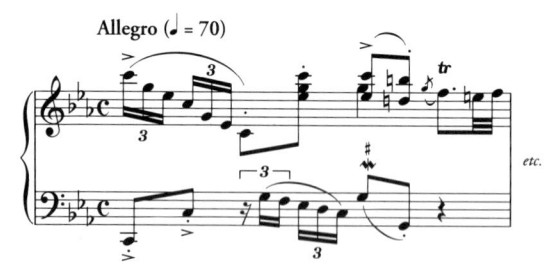

Example 3 beginning with an ascending **F** minor arpeggio [starting on the note C] and, in bars 3 and 4, an ascending arpeggio of the dominant seventh – **C7** – [starting on the note G]:

Track 90

Sonata Op. 2 No 1 Ludwig van Beethoven [1770–1827]

Understanding Arpeggios

Example 4 illustrates the use of an arpeggiated accompaniment over the melody:

Liebestraum No. 3 Nocturne Franz Liszt [1811–1886]

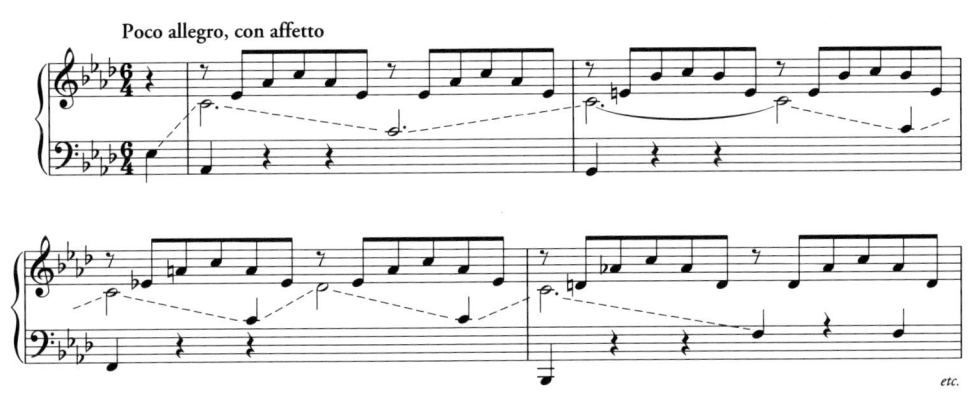

Poco allegro, con affetto

etc.

Appendix 4

Composing and Arranging Assignments – Some Suggestions

Starting points: basic skills

Assignment 1: Harmonising scales

Using a piano or electronic keyboard, experiment with harmonising a major scale, both ascending and descending.

- Your harmonisation could be improvised and remembered, notated on a piano stave or written on a single treble stave with chord symbols.

- When you have arrived at a successful harmonisation, experiment with transposing your harmonisation into a different major key and/or try harmonising a minor scale.

Assignment 2: Creating an increasingly complex rhythm over a basic pulse

- Choose a time signature – say, $\frac{4}{4}$

- Map out 8 or 16 empty bars on a sheet of manuscript paper, or use your music software programme.

- Write/enter an opening bar of, say, four crotchets:

- Now, make each bar a development of the previous one, perhaps by converting one of the crotchets into a quaver pair:

- Continue the process, always ensuring that you can tap or clap your growing rhythm, making use of rests, dotted rhythms, semiquavers, *etc.*

Assignment 3: Using parts of your rhythm from assignment 2 as a basis for a melody

- Although the rhythm which you created in *Assignment 2* will probably prove unsuitable as a basis for a melody in its entirety, you may well be able to use parts of it – perhaps a modified four-bar section.

Composing and Arranging Assignments – Some Suggestions

- Because your rhythm was developed sequentially, you may be able to employ melodic sequence too. [see *Section 6: The Composer's Toolkit*]

- Remember, however, that a successful melody will fall into phrases and the melodic line will want to come to rest, no matter how briefly at the end of each phrase.

- Be prepared to improvise and to experiment; a successful result is seldom achieved at the first attempt although further ideas may well occur as you gain in experience.

- Once your melody is finished, you might consider developing it into a simple piano arrangement:

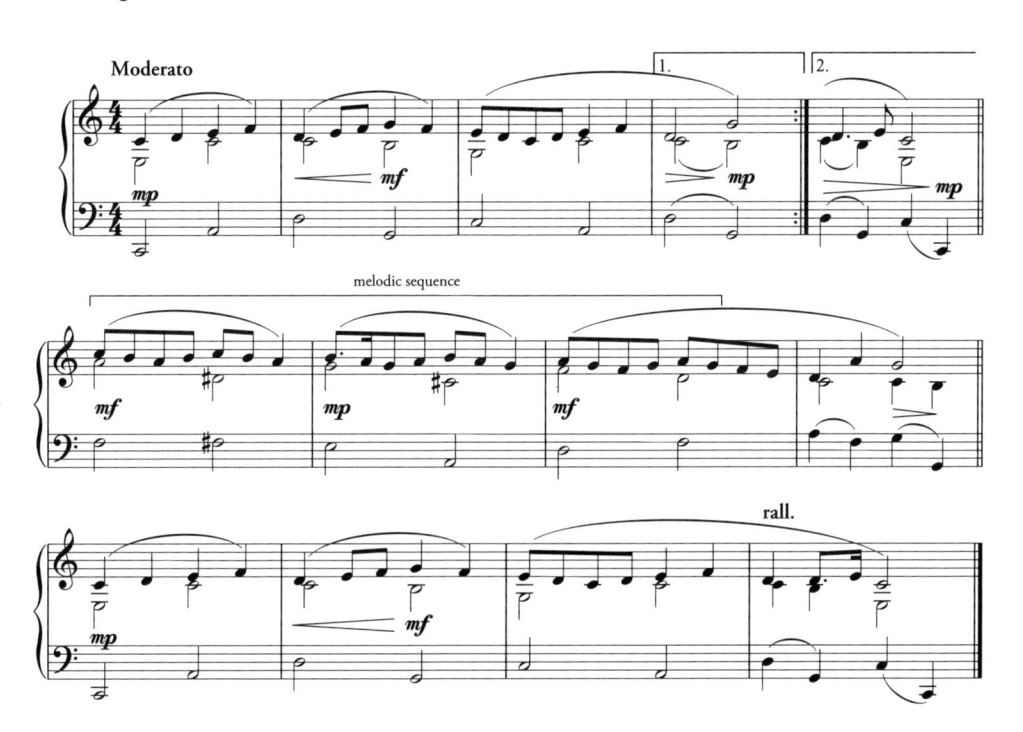

Assignment 4: Composing a melody which only moves by step or by an octave leap

- Choose a suitable scale, major or minor and select a time signature.

- The rule governing this melody is quite straightforward, although the assignment is by no means easy: the next note in the melody can only be one step away within your chosen scale, and the only permitted leap is an octave.

- Work through improvisation, either vocally or on your chosen instrument. Think in terms of four-bar units and try to give your melody some structure, creating arches. This example is in $\frac{6}{8}$ [compound duple time] e.g.

- You will quickly discover that rhythmic variation, when working within these limitations, is essential to offset the constant scalic movement.

Assignment 5 Word setting
Set the following words to a melody:

A Brand New Song

Isn't it amazing,
How very stimulating,
Composing a song can be?
You wake up in the morning,
Half asleep and yawning,
And dreaming as you sip your tea.

And then perhaps it strikes you,
A word or phrase delights you,
The start of a brand new song,
It may be just a lyric,
But man, it sounds terrific,
You feel as if you can't go wrong!

Composing and Arranging Assignments – Some Suggestions

- Begin by working out a rhythm-only setting which comfortably accommodates the words. [see *Section 10: Writing for Voices*].

- In the version given below, a swing rhythm in 4/4 has been used with many syncopations, but this is, by no means, the only possibility. In fact, it might be better to give your own ideas a chance before looking at the following example which uses notes from the blues scale on **F**:

A Brand New Song

Medium swing tempo

Is-n't it a-maz-ing, How ver-y stim-u-lat-ing, Com-pos-ing a song can be?
then per-haps it strikes you, A word or phrase de-lights you, The start of a brand new song?

You get up in the morn-ing, You're half a-wake and yawn-ing, And
It may be just a lyr-ic, But man, it sounds ter-rif-ic, You

1. dream-ing as you sip your tea.
2. And feel as if you can't go wrong!

Assignment 6: Scoring a round or canon

As an exercise in scoring, notate a well-known round or canon [see *Section 7: Thinking Horizontally* and also *Section 8: Instruments and their Characteristics*].

You could base your arrangement on the short-score version of *Row, Row, Row Your Boat* [which is given in *Section 7*] or better still, choose a different one.

- Set up your score for four identical instruments – say, four clarinets.

- Begin by checking the comfortable range of your chosen instrument and select the key accordingly [see *Section 8: Instruments and Their Characteristics*].

- Remember, in a round or canon, all voices or instruments play or sing exactly the same melodic line but enter in succession.

- Begin by notating the first voice or instrument in its entirety, remembering that additional bars will be required for the second, third and fourth voices.

- Complete your score by adding dynamics, a tempo direction and any articulation [see Section 11: *Adding Important Instructions to Your Score*] that will help the players to perform the piece musically.

More Advanced Assignments

Assignment 7: Composing a miniature suite
Compose a miniature suite of descriptive pieces for solo flute, saxophone or clarinet. On the face of it, this would seem to be a comparatively easy project, but the main challenge is to maintain the listener's interest without the assistance of harmony or any variety of timbre apart from that provided by the solo instrument itself.

- Aim for contrast between each of the short movements by using differing tempi, dynamic ranges, pitch ranges and time signatures. Historically, the origins of the suite are to be found in the grouping of contrasting dances and this could provide a model for your own composition.

- You may find inspiration in choosing to make each movement descriptive, perhaps of a journey or of differing aspects of a particular place. An exotic location may help to give a stylistic focus to this; a Latin American suite for example.

- If you are not a performer on your chosen instrument, try to talk to someone who is; they should be able to help you to explore the possibilities of the instrument and avoid its particular difficulties or weaknesses. It's always better, too, to have someone in mind who can play your work through to you. [see *Section 8: Instruments and their Characteristics* for specific information concerning your chosen instrument]

- Don't forget that brass and woodwind performers will need to breathe between phrases and avoid overly long notes.

Assignment 8: Composing a 12-bar blues for voice and piano [or keyboard or guitar]
A sure-fire way to begin composing an authentic sounding blues is to draw the melodic phrases from the blues scale, shown here beginning on the note **C**. Play or sing this scale until you become comfortable with it.

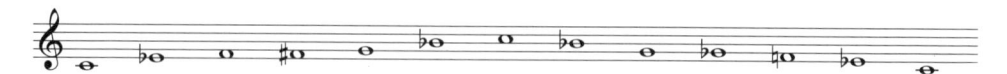

- Listen to some authentic blues to help you to get a 'feel' for the style. You will probably find that the listening examples 'swing' and that the tempo is slow and that the form of the song is dictated by the structure of the simple lyrics.

for *e.g.*

My baby left me, she left me all alone,
Yes, my baby left me, she left me all alone,
I spend my evenings, just sittin' by the 'phone.

Composing and Arranging Assignments – Some Suggestions

- Frequently, the first and second lines of a 12-bar blues are very nearly the same. In the example above, the accommodation of the extra syllable at the beginning of the second line may provide the only difference.

- The third line of the blues will frequently take a new direction, perhaps a descending phrase beginning at a higher pitch than has been heard in the previous phrases.

- The harmonic accompaniment might well consist of simple repeated four-in-a-bar, on-beat chording following the conventional chord structure:

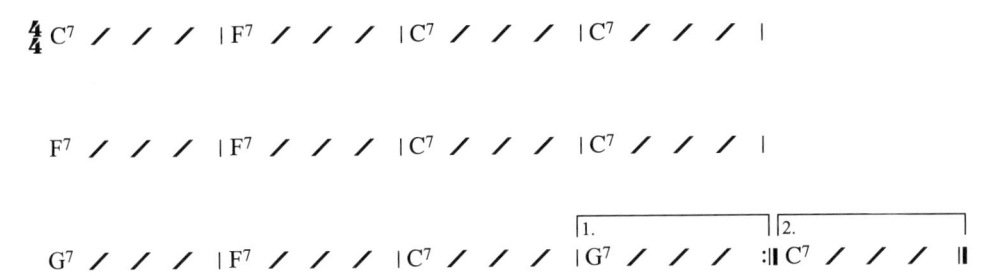

$\frac{4}{4}$ C⁷ / / / | F⁷ / / / | C⁷ / / / | C⁷ / / / |

F⁷ / / / | F⁷ / / / | C⁷ / / / | C⁷ / / / |

G⁷ / / / | F⁷ / / / | C⁷ / / / | [1. G⁷ / / / :|| [2. C⁷ / / / ||

- Finally, take a look at a possible first line for this blues and note where the vocal phrase ends, leaving the last bar in each four-bar line to the accompanist who may choose to play a *fill* here.

Slow blues tempo in swing quavers

"Fill"

My ba-by left me,   She left me all a-lone___   etc.

Assignment 9: Composing a set of variations

Compose a set of variations using a simple melody that you know very well – *Twinkle, Twinkle Little Star* is an obvious choice – and examples of a range of treatments of this tune can be found in *Section 9: Writing for the Piano*.

- Begin by playing or singing your chosen theme many times and then experiment with simple improvised alternative treatments of the melody. Compose each different treatment as a separate little movement.

- Create your variations by exploiting every variable element of the piece to create contrast from one movement to the next: major to minor, fast to slow or slow to fast, simple four-in-a-bar to three-in-a-bar, loud and energetic to quiet and lyrical, and so on.

- If your variations are to be accompanied, establish an obviously correct-sounding harmony for the opening statement of the theme. Now be prepared to think of alternative harmonies [chord substitutions] which will change the "feel" or the musical sense of a particular phrase:

Twinkle, Twinkle Little Star

[Musical notation showing three harmonizations:

First: C — C/E — F — C/E etc.

Second: C — Gm7 — C7 — F — G9 — Em7 — Am7 etc.

Third: C — Csus2/E — C/E — Fma7 — G9/F — Em7♭5 — A7 etc.]

- Conclude with a bold re-statement of the theme, bearing in mind that your listener should have learned quite a lot about the potential of your chosen musical subject in the process of listening to your piece.

Assignment 10: Composing film music

Compose the accompanying music for a short film sequence, real or imagined. Choose an obvious mood: suspense, chase, creepy, *etc.* and decide on the length of your sequence. The secret, here, is to keep the sequence short – perhaps 30 seconds or so – and not to be afraid of the obvious.

- How you respond to this challenge will depend greatly on the resources at your disposal. If you are working in a group context and have access to a range of instruments, then your response may be more colourful. But remember that in the days of the silent cinema, the pianist had to improvise everything. It may be worth considering some of those silent cinema *clichés* before you start.

- So what are the obvious responses? Think in terms of tempo, dynamics, pitch, tonality and timbre. Creepy sequences may well use slow, quiet, low-pitched, minor and dark sounds. Suspense sequences may well build to a climax, and so on. Choose an effective sequence from a film and try to discover what the professionals have done.

- Think about exploiting different and unusual sounds from your chosen instrument. A wealth of sounds can be produced from a piano, for example, by playing directly onto the strings – with or without use of the sustain pedal – using beaters and other objects. The sound of the 'take off' of the 'Tardis' in the original *Doctor Who* television series was produced, initially, using a coin on the wire-wound lower strings of the piano. The sound was then enhanced in the BBC Radiophonic Workshop.

- If you have the means to add your soundtrack to a video sequence or, at least, to play the sequence in conjunction with the video you will gain a very good idea of how successful you have been.

Assignment 11: Composing a pastiche folk song

Compose a *pastiche* folk song, using a particular scale or mode [see *Section 4: Understanding Key Signatures*].

Copying the style of a folk song from the western European tradition may well be an appropriate choice, perhaps using compound time [see *Section 3: Understanding Pulse, Time Signatures and Rhythm*] in the Dorian mode.

- The Dorian mode can begin on any chosen note but the example given below begins on the expected note **D**:

- Choose a suitable lyric, one which scans easily and has a natural simplicity and this will give form and structure to your song.

The following example is by A. E. Housman [1859–1936] and is Number LVIII from his collection *A Shropshire Lad*. It displays many of the appropriate characteristics:

When I came last to Ludlow
Amidst the moonlight pale,
Two friends kept step beside me
Two honest lads and hale.

Now Dick lies long in the churchyard,
And Ned lies long in jail,
And I come home to Ludlow
Amidst the moonlight pale.

- Whichever lyric is chosen, the composer needs to capture the mood which, in this instance, is certainly reflective and somewhat sad. For this purpose, the Dorian mode is quite appropriate.

- Stylistically, it would also be appropriate to use the same melody for both verses. Such a setting may be referred to as *strophic* or verse-repeating.

Assignment 12: Making a duet arrangement

Make a duet arrangement of an existing song or piece for two identical or two different instruments from the same family group *e.g.* two flutes, two clarinets, violin and cello, trumpet and trombone.

Unless you are using a computer software programme which allows you to hear what you write, try to choose instruments for which players are available and write only what you know they will be able to play.

- Much of the composing skill in this assignment will be to write contrapuntally [see *Section 7: Thinking Horizontally*] so that the harmonies arise through the weaving melodic lines of each part.

- Ensure that you have a strong grasp of the song or piece which you are going to arrange. Play or sing it through many times and try to imagine how it will sound on your chosen instruments. Don't be afraid to improvise and experiment to find workable ideas.

- Think about how the lower instrument will complement the upper instrument which will probably carry the melody for the most part. Some passages may harmonise happily in thirds or sixths, but try to avoid constant parallel movement [*i.e.* both instruments moving up or down in pitch together]. Much harmonic strength can be derived from the use of contrary or opposite movement; when the melodic line ascends then think about making the lower voice descend and *vice versa*. Some rhythmic independence of parts is also important: if one instrument is holding a sustained note [*i.e.* is stationary] then it will often be appropriate to give some movement to the other part.

- Remember that both instruments may not need to be playing together all the time. Don't overlook the possibility of using imitation as in the opening bars of the following example, and once again, if they're brass or wind instruments allow time to breathe:

Barbara Allen – English folksong

- Remember that, just as in Assignment 1, that working with limited resources may seem to be a simpler proposition but, in reality, makes achieving a convincing result more difficult. Be prepared to re-work and to modify; you may find that the first answer is not always the best one!

Assignment 13: Composing a piece for a small group of unpitched percussion instruments

- Again, think about the resources and players at your disposal and try to plan a piece which you will actually be able to hear performed.

- Make a selection of instruments which are suitably contrasting in sound: *i.e.* skins, metal and wood in the form of a drum, a triangle or cowbell and claves, for example.

- Remember, the interest in such a piece will be restricted principally to rhythmic pattern, changes of tempo and dynamics, and timbre.

- It might be interesting to give the whole piece a specific overall unity by working within a prescribed rhythmic pattern which is sustained throughout – perhaps by alternating bars of $\frac{3}{4}$ and $\frac{6}{8}$ [think of *I Like to be in America* from Bernstein's *West Side Story* to get the effect of this] which gives a three-in-a-bar/two-in-a-bar pattern, or maybe to choose a five-in-a-bar or seven-in-a-bar time signature.

- Aim for a short but clearly structured piece. The listener will need to feel that the piece is 'going somewhere' and don't play all your cards at once.

Select Bibliography

1791: Mozart's Last Year – H.C. Robbins Landon [2nd Edition – 1990]: Fontana Paperbacks. First published by Thames & Hudson. ISBN 0-00-654324-3

An Introduction to Music – Martin Bernstein & Martin Picker [4th Edition]: Prentice Hall Inc., Eaglewood Cliffs, New Jersey, USA. ISBN 0-13-489559-2

George Gershwin – Rodney Greenberg [1998]: Phaidon Press Ltd. ISBN 978-0-7148-4772-6

Letters of Wolfgang Amadeus Mozart – Ed. Hans Mersmann [1972]: Dover Publications, Inc. New York. ISBN 0-486-22859-2

Mozart: The Golden Years [1781–1791] – H.C. Robbins Landon [1990]: Thames & Hudson, London. ISBN – 0-500-27631-5

Murmurs of Earth – Carl Sagan [1978]: Random House, New York. ISBN 0-394-41047-5

Oh, What A Circus – Tim Rice [1999]: Hodder and Stoughton. ISBN 0-340-65459-7

Orchestral Technique – Gordon Jacob: [2nd Edition 1968]. Oxford University Press

Peter Warlock, The Life of Philip Heseltine – Barry Smith [1994]: Oxford University Press. ISBN 0-19-816310-X

Saxophone – Paul Harvey [1995]. Kahn and Averill: ISBN 1-871082-53-6

The AB Guide to Music Theory – Part 1 – Eric Taylor [1993]: The Associated Board of the Royal Schools of Music (Publishing) Ltd. ISBN 1-85472-446-0

The AB Guide to Music Theory – Part 2 – Eric Taylor [1993]: The Associated Board of the Royal Schools of Music (Publishing) Ltd. ISBN 1-85472-447-9

The New Oxford Book of Carols – Ed. Hugh Keyte & Andrew Parrott [1998]: Oxford University Press. ISBN 0-19-353322-7

The New Oxford Companion to Music – Ed. Denis Arnold [1991]: Oxford University Press. ISBN 0-19-311316-3

The Oxford Companion to Music – Percy A. Scholes [9th Edition 1967]: Oxford University Press

The Oxford Dictionary of Music – Michael Kennedy [1985]: Oxford University Press. ISBN 0-19-311333-3

The Street Where I Live – Alan Jay Lerner [1978]: Hodder and Stoughton. ISBN 0-340-22838-5

Postscript

Here are a few final words of advice arising from our own experiences as composers:

- Never discard anything you write. Sometimes, even the smallest fragments or ideas may prove to be useful when revisited later.

- Consider making new arrangements of your own finished compositions. A piano piece, for instance, might be arranged for a solo instrument with piano accompaniment. Many composers have recycled their work in this way.

- A great deal of useful experience can also be gained by making arrangements of the work of other composers.

- Develop your keyboard harmony skills, whether or not you are a pianist/keyboard player and evolve your own impromptu arrangements of simple melodies in a range of keys. You may be surprised to find that different harmonisations occur to you as you move from one key to another.

- Do not neglect your own performance skills and, as has been mentioned elsewhere in this book, try not to divorce your musical experiences as a performer from your work as a composer. Very often, a piece which you have enjoyed playing can serve as a model for a new piece of your own.

- Devote as much time as you can to improvisation, both within a set framework/genre or completely freely.

- If you encounter a problem with a particular bar or section of a piece which you are writing, leave it incomplete and push on with the piece. When you return to the problem at a later stage, you may well find the answer.

- Never be afraid to ask for help or advice from someone who has more experience. This might apply to specific technical questions or to more general issues concerning the piece as a whole.

- Always try to organise a 'play through' of your piece. Sometimes, problems will arise in performance which you may not have foreseen and these can then be addressed.

- Lastly, and we make no apology for reiterating this essential piece of advice, try to continue broadening your musical experience through listening. Most of us have a tendency to stay within our 'comfort zone' when it comes to preferences in listening but, as composers, we are not simply 'consumers' of music. We are now also creators of music and we need to constantly add to our musical 'memory banks', drawing on the vast wealth of music that exists in the world.

Glossary

8va [*ottava*]*:* to be played one octave higher/lower than notated according to the placing of the sign.

8vb: to be played one octave lower than notated.

a cappella [*Italian*]*:* meaning unaccompanied [with reference to choral music].

accent: the placing of an emphasis on a particular note or chord and usually marked by a range of symbols where this emphasis is not determined by the usual pattern of strong beats in the bar/measure.

accidental: any sign preceding a note which affects its pitch: *e.g.* a sharp, flat, or natural.

ad lib [*Latin*: *ad libitum*]*:* meaning 'at will', a direction to the player which allows a degree of freedom in performance

added note [to a chord]*:* a note which is added to a chord which is not in the triad.

Alberti bass: a term used to describe a style of left-hand piano accompaniment which uses broken chords; so named as a result of its frequent use by Domenico Alberti [1710–1740].

aleatory [from Latin]*:* a term which describes music containing elements, the performance of which is determined by chance.

alto clef [see *clef*]*:* a clef which places the note middle C on the middle line of the staff or stave.

amanuensis: one who writes/notates from dictation.

anacrusis: a note or group of notes preceding an accented beat, commonly arising on the last beat/beats of a bar/measure.

appoggiatura [*Italian*]*:* a 'leaning' note. A note which does not belong to the chord and which is resolved – by rising or falling – onto a note which does belong. If the note has been heard in the previous chord, its effect is similar to a suspension. If not heard in the previous chord, its effect is similar to an unprepared suspension.

arco [*Italian*]*:* an instruction to string players indicating that they should play with the bow (as distinct from *pizzicato*).

aria [*Italian*]*:* a solo song, often in the context of opera.

arpeggiation [from *Italian*]*:* the spreading of the notes of a chord, upwards or downwards, in a harp-like fashion.

arpeggio [from *Italian*]*:* the notes of a chord played in succession, rising and/or falling.

articulation: the way in which a note or notes are played in a passage in terms of their connection or separation as indicated by articulation marks such as slurs, staccatos, tenutos, etc.

atonal: not tonal. *i.e.* not belonging to a key.

augmentation [durations]*:* the doubling of the durations of the notes in a subject/theme.

augmented [chord]*:* a triad consisting of two major 3rds. *e.g.* C to E and E to G♯.

augmented [interval]*:* literally – made larger. *e.g.* an augmented 5th is an interval which is a semitone larger than a perfect 5th.

b.p.m./bpm: an abbreviation for *beats per minute*.

Glossary

barlines: vertical lines which divide music into bars/measures, each containing the number of beats indicated by the preceding time signature.

Baroque [style/period – from *Portuguese*]***:*** a term used to describe the predominantly contrapuntal style of Western European music in, very broadly, the 17th and early 18th centuries.

bars/measures: in notated music, units of a number of beats, separated by barlines, as determined by the time signature.

bass clef [see *clef*]***:*** a clef which places the note middle C on the first ledger line above the stave. (also known as the 'F' clef).

beaming: the connecting of notes of fractional duration by one or more lines joining the stems, indicating their value as quavers, semiquavers, demisemiquavers, *etc.*

beat: a synonym for pulse.

bel canto [*Italian* – literally *beautiful song*]***:*** Commonly used to describe a style of operatic aria in which the lyrical qualities are particularly evident.

binary form: a musical form consisting of two elements or sections.

blues/12-bar blues: originally, a song form of Afro-American origin which uses the primary chords I, IV and V with added minor 7ths. The form of the blues is essentially a three-line lyric, each consisting of four bars where the first two lines are broadly similar. The use of the dominant chord is reserved for the final line which often contains the climax of the piece. The rhythm of the blues is often swung and the melodic line draws on the notes of the blues scale. The form has been, and continues to be, exploited in jazz, rock and roll and popular song.

bossa nova [*Portuguese*]***:*** a style of Latin-American music which bears some rhythmic similarity to the samba. The development of the style is largely attributed to João Gilberto in the late 1950s and was quickly taken up by jazz musicians including Charlie Byrd and Stan Getz. Bossa Nova has a characteristic 'laid-back' feel, softly sung and, initially, unobtrusively accompanied by an acoustic guitar. Like modern jazz, the harmony is often sophisticated although the mood and sentiments are very much those of the Rio de Janeiro good life. The Getz/Gilberto version of *The Girl From Ipanema* is probably the most successful recording of a bossa nova.

cadence [from *Latin*]***:*** a two-chord progression which harmonises a phrase ending. *e.g.* a perfect cadence, which uses the progression V–I.

call and response: a style of music commonly, although not exclusively, thought of as African or Afro-American in origin, usually vocal, in which a phrase is followed by an answering phrase. *e.g.* the voice of a preacher followed by the response of the congregation or, the voice of a work-gang leader and the response of the work-gang.

calypso: a genre of Afro-Caribbean [Trinidadian] song characterised, in authentic performances, by the improvised character of its music and lyrics.

canon [from *Greek*]***:*** see *round*.

chord substitution: the substitution of a chord in place of the one expected or previously used in that context.

chord voicing: particularly, but not exclusively, in jazz piano playing, the way in which the chords are laid out in terms of their inversions and vertical spacing and how these progress from chord to chord.

chromatic [from *Greek* – chromatic note]***:*** a note which does not belong to the key.

Glossary

chromatic [from *Greek* – chromatic scale]*:* a scale ascending or descending in semitones.

chromaticism [from *Greek*]: usually used to describe a style which makes considerable use of chromatic notes [*i.e.* those not belonging to the key] especially with reference to harmony.

Classical [style/period]: a term used to describe the highly structured style of Western European music in, very broadly, the latter half of the 18th century and the early years of the 19th century. Commonly misused to describe any music of so-called serious intention as distinct from '*pop*' or *popular* music.

clef [*French*]*:* the sign placed at the beginning of each stave which defines the pitch of the lines and spaces.

cliché [*French*]*:* an idea which has suffered a loss of impact as a result of overuse.

click track: a regular pulse audible only to the performers through headsets which is often used in theatre or recording situations where they may need a guide to ensure playing in strict time.

close position/harmony: where the voices in a chord are closely spaced, as in a root position triad.

coda [*Italian*]*:* Literally, a 'tail'. A section added at the end of a composition which, in a short piece, might simply provide an extended or different ending. In longer and more highly structured compositions, the coda may contain further development.

compound [interval]: an interval which exceeds an octave.

compound [time]*:* a time signature where the beat is a dotted note and therefore divisible by three.

con sordino/senza sordino [*Italian*]: with mute/without mute.

concert pitch: the generally agreed standardised pitch where the A above middle C = 440 cycles per second.

consonant [the opposite of dissonant]*:* concordant. Sounding well together, and as such, a matter of judgement and taste which will always remain subjective. Predominant views, especially with regard to concordant and discordant intervals, have clearly changed through history.

contrapuntal: using counterpoint: polyphonic.

contrary motion: voices/lines which move in opposite directions.

countermelody: A melody which runs counter [*i.e.* in counterpoint] to the principal melody.

counterpoint: note against note. A musical style where the combination of melodic lines gives rise to the harmony as distinct from a homophonic approach where a melodic line is accompanied by chords.

cycle-of-fifths: a succession of chords where the root notes follow a sequence of descending fifths/rising fourths.

decay [of sound]*:* the time taken for a sound to die away.

descant: the addition of another part/voice/melodic line, usually above the melody.

development: the section of an extended composition in which the musical potential of the subject material is exploited.

diminished [chord]: a chord which, in a root position triad from the root upwards, consists of two minor 3rds. *e.g.* C to E♭ and E♭ to G♭.

Glossary

diminished [interval]***:*** the interval created by lowering the upper note of a perfect or minor interval by a semitone or a major interval by two semitones.

diminution: [durations]***:*** the halving of the durations of the notes in a subject/theme.

dissonance [the opposite of consonant]***:*** discordant. Not sounding well together, and as such, a matter of judgement and taste which will always remain subjective. Predominant views, especially with regard to concordant and discordant intervals, have clearly changed through history.

divisi [*Italian*]***:*** divided. A direction, where there is more than one player to a part, to divide in order to play separate parts.

dodecaphony [see serialism]***:*** 12-note music.

dominant [key]***:*** in modulation, a new key which has as its tonic the dominant note of the old key.

dominant: the 5th degree of a major/minor scale.

dot [articulation]***:*** as placed at the head of a note to indicate staccato.

dot [note duration]***:*** as placed after the notehead to lengthen its duration by 50%.

double dotting [note duration]***:*** the first dot extends the note duration by 50% whilst the second dot further extends it by 50% of the value of the first dot. *e.g.* a dotted crotchet has a duration of 3 quavers and a double-dotted crotchet has a value of three quavers + a semiquaver.

double flat: [♭♭] sign placed before a note which lowers the pitch by a tone [or two semitones].

double sharp: [x] sign placed before a note which raises the pitch by a tone [or two semitones].

double stopping: the playing of two notes simultaneously on a bowed string instrument by bowing two strings.

double/doubling: the duplication of a note or of a part at the octave or multiples of the octave.

duple [time]***:*** having two beats in a bar/measure.

duplet: Two notes to be played in the time of three of the same kind. *e.g.* in $\frac{6}{8}$: ♪♪ in the time of ♪♪♪

duration [notes]***:*** the length of a musical sound.

elision: the omission of an unaccented letter or syllable in a word, commonly used in song lyrics to accommodate the rhythm of the melodic line.

enharmonic [keys]***:*** those keys which, although notated differently, sound the same on instruments of fixed pitch *e.g.* C♯ major and D♭ major.

enharmonic [notes/intervals]***:*** notes or intervals which sound the same on instruments of fixed pitch *e.g.* the notes: G♯ and A♭ and the intervals of an augmented 4th and a diminished 5th.

entry [in contrapuntal writing]***:*** the first appearance or sometimes re-appearance of a voice part in a fugue or other contrapuntal piece

episode [in counterpoint]***:*** a passage based on previously heard material which often will lead to a cadence in a new key.

Glossary

equal temperament: a method of tuning instruments of fixed pitch so that the octave is divided into 12 equal intervals, so facilitating performance in every key.

exposition: the opening section of an extended composition, such as in sonata form, where the subject material of the piece is first heard.

fermata: a pause; a sign indicating that a note/chord can be sustained beyond its written length.

fill [in jazz/blues]: usually, but not exclusively, applied to the *ad lib* drum 'breaks' which are played to create rhythmic interest between phrases or longer musical sections.

fine/fini [*Italian*]: end.

flat [intonation]: sounding lower than the correct pitch.

flat [sign]: a symbol placed before a note which lowers its pitch by a semitone.

form: the structural organisation of a piece of music.

fugato [*Italian*]: a term used to describe a contrapuntal passage in a composition which is written like a fugue although the piece, as a whole, is not a fugue in the formal sense.

fugue/fuga/fuge [*French/Italian/German*]: a highly structured contrapuntal composition for two or more voices which is based on a melodic subject. The fugue, as a compositional form, is thought to have reached the peak of perfection in the late Baroque period and especially in the works of J. S. Bach.

functional harmony: harmony which serves to reinforce the tonality of a melody.

gapped scale: a scale in which the sequence of notes are not are not all consecutive letter names. *e.g.* a pentatonic scale.

glissando [from *French*]: strictly, a rising or falling slide across a number of pitches where individual notes are not discernible, as can be achieved on a trombone or violin, for instance.

grace note[s]: a note or notes which are added for ornamental purposes, usually denoted by being printed in smaller notation.

ground bass: a bass line which is repeated through all or part of a composition.

grouping: in the notation of rhythm, the combining of fractional note durations by beaming them together according to the rules which govern this process [see *beaming*].

half-diminished [chord]: a term used, especially by jazz musicians, to describe a minor chord with a flattened 5th and an added minor 7th.

harmonic minor: the scale formed by the intervals: tone, semitone, tone, tone, semitone, 3 semitones, semitone. Unlike the melodic minor scale, the descending form simply reverses this order of pitches.

harmonic/chord progression: a sequence of chords which conveys a sense of forward movement, usually to a cadence.

harmonics: the overtones which are present in all musical pitches and which determine their timbre. Harmonics can be utilised as distinct notes on many instruments.

homophonic: where the harmony moves in the same rhythm as the melody [hymn-like], as distinct from counterpoint.

imitation: the passing of melodic phrases or fragments from one voice/part to another, whether exactly or otherwise.

Glossary

interval [harmonic]*:* the interval between two notes sounding together.

interval [melodic]*:* the interval between two notes sounding consecutively.

inversion [of a subject]*:* the inversion of the intervals of a melody or sequence of notes to produce a new melody or sequence.

inversion [of a triad/chord]*:* the rearrangement of the notes of a triad so that the root moves to become either the middle or the upper note. A triad may therefore be in root position [*e.g.* C E G], 1st inversion [E G C] or 2nd inversion [G C E]. Triads with an added note [*e.g.* C E G B♭] are capable of a 3rd inversion [*e.g.* B♭ C E G] which is sometimes referred to as the last inversion.

key signature: sharps or flats placed at the beginning of a piece [and repeated on each new system] which indicate the key.

leading note: the 7th degree of a major or minor scale.

ledger/leger lines: additional stave lines for specific notes which are pitched above/below the stave.

legato [*Italian*]*:* a direction to play smoothly.

Leslie speaker: a loudspeaker used on some electric organs which uses a rotating baffle to produce a kind of tremolo effect.

loco: a direction to play at the written pitch [following a previous direction to play an octave higher/lower, or similar].

lyricist: one who writes the lyrics for songs.

major [chord]*:* a chord which, as a root position triad from the root upwards, consists of a major 3rd and a minor 3rd. *e.g.* C to E and E to G.

major [interval]*:* the intervals above the tonic of a 2nd, 3rd, 6th and 7th in a major scale and the 6th and 7th degrees of the ascending melodic minor scale.

major [key/scale]*:* the scale formed by the sequence of intervals: tone, tone, semitone, tone, tone, tone, semitone.

measures: see *bars*.

mediant: the 3rd degree of a major/minor scale.

melodic minor: the scale, ascending, formed by the intervals: tone, semitone, tone, tone, tone, tone, semitone, and descending: tone, tone, semitone, tone, tone, semitone, tone.

melody: a succession of notes which, in terms of their tonal centre, rhythmic pattern, phrasing, *etc.* convey a musical coherence to the listener. In simple terms, a tune.

metronome: a device, mechanical or electronic, which provides a regular pulse across a range of pre-set tempi.

middle eight or 'bridge': the eight-bar middle section commonly encountered in a popular song which is often in a closely related key to the tonic of the song.

midi: an acronym for musical instrument digital interface.

minimalism: a modern style of composition in which simple rhythmic, harmonic and melodic figures are organically developed through extensive repetition. Composers who have exploited and developed this style include Steve Reich, Phillip Glass and John Adams.

minor [chord]*:* a chord which, as a root position triad from the root upwards, consists of a minor 3rd and a major 3rd. *e.g.* C to E♭ and E♭ to G.

minor [interval]*:* the interval created by lowering the upper note of a major interval by a semitone.

minor [key/scale]*: see* harmonic minor

minor 3rd pentatonic/♭ 3rd pentatonic [scale]*:* one in which the third note is flattened. *e.g.* G, A, B♭, D, E.

mode(s): Scale forms which originated in the 10th century which, although subsequently largely superseded by major/minor tonality in Western European art music, continue to be exploited in a range of musical genres.

modulation: changing key.

mute: a device which can be fitted to a musical instrument which quietens or otherwise affects its sound.

N.C./NC: an abbreviation for *no chord* used in conjunction with chord symbols.

natural: the symbol placed before a note which cancels the effect of a previous accidental.

notehead: the part of a written note which indicates its pitch by being placed on a line or in a space.

octave/perfect octave: an interval of an eighth. The interval created by two notes where one is double or half the frequency of the other.

open harmony: harmony in which the notes are spread widely as opposed to close harmony where they lie together.

organum [*Latin*]*:* the earliest form of harmony dating from the 9th century where the vocal lines moved in parallel 4ths or 5ths.

ostinato/basso ostinato: a repeated musical pattern/a repeated bass figure or, even, a repeated bass line as in *ground bass*.

overstrung: a term applied to piano design which describes the layout of the strings, such that one set of strings overlays another, diagonally. This layout allows for the accommodation of longer strings than would otherwise be possible with parallel stringing.

parallelism: harmony in which each voice moves in parallel with the others.

partita [*Italian*]*: see suite.*

passing note[s]: notes which pass between those which belong to the chord.

pastiche: literally, a piece put together from portions of other pieces, as in a medley for example. Now, more likely to be used to describe a piece which sets out to imitate a particular composer, style or genre.

pause: see *fermata*

pedal [note] [in a harmonic context]*:* a repeated or sustained bass note over which the harmony changes. The term derives from the practice of sustaining organ pedal notes.

pentatonic : music derived from a pentatonic scale.

pentatonic [scale]*:* a scale using five notes.

perfect [interval]*:* the intervals of a 4th, 5th or octave.

perfect cadence/final cadence: the sequence of chords V–I used to harmonise a phrase ending.

Glossary

perfect/absolute pitch: the ability to remember pitch so exactly that those possessing this facility can sing or name any requested note or name the key of any tonal piece heard.

perpetual canon: a canon or round which may be repeated indefinitely.

phrase: a melodic statement which can vary in length but which, in classical music, is often of 2 to 4 bars, leading to a cadence.

phrasing: the manner in which phrases are performed or shaped. Also the way in which phrases are indicated in musical notation.

pitch: the frequency of a note [in cycles per second]. How high or low it is.

pizzicato [*Italian*]***:*** an instruction to string players meaning: to pluck the strings (as distinct from *arco*: to play with the bow).

plainsong [chants]***:*** term used from the 13th century to describe Gregorian chant

polyphony [from *Greek*]***:*** many sounds/voices. Usually used to describe the contrapuntal vocal compositions of the 16th century, but is sometimes applied to the contrapuntal writing of the Baroque period and occasionally of later works.

prepared piano: a term used by the American composer John Cage to describe placing specific objects on specified piano strings to alter the sound of the instrument.

primary chords: chords/triads constructed on the 1st, 4th, or 5th degrees of a major/minor scale.

programme music: music which relates to a storyline, a sequence of events or, indeed, anything which is not entirely abstract.

pulse: a regular beat.

quadruple [time]***:*** having four beats in a bar/measure.

quantizing: in sequencing music, the process of determining the shortest note duration which the software programme will recognise. Its purpose is to eradicate slight irregularities of timing.

real [in the context of sequence/transposition]***:*** an exact transposition of a phrase in a sequence, for example, as distinct from a *tonal* transposition which remains within the context of the key/harmony.

real [time]***:*** usually, the process of playing music into a sequencing system against a 'click track'.

recapitulation: that part of an extended musical form [*i.e.* sonata form] where the opening section or subjects are reprised, usually with some modification.

relative major: a major key which has the same key signature as a specific minor key.

relative minor: a minor key which has the same key signature as a specific major key.

relative pitch: the ability to pitch or name a note with reference to another identified pitch.

resolution: in harmony, the progression from dissonance to consonance.

rest: a sign which indicates a silence of a specific duration. There is an equivalent rest for every note duration.

retrograde inversion: a sequence of pitches which is inverted and reversed.

retrograde: a sequence of pitches in reverse order.

rhythm: everything pertaining to the time and note length elements of music.

riff: particularly in jazz, a short repeated phrase which recurs through part or all of a piece.

Glossary

rock: a style of pop music derived from the 12-bar blues and which evolved through 'rock-and-roll' into a plethora of sub-styles and fusions which include 'glam'-rock, punk rock, hard rock and jazz rock to name a few.

Romantic/Romanticism [style/period]***:*** very broadly, the style prevailing in Western European art music from 1820–1920.

root [note]***:*** the note on which a triad is constructed. The root of the triad [as distinct from its bass or lowest note] remains the same even when the triad is inverted. *e.g.* in the root position triad C E G, the note C is described as the root and continues to be so described even as it changes octave and/or position in the inversions E G C and G C E.

root [position]***:*** a triad in which the root note is the lowest.

round: a canon – a piece in which voices enter in exact imitation, either in unison or at the octave.

scat: a style of singing used by jazz singers when improvising where invented syllables replace words. *e.g.* "doo-bee-doo-bee", or "doo-wah". Scat is sometimes used by singers in improvised sections of jazz/jazzy performances in imitation of instrumental sounds.

semitone: a difference in pitch of one-twelfth of an octave. Generally the smallest interval in Western music.

senza [Italian]***:*** without *e.g. senza ped.* – without pedal.

sequence/sequential: a specific kind of repetition where a phrase or fragment of a phrase is repeated, perhaps several times ascending or descending, at different pitches.

serialism: a process of creating atonal music devised by composers of the Second Viennese School and particularly Arnold Schönberg [1874–1951].

sharp [intonation]***:*** sounding higher than the correct pitch.

sharp [sign]***:*** a symbol placed before a note which raises its pitch by a semitone.

short score: the reduction of a score so that it is written on two staves, as used for piano notation.

simile: a direction to continue playing in the same manner, with reference to articulation for instance.

simple time: time signature in which the beat or pulse is an un-dotted note. *e.g.* $\frac{3}{2}$, $\frac{3}{4}$, $\frac{3}{8}$ *etc.*

slur: a curved line over or under a pair or group of notes which indicates that they are to be played *legato.*

solo [in jazz]***:*** that part of a performance where an individual player improvises.

sostenuto [*Italian*]***:*** sustained.

sostenuto pedal: the middle pedal provided on some pianos which allows the player to sustain specific notes.

staff/stave: the system of five lines on which music is notated.

standards [with reference to songs]***:*** songs, often from musical shows, which have become part of a repertoire; a term used by jazz musicians to describe these well-established songs as vehicles for improvisation.

step time: usually, in sequencing music, the process of inputting notes/chords from a keyboard but not in real time.

Glossary

stops [speaking stops: the pipe organ]***:*** the means by which different ranks of organ pipes are brought into play.

stride [jazz piano]***:*** A left-hand 'vamping' solo jazz piano style, developed from ragtime, in which octaves or even tenths were played on the first and third beats of a $\frac{4}{4}$ bar/measure alternating with chords on the second and fourth beats so providing both a powerful rhythmic and harmonic accompaniment. Sometimes called *Harlem Stride*, the style is closely associated with James P. Johnson and Thomas 'Fats' Waller in the 1920s.

string quartet: an ensemble usually comprising two violins, a viola and a cello.

strophic [from *Greek*]***:*** verse-repeating. In a song/hymn, the use of substantially the same musical setting for each verse.

subdominant: the 4th degree of a major/minor scale.

subject [in context of form]***:*** the melody or other musical material of a composition which is subsequently developed.

submediant: the 6th degree of a major/minor scale.

suite: in music of the romantic period and later, a set of pieces linked by a common thread, often programmatic [*e.g. The Planets* – Gustav Holst: 1914–16]. The suite as a form of musical composition evolved from the practice of playing successive dances in different tempi and time signatures and earlier examples consist of such dance movements, following a conventional sequence. In the latter half of the 17th century, the term *partita* is used by some German composers to describe a suite.

supertonic: the 2nd degree of a major/minor scale.

swing quavers: in jazz, the playing of quavers in an unequal fashion so that, very broadly speaking, in each pair of quavers, the durations are two-thirds to one-third. In practice, the playing of swing quavers is a matter of interpretation rather than one of mathematics and calls for an understanding of, or a so-called 'feel' for the style.

syncopation: the displacement of accentuation from that which is expected, or sometimes, the anticipation or delay of an accented note within the divided beat. *Ragtime* is a genre which provides obvious examples of these forms of syncopation.

tempo: the speed of the pulse or beat of a piece of music.

tenor clef [*see clef*]***:*** a clef which places the note middle C on the fourth line of the stave.

tessitura [Italian]***:*** the predominant range of a melodic line within the overall compass of an instrument or voice.

thematic metamorphosis: describing the process whereby a theme undergoes changes of character in the course of a piece. Commonly used in programme music.

tie: a slur joining notes of the same pitch so that no break is perceptible.

time signature: the figures placed at the opening of a musical composition which inform the player of the number and value of the beats in each bar/measure.

tonal/tonality: belonging to a key or having a tonal centre.

tone [French - *timbre*]***:*** the quality of an instrumental or vocal sound; that aspect of the sound which allows the listener to distinguish one instrument or voice from another.

tone [interval]***:*** an interval of two semitones.

Glossary

tone row: the sequence of 12 different pitches which forms the basis of the matrix in serial [*dodecaphonic*] music.

tongued: non-slurred notes produced by woodwind and brass players using a technique whereby they are articulated by the rapid release of the tongue.

tonic: the first note of a major/minor scale.

transposing [instruments]**:** instruments which sound a different note from the one which is written. *e.g.* a B♭ clarinet when reading the note C will sound the note B♭.

transposition [in the context of key]**:** the movement of a note/chord/melody to a new pitch/key.

treble clef [*see clef*]**:** a clef which places the note middle C on the first ledger line below the stave [also known as the G clef].

triad: a three-note chord which, in root position, consists of the root note, a note which is a third above the root and a third note which is a fifth above the root. *N.B.* the exact nature of the intervals of a third and a fifth above the root define the triad as major, minor, diminished or augmented.

triple [time]**:** having three beats in a bar/measure.

triplet: Three notes to be played in the time of two of the same kind. *e.g.* in $\frac{2}{4}$: ♩♩♩ in the time of ♩♩

tritone [interval]**:** an interval of three tones. *e.g.* C to F♯: an augmented 4th.

tritone substitution: the substitution of one chord by another, the root of which is three tones above/below the root of the chord which it replaces. *e.g.* substituting a dominant 7th in C major [G7] with the chord on the flattened supertonic [D♭7/ C♯7].

una corda [Italian]**:** literally, one string; an instruction to pianists to use the left ['soft'] pedal.

upbeat [see also *anacrusis*]**:** the last beat of a bar or measure.

voicing: see *chord voicing*

whammy bar: a device fitted to some electric guitars which allows the player to bend the pitch.

word painting: in vocal music, the practice of interpreting literally the meaning of the words in the music; *e.g.* composing a rising melodic line to words which, in one way or another, are concerned with ascent.